David Jones and the Craft of Theology

T&T Clark Studies in English Theology

Series Editors
Karen Kilby
Mike Higton
Stephen R. Holmes

David Jones and the Craft of Theology

Becoming Beauty

Elizabeth R. Powell

LONDON • NEW YORK • OXFORD • NEW DELHI • SYDNEY

T&T CLARK
Bloomsbury Publishing Plc
50 Bedford Square, London, WC1B 3DP, UK
1385 Broadway, New York, NY 10018, USA
29 Earlsfort Terrace, Dublin 2, Ireland

BLOOMSBURY, T&T CLARK and the T&T Clark logo are trademarks of
Bloomsbury Publishing Plc

First published in Great Britain 2020
This paperback edition published in 2022

Copyright © Elizabeth R. Powell, 2020

Elizabeth R. Powell has asserted her right under the Copyright, Designs and Patents Act,
1988, to be identified as Author of this work.

For legal purposes the Acknowledgements on p. xv and the List of Figures on p. ix
constitute an extension of this copyright page.

Cover design: Terry Woodley
Cover image: clairevis/iStock

All rights reserved. No part of this publication may be reproduced or
transmitted in any form or by any means, electronic or mechanical, including
photocopying, recording, or any information storage or retrieval system,
without prior permission in writing from the publishers.

Bloomsbury Publishing Plc does not have any control over, or responsibility for, any
third-party websites referred to or in this book. All internet addresses given in this
book were correct at the time of going to press. The author and publisher regret any
inconvenience caused if addresses have changed or sites have ceased to exist, but can
accept no responsibility for any such changes.

A catalogue record for this book is available from the British Library.

Library of Congress Cataloging-in-Publication Data
Names: Powell, Elizabeth R., author.
Title: David Jones and the craft of theology : becoming beauty / Elizabeth R Powell.
Description: London ; New York : T&T Clark, 2020. |
Series: T&T Clark studies in English theology |
Includes bibliographical references and index.
Identifiers: LCCN 2020022397 (print) | LCCN 2020022398 (ebook) |
ISBN 9780567691637 (hardback) | ISBN 9780567696427 (paperback) |
ISBN 9780567691651 (pdf) | ISBN 9780567691644 (epub)
Subjects: LCSH: Jones, David, 1895–1974–Criticism and interpretation.
Classification: LCC PR6019.O53 Z84 2020 (print) |
LCC PR6019.O53 (ebook) | DDC 821/.912–dc23
LC record available at https://lccn.loc.gov/2020022397
LC ebook record available at https://lccn.loc.gov/2020022398

ISBN: HB: 978-0-5676-9163-7
PB: 978-0-5676-9642-7
ePDF: 978-0-5676-9165-1
eBook: 978-0-5676-9164-4

Series: T&T Clark Studies in English Theology

Typeset by Newgen KnowledgeWorks Pvt. Ltd., Chennai, India

To find out more about our authors and books visit www.bloomsbury.com
and sign up for our newsletters.

To Ma and Da

Contents

List of Figures	ix
Preface	xi
Acknowledgements	xv
Introduction: The art of David Jones and the craft of theology	1

1. **The quest for sacrament: 'A, a, a, DOMINE DEUS' poem** — 11
   - Introduction: 'Asking the question' and the myth of Peredur — 11
   - Asking the question of 'A, a, a, DOMINE DEUS' — 17
   - The art of writing in the age of mechanical reproduction — 20
   - Performing the quest of 'A, a, a, DOMINE DEUS' — 26
   - Conclusion: Wounds that bless and defeats that revive — 48

2. **The art of the incarnate word: '*Quia per Incarnati*' painted inscription** — 51
   - Introduction: Epiphany — 51
   - 'A living lettering': Painted inscriptions and the art of the incarnate word — 54
   - Journeying through the inscription of the preface to the Christmas Mass — 60
   - *Claritas, Caritas* and the analogy of the *Verbum Cordis* — 72
   - Conclusion: *Poiesis* as Christological participation — 80

3. **'The Vessel of the *Ecclesia*': '*Bride*' wood engraving** — 83
   - Introduction: Wedding guests — 83
   - Following the furrowed line: The craft of wood engraving — 90
   - 'A flowery, starry, intertwined image': The liturgical character of *Bride* — 97
   - The figures of *Bride* — 103
   - Conclusion: 'Magdalenian splendours' — 126

Conclusion	129
Bibliography	137
Index	149

Figures

1. 'A, a, a, DOMINE DEUS', in *The Sleeping Lord and Other Fragments*, London: Faber & Faber, 1974. Reproduced with permission of Faber & Faber 18
2. *Quia per Incarnati*, 1950, watercolour and graphite on paper, 500 × 380 mm, Kettle's Yard, University of Cambridge. Estate of David Jones (Bridgeman Copyright). Used with permission 61
3. *Bride*, 1931, wood engraving on paper, 140 × 110 mm, Kettle's Yard, University of Cambridge. Estate of David Jones (Bridgeman Copyright). Used with permission 86

Preface

This work began by accident. Having fallen into a hole in the process of writing a dissertation on that most sublime and speculative of doctrines, the Trinity, months passed tediously translating from the Latin a twelfth-century text – an exercise made doubly difficult, if not dubious, by the need to learn Latin itself along the way. Finding oneself in a ditch seems to be a familiar experience for most PhD students I've met, and I was deeply ensconced in this initiation rite. During these long hours at my desk, a postcard I had picked up on a visit to Kettle's Yard House became a frequent reprieve for my attention. It was of David Jones's Preface of the Christmas Mass, the original acquired by Jim Ede, a friend to Jones, and still on display in the House at the bottom of a long staircase. Looking up repeatedly from the black and white papers on my desk, trying to discern the marks there as one learning to read for the first time, the colours and shapes of Jones's image, stuck to the wall with blue tac, constituted what one might resolutely class as a distraction. But sometimes distractions, it turns out, may not be what we want, but what we need.

My dutiful work on the Latin text had itself been a kind of waylay, a retreat into what felt objectively as serious theological labour and away from questions which I had set out to answer but struggled to even articulate. The previous few years I had been steeped in Christian classics from the premodern period – Augustine's *Confessions*, Julian of Norwich's *Revelations*, Dionysius's *Divine Names*. Though I had been a theology student for a long time, my encounter with these works was markedly different. They welcomed me into their life and reshaped mine. I wept with Augustine in the garden scene; I wondered at the pressures of bearing life with Julian; I walked the scale of being with Dionysius from rocks to angels. Here theology, spirituality, intellect, emotion were not divisible, and their writing, like my reading, conducted the philosophy. I had read, too, of the struggle represented by the Victorine school in the twelfth century to bring together the burgeoning scholastic and settled monastic modes of doing theology during the rise of the university in Paris, and how these tensions were accompanied by changes in the very technology of books – the invention of tables of content and the like to accommodate use of the book as an accessible resource rather than a place to willingly get lost.

Over eight hundred years later, these tensions within theology as a discipline and its place within the university are, of course, far from finished. The university has nourished and sustained theology if at other times or ways had a narrowing or even threatening effect. But perhaps one of the ongoing gifts of this exchange has been a mutual spurring towards meta-disciplinary and institutional questions about practices, habits and ends. My own awkward questions took these forms: Where is the beauty and power of these classical texts residing within works of academic theology today? What had happened to the production of texts that set out to not just articulate ideas but to praise, repent or simply persevere? How to cultivate this awareness that the meaning of *what* we write is indelibly shaped by *how* we write it, whether we like it or not?

When giving an account of the trajectory of his own life and work, David Jones startled his friend Saunders Lewis with this interjection: '… By accident. Everything that has ever happened to me is by accident, and it's never been by design.' Lewis playfully rebuffed him: 'That's a strange thing for a Catholic to say!' Chuckling at the jab, Jones mumbled his defence: 'Well, I mean ….' Lewis pressed further, revelling in the friendly spar: 'You're awfully unorthodox, David.' David: 'No, I'm not. I'm not!'[1] If his insistence on the 'accidental' sounds at first blush as either a denial of divine providence or abdication of human responsibility, I've learned that Jones is a poet best taken at his word, though these often come in strange packaging and one has to do not a small amount of unwrapping. In many ways, Jones is simply claiming here what is true for any life – it is not by choice that one is born in a particular place within this particular line of ancestors, with a set of particular gifts and weaknesses. One does 'fall' into the world in this sense and, not incidentally, 'to fall' is the root meaning of the word, 'accident': from the Latin, *accidere* (*ad* + *cadere*), it means, literally, to fall towards.

In his 1959 talk for the BBC, titled, 'A London Artist Looks at Contemporary Wales', Jones colourfully describes himself as 'an English monoglot, born, bred, and for practically all my life, have lived near where Thames runs softly'.[2] And yet, with Welsh ancestry on his father's side, Jones's heart always longed or tended towards the land, history and culture of Wales. He articulates this longing at the heart of his sense of place by drawing an analogy with the fourth-century theologian, Augustine:

> There is a well-known saying, attributed, I think, to St. Augustine of Hippo, which seems to me as true in content as it is concise in form: *Amor meus pondus meum*, 'My love is my weight'. … If this Latin saying *is* from the pen of the author of *The City of God* then it was written down in Roman Africa by a passionate man who, though so very Roman in culture, betrays a warmth of feeling for his Carthaginian *patria* and ancestry.[3]

So, too, Jones betrays this 'warmth of feeling' increasingly throughout his life for his Welsh *patria* and ancestry, a relation he considered essential not only to his own identity but for the whole of the British Isles. The phrase, 'my love is my weight' – *amor meus pondus meum* – is one of Augustine's favoured images for the nature of love. The imagery arising from Aristotle's metaphysics – rocks, bubbles, stars – all carry this kind of natural weighting within them, upwards or downwards, depending on their material make-up. In Augustine's hands, this metaphysics of the natural world becomes an analogy for the human heart and all creatures in their relation to the Creator. If all

---

[1] For a full transcription of this interview, see Jasmine Hunter-Evans, 'You're Awfully Unorthodox, David', *New Welsh Review* no. 104 (2014): 24–31.
[2] Jones, David, *The Dying Gaul and Other Writings*, ed. Harman Grisewood (London: Faber & Faber, 2008), 35.
[3] Ibid., 36.

creatures are brought into being and sustained in existence by the love and wisdom of God, it is this invisible and immeasurable relation that constitutes their most elemental make-up and by which finite loves, too, find their natural place. When creatures fall in the direction of their Creator, they flourish and unfold according to this right order, that is, in truth, beauty and goodness. If human loves are known for being fickle and prone to accidents, the saying is no less true that we move in the direction of our loves. No wonder Jones ends his talk with this rejoinder:

> I try to continue to say *Dewi Ddyfrwr, gweddia dros Cymru*, 'David the Waterman, pray for Wales', and even if you don't hold with the invocation of saints, I ask you to make this exception. Or, if you can't run to that, then remember Augustine's (if it was his) 'My love is my weight'. For whether your heart's love is *Cymru Fawr* or something or someone quite other, those words, being true, can do you no possible harm to contemplate.[4]

If the deepest orientation of any creature resides, ultimately and primordially, in this 'something or someone quite other' that is the love of God, then there is no such thing as dead, mute matter and no form beyond the possibility of inflection by grace. All things may be channels of the love of God in which truth, goodness and beauty find their source.

Words are the primary channels with which the theologian works in the modern academy, and they too will bear the imprint of our loves. They may also yet surprise us by their capacity to bend as grace-inflected forms, even – if awkwardly – that most formidable of forms, the PhD dissertation. The questions about the craft of theology with which I began persist, but this vulnerability to 'ask the question' is itself, as Jones insists, a way of life and of the most perennial import. I hope I have learned something of what this means by my accidental fall into doing theology with the artefacts of David Jones. For though our works are inseparable from the accidents of our lives, this too may be a 'happy fault'. It is, after all, only by accident that we learn the word for grace.

---

[4] Ibid., 40.

Acknowledgements

My first thanks must go to Janet Martin Soskice whose theological writing was an early source of kinship and who always trusted in the process, even when the odds seemed against it. For teaching me the value of insight over just being clever I remain in her debt. I am grateful to the Faculty of Divinity at Cambridge for the Burney Studentship and to Fitzwilliam College scholarships for funding through the course of the PhD in which this book had its beginnings. Incidentally, much of it was originally written while living above a pub where the punters' daily resurrections of John Barleycorn also contributed to my subsistence. My gratitude to Jacob Holsinger Sherman for persevering in reading my first drafts with characteristic enthusiasm and without whose encouragement and editing they never would have left the orbit of my desk. Vittorio Montemaggi and Andrew Davison provided friendship through collaborative, constructive conversation and I am particularly thankful for their hospitable reception as examiners.

If footprints of kindness track the genesis of this work, its journey to publication would not have been possible without the patience and solidarity of my colleagues at the Centre for Catholic Studies at the University of Durham and the Sisters of La Retraite. The Sisters' creation of the La Retraite Fellowship in Theology and Spirituality has given me the means and time needed to bring this work to full term. I will be content if it bears even a trace of that 'continual loving attention to God present in the depths of the heart' which guides their life and vocation. Many thanks to Karen Kilby for giving it a home in the *Studies in English Theology* series and for accompanying me with an ever steady hand and healthy doses of realism along the way. My gratitude also to the research associates at Margaret Beaufort Institute and to Tim Harling, dean of Chapel at Queen's College, Cambridge, for giving me a home away from home. For persevering with me through the final throes of this project and believing in its worth, my thanks to Olly; his innate sense of craft teaches me more than all my books what it means to take care. My sisters, Amanda and Katie, with their good sense of humour and eagle insights have also grounded me throughout as always. Finally, thanks go to my dad whose fierce determination and gentle heart have taught me so much of what it is to be human, and to my mom whose understated big-heartedness has pulled me out of not a few ditches. This book is for them.

A refined version of Chapter One appeared as the article 'The Quest for Sacrament in David Jones's Poem, "A, a, a, DOMINE DEUS"' in the journal *Religion and Literature* 49, no. 1 (2017): 150–9. Elements of this book also appeared in the Forum on Grace and Poetry in *Religion and Literature* 49, no. 2 (2017): 260–5. Scholarly writing on David Jones is bursting with new life and the past few years have seen the publication of studies of exceptional calibre. I have tried to incorporate these to the best of my ability, but in many cases, adequate response will only be through the beginning of new works. The David Jones Society continues to be not only essential for fine scholarship but also a place to practice friendship, forgiveness and faithful listening – thanks especially to Thomas Berenato, Tom Villis and Anna Svendsen for accompanying my engagement with Jones at different stages. As tutelars of his legacy, the trustees of the Estate of David Jones have shown generosity in their sharing of his artefacts for publication here; thanks are also due to Kettle's Yard, Cambridge and Faber & Faber for allowing and facilitating their reproduction. Unless indicated otherwise, Scripture quotations are from the New Revised Standard Version Bible, copyright © 1989 National Council of the Churches of Christ in the United States. Used by permission. All rights reserved worldwide.

Introduction: The art of David Jones and the craft of theology

'The issue is this: we are faced by the situation of living in a civilization that has particularly incapacitated one of the normal faculties of man – that of making, without conscious effort, works possessing the quality called "beauty".'[1] This bold pronouncement made by artist David Jones at the young age of 30 speaks to our contemporary culture as much as it did his own.[2] Writing for the burgeoning Dominican journal, *Blackfriars*, in July 1926, Jones has within his sights a surprising demographic: 'Among those people who are conscious of and annoyed by the complete badness in the building and decoration in use in the Catholic Church in our days, there are very few who regard the matter as anything more than a superficial defect that can be, with care, remedied.'[3] He critiques attempts to redress this apparent aesthetic problem by 'educating people up to this or that notion' or filling the churches with reproductions from earlier 'more civilized periods than our own'.[4] These efforts, he contends, fail to get to the root of the matter. 'There is not,' he writes, 'a scale of beauty, extending from the merely useful objects required for a church (like shelves or pipes or rubber door-mats) to the culminating point in the vestments and the sacred vessels. It is subconsciously felt,' he still more colourfully argues, 'that the searching eye of Almighty God will overlook the radiator casing and the electric button so long as the priest's chasuble is graceful and costly.'[5] For Jones, to go to the root of the matter is to question no less than our entire form of life. As his conclusion makes clear: 'If we

---

[1] David Jones, 'Beauty in Catholic Churches', *Blackfriars: A Monthly Review* (July 1926): 438–41.
[2] Thomas Dilworth, *David Jones: Engraver, Soldier, Painter, Poet* (London: Jonathan Cape, 2017). Other overviews of Jones's life and works include Keith Alldritt, *David Jones: Writer and Artist* (London: Constable & Robinson, 2003); Ariane Bankes and Paul Hills, *The Art of David Jones: Vision and Memory* (Farnham: Lund Humphries, 2015); H. S. Ede, 'David Jones', in *A Way of Life: Kettle's Yard* (Cambridge: Cambridge University Press, 1984); René Hague, *David Jones* (Cardiff: University of Wales Press, 1975); Merlin James, *David Jones 1895–1974: A Map of the Artist's Mind* (London: Lund Humphries Publishers in association with National Museums & Galleries of Wales, 1995).
[3] Jones, 'Beauty in Catholic Churches', 438.
[4] Ibid.
[5] Ibid., 438–9.

do not like our churches to reflect the sort of life we have, let us have a different sort of life, and the churches will change inevitably.'⁶

Jones is writing in a time of cultural upheaval when England was reeling from the rapid changes set in motion by the Great War. Even the Arts and Crafts movement which had, in the nineteenth century and in response to an industrialized and automated Britain, sought to salvage the making of artefacts as essentially a human activity – as a practice and not merely a production – had become by Jones's time a factory-based commercial industry. Jones and his contemporaries felt they were on the other side of what they called 'The Break' – this radical sense of disjunction or loss of continuity with the cultural treasure troves of the past, a situation in which the artist himself could no longer take it for granted that his use of signs like 'water' or 'wood' or 'chair' would call up for readers a rich stream of meanings or referents they once did.⁷ It is from within this vortex of cultural change that Jones issues his prophetic call to the Church: leave aside your 'aesthetic welfare work' and return first to the wisdom of your very own teaching, namely, that 'the beauty of God is the cause of the being of all that is' (*ex divina pulchritudine esse omnium derivatur*).⁸

Jones first encountered this *sacra doctrina* in the early 1920s through the writings of the Thomist philosopher, Jacques Maritain. These were deeply influential for him. Here he found an understanding of the world, set forward as one reaching back to the time of the Church's foundation, which saw the world as gratuitous gift, brought into being and sustained in being by the Creator who alone is wholly Good, True and Beautiful in Godself.⁹ All things only are by their participation in this One. Insofar as a thing *is*, it has a share in the goodness, truth and beauty of the divine artist. Conversely, insofar as a thing lacks goodness, truth or beauty, this is a deprivation in being. It is from within this venerable tradition that Jones admonishes his early-twentieth-century readers: the beautiful is not the sole possession of the well-educated, the wealthy or even the holy, nor is it a specially curated product of artistic genius. It's a matter of being.

This understanding of the real resounds as a clarion call throughout Jones's life, even though he would come to speak less directly of beauty and more of the human being as the gratuitous sign-maker: 'It is the intransitivity and gratuitousness in man's art that is

---

⁶ Ibid., 441.
⁷ For Jones's account of 'The Break' see his preface to *The Anathemata* (London: Faber & Faber, 1952), esp. 14–24. See also Tom Villis, 'When Was "the Break"? David Jones and Catholic Ideas of Rupture in British History', *Religion and Literature* 49.1 (2017): 9–18.
⁸ Jones, 'Beauty in Catholic Churches', 440. Cf. Jones's essay, 'Art in Relation to War' where he regards these words as 'that best of sayings', in *The Dying Gaul and Other Writings*, ed. Harman Grisewood (London: Faber & Faber, 2008), 134.
⁹ Jones read and discussed at length Jacques Maritain's *The Philosophy of Art: being 'Art et scholastique'*, trans. John O'Connor (Ditchling, Sussex: St. Dominic's Press, 1923) while living at Ditchling Common with the community of craftsmen and women. As Thomas Dilworth recounts, 'Jones would read and reread Maritain's book, urging friends to buy it. It was, one of them, Ernest Hawkins, said, his "bible" – no book influenced him more. By 1924, it would be to his mind as a map to a place', in *David Jones*, 76. For works that expound the centrality of this participatory metaphysics for Jones's poetics, see especially Romana Huk, 'Sacrament as *ars* in the down-to-earth poetics of David Jones (pursued through a reading of his ars[e]-poetica, "A, a, a, Domine Deus")', *Religion and Literature* 49.1 (2017): 181–201; Thomas Whitaker, 'Homo Faber, Homo Sapiens', in *David Jones: Man and Poet*, ed. John Matthias (Orono, Maine: National Poetry Foundation, 1989); and Rowan Williams, *Grace and Necessity: Reflections on Art and Love* (London: Continuum, 2005).

the sign of man's uniqueness; not merely that he makes things, nor yet that those things have beauty.'[10] Many creatures make things of beauty often far surpassing those contrived by human hands – he cites the honeybees, 'the agger-making beaver, the ant and the nuthatch', even 'the hoar-frost on the pane or the leaf vein'.[11] That which marks human beings out among creatures is the habit, the compulsion even, to freely make things that are significant of something other. This sign-making activity springs not from mere necessity, the meeting of immediate ends, but from this innate desire to 're-present', to show something again under a new form.[12] In this gratuitous activity, he says, we have the first inkling that human beings are themselves meant for something other, that the 'natural end of men (i.e., the end conformable to man's nature) is eternal felicity'.[13]

In this later, most well-known of Jones's essays, 'Art and Sacrament' (1955), his feeling thought penetrates once more like a laser to the root of things. Though written in response to an invitation to reflect on the relationship between his practice as an artist and as a practising Catholic, the profundity of Jones's conclusions stems precisely from his refusal to treat 'art' and 'sacrament' as two alien categories between which one must construct an artificial bridge. To be human, Jones will argue, is to be an artist, which in turn is to be a sign-maker, and this, more surprisingly, is to be a sacramentalist. Jones's revealing of the inherent connections between these terms is the essence of his thought. He argues that art *is* sacrament and sacrament – even *the* sacrament of the Church, the Eucharist – is art. The Eucharist and the sacrifice of Christ on the cross itself, which it re-presents, presuppose the whole sign-world and inflects this sign-world with this redemptive presence.[14]

Jones illustrates his thesis with an unforgettable portrait of a putatively secular man, one disavowed 'of all that is commonly or vulgarly meant by the "sacramental"'. And yet, writes Jones,

> no sooner does he put a rose in his buttonhole but what he is already in the trip-wire of sign, and he is deep in an entanglement of signs if he sends that rose to his

---

[10] Jones, 'Art and Sacrament', *Epoch and Artist* (London: Faber & Faber, 1959), 149.
[11] Ibid.
[12] I use this hyphenated form 're-presents' following David Jones's own usage which he learned from the liturgist, Gregory Dix, *The Shape of the Liturgy* (London: Dacre, 1945). Jones discerned a crucial analogy between the doctrine of the real presence of Christ in the bread and wine of the Eucharist with the Post-Impressionist insight that an art work re-presents, that is, really *is* a thing under another mode, and not just a picture or representation of another thing. Cf. 'Art and Sacrament', 171–5. We will return to this understanding of re-presentation and the analogy between art and the Eucharist throughout the following chapters.
[13] Jones, 'Art and Sacrament', 148. That gratuitous sign-making is not limited to the human but shared by other animals in some degree is a possibility Jones allows for in his interview from 1973:

> I suspect it goes beyond human beings too. It's becoming, I understand from certain biologists, that certain creatures, not human, also in a very elementary way as far as we can see … I believe they have found that a certain kind of ape in India, that they carry away dead ones and *howl*. It is getting sort of near … it isn't a chant, or Michelangelo, but at least it isn't purely *utile*.

in 'David Jones, Mabon Studios Interview, 31 August–3 September 1973', ed. Jasmine Hunter-Evans and Anne Price-Owen in *Unpublished Prose*, ed. Thomas Berenato, Anne Price-Owen and Kathleen Henderson Staudt, 296.
[14] Jones, 'Art and Sacrament', 168.

sweetheart, Flo; or puts it in a vase by her portrait; and he is hopelessly and up to his neck in that entanglement of Ars, sign, sacrament should he sit down and write a poem 'about' that sweetheart. Heaven knows what his poem will really be 'about'; for then the 'sacramental' will pile up by a positively geometric progression. So that what was Miss Flora Smith may turn out to be Flora Dea and Venus too and the First Eve and the Second also and other and darker figures, among them no doubt, Jocasta. One thing at least the psychologists make plain: there is always a recalling, a re-presenting again, anaphora, anamnesis.[15]

This turn to the semiotic in Jones's later thought remains wedded, crucially, to the classical metaphysics of being (or, more precisely, of participation in being) to which he was first introduced through Maritain.[16] 'Why, granted the sign-making nature of man's art must those signs be "sacred"? Is "sacredness" implicit in "sign"? I think it to be so if we assent to what philosophers say about "being", *esse*. I understand them to say that for anything to be real it must have *esse*.'[17] Signs themselves are real and, as well, point to other things that are real. But the real participates in the divine goodness, truth and beauty and so is always in excess of itself; there is this ecstatic 'more than' presence in the very heart of things.[18] As a consequence of this metaphysics of participation, Jones concludes, 'a sign then must be significant of something, hence of some "reality", so of something "good", so of something that is ' "sacred". That is why I think the notion of sign implies the sacred.'[19]

Jones can apply this not only to radiant works of art such as the Venus de Milo or Van Gogh's *Sunflowers*, but also to everyday craft – the ritual baking and decorating of birthday cakes or even – to make his point as provocatively as possible – war strategy. He argues that the latter shows forth the form-making capacities of human beings, however much we justly query the ends to which it is devised. The central elements of art are present:

---

[15] Ibid., 167.
[16] Aidan Nichols argues that Jones grasped from his reading of Maritain's *Art and Scholasticism* precisely this semiotic importance of the art work: 'Jones drew ... not only (with [Eric] Gill) Maritain's view of the artistic object as something made "according to right reason" but also, in the case of the fine arts, the artwork's semiotic importance – its status as a sign of realities beyond itself', in *Redeeming Beauty: Soundings in Sacral Aesthetics* (Aldershot, Hampshire: Ashgate, 2007), 139.
[17] Jones, 'Art and Sacrament', 157.
[18] As Regina Schwartz reflects,

> Somehow, a sign seems to inevitably evoke the sacred. But how? First, because it works by evoking something beyond itself, something that transcends the sign. Insofar as it evokes something beyond, the sign participates in transcendence, and transcendence – whether vertical or horizontal, above or beyond our comprehension, control, and use – is the realm of mystery. We can point to it, sign it, and by doing so evoke it, and sometimes even more, manifest it.

in *Sacramental Poetics at the Dawn of Secularism: When God Left the World* (Stanford, CA: Stanford University Press, 2008), 4.
[19] Jones, 'Art and Sacrament', 157. As Romana Huk summarizes, 'The "signs" we learn, reinterpret and make *become real things*, become "facts" that, like such material "accidents," nonetheless *change* things, and us – sometimes utterly – like real, locating history', in 'Sacrament as *ars*', 185–6; italics in original.

That is to say a number of existing shapes (which themselves may or may not require re-shaping) are shifted about; by which activity a form, not previously existent, is created. Insofar as form is brought into being there is reality. 'Something' not 'nothing', moreover a new 'something', has come into existence. And if, as we aver man's form-making has in itself the nature of a sign, then these formal realities, which the art of strategy creates, must, in some sense or other, be *signa*.[20]

We will have opportunity to unfold more thoroughly the intricacies of Jones's argument and, in particular, his theology of form and what (or better, who) such formal realities may ultimately signify. For now it is sufficient to see that for Jones, to be *human* is to be an *artist*, a participant in the gratuitous sign-making begun with the first gratuitous act of creation itself. The central point is this: What you do *is* sacred; it matters. To be human is to be a sign-maker, an artist, and in this way human beings participate in the gratuity of creation and further *being* itself.

The craft of theology

The relevance of Jones's penetrating comments extends well beyond the matters of church fabric and architecture raised in his *Blackfriars* essay; it extends, I suggest, to the practice of theology itself. Since at least Balthasar's *The Glory of the Lord*, the academic discipline of theology has been newly invested in aesthetic matters. Yet insofar as the beautiful remains merely a category to be restored or a special branch of theological discourse, we have failed, Jones might admonish, to reach the root of the matter. We are still in need of addressing theology itself. What is the purpose of theology? Is the writing of theology itself a craft or a practice? If the purpose of theology is formative, or even performative, do the prevalent styles of theological writing assist or detract from this purpose? Can we, should we, insist that theology itself should be beautiful? The question of how to address this problem remains with us.[21]

---

[20] Jones, 'Art and Sacrament', 159.
[21] A great deal of theological literature in recent times has been concerned with questions regarding the very nature and practice of theology. Contemporary works which have been relevant to my own reflections on these meta-theological issues include Ann W. Astell, *Eating Beauty: The Eucharist and the Spiritual Arts of the Middle Ages* (Ithaca, NY: Cornell University Press, 2006); Stratford Caldecott, *Beauty for Truth's Sake: On the Re-enchantment of Education* (Grand Rapids, MI: Brazos Press, 2009); Peter Candler, *Theology, Rhetoric, Manuduction or Reading Scripture Together on the Path to God* (London: SCM Press, 2006); Pierre Hadot, *Philosophy as a Way of Life* (Oxford: Blackwell, 1995); Matthew Levering, *Scripture and Metaphysics: Aquinas and the Renewal of Trinitarian Theology* (Oxford: Blackwell, 2004); Karen Kilby, 'Beauty and Mystery in Mathematics and Theology', in *God, Evil and the Limits of Theology* (London: T&T Clark, 2020); Robin Kirkpatrick, 'Polemics of Praise: Theology as Text, Narrative, and Rhetoric in Dante's *Commedia*', in *Dante's Commedia: Theology as Poetry*, ed. Vittorio Montemaggi and Matthew Treherne (Notre Dame, IN: University of Notre Dame Press, 2010), 14–35; Robert McMahon, *Understanding the Medieval Meditative Ascent: Augustine, Anselm, Boethius, & Dante* (Washington, DC: Catholic University of America Press, 2006); Vittorio Montemaggi, *Reading Dante's Commedia as Theology: Divinity Realized in Human Encounter* (Oxford: Oxford University Press, 2016); Ben Quash, *Found Theology: History, Imagination and the Holy Spirit* (London: Bloomsbury, 2013); Fáinche Ryan, *Formation in Holiness: Thomas Aquinas on Sacra Doctrina* (Leuven – Dudley,

Jones argues we need to change our lives to change our churches. So too might we need to change our integrally spiritual and aesthetic practices to change our theology. But how do we change? One route, I suggest, is by attending to a different way of comporting ourselves, by being formed through a deep engagement with theology in material form. These sorts of meta-theological questions – that is, theological questions about what it is we are doing when we are doing theology – may be best addressed by those whose own theological voices are less direct. Reflecting on theology pursued in different media forces us to ask what theology's vocation is, and this may in turn aid the recovery of our own original relationship to the search for wisdom. I thus propose to further this conversation not by directly mounting an argument as to why theology needs the arts, but rather by doing theology through a close, attentive engagement with the art of David Jones.[22]

What might it look like to 'do theology' in this manner? There is a very real sense in which that answer can only be given through the practice itself and so must await the close readings I attempt in the chapters that follow. It is helpful at the outset, however, to consider a distinction that Rowan Williams has put to good use. In his essay, 'Theology among the Humanities', he draws on the contrast made by Mikhail Bakhtin between monologic and dialogic forms of knowing as a way of talking about scholarly interpretation.[23] On the former model, the relationship between reader

MA: Peeters, 2007); Jacob Holsinger Sherman, *Partakers of the Divine: Contemplation and the Practice of Theology* (Minneapolis, MN: Fortress Press, 2014); Robert Louis Wilken, *The Spirit of Early Christian Thought: Seeking the Face of God* (New Haven, CT: Yale University Press, 2003); and Rowan Williams, '"New Words for God": Contemplation and Religious Writing', in *A Silent Action: Engagements with Thomas Merton* (Louisville, KY: Fons Vitae, 2011), 43–51.

[22] Ben Quash in 'Wonder-Voyaging: The Pneumatological Character of David Ford's Theology', in *The Vocation of Theology: A Festschrift for David Ford*, ed. Tom Greggs, Rachel Muers and Simeon Zahl (Eugene, OR: Cascade Books, 2013) and Rowan Williams in *Grace and Necessity* also suggest this potentially fruitful relationship between Jones's art and reflection on theological method or practice. Cf. also John Drury, *The Painting of the Word: Christian Pictures and their Meanings* (New Haven, CT: Yale University Press/The National Gallery, London, 1999); Malcolm Guite, *Faith, Hope and Poetry: Theology and the Poetic Imagination* (Farnham: Ashgate, 2012); Alison Milbank, *Chesterton and Tolkien as Theologians: The Fantasy of the Real* (New York: T&T Clark, 2008); and Chloë Reddaway, *Transformations in Persons and Paint: Visual Theology, Historical Images, and the Modern Viewer* (Turnhout: Brepols, 2016). Though working with very different art forms and writing themselves in very diverse styles, these authors all approach the artists they study as themselves doing theology, not merely illustrating prior theological theses. That Jones's art is itself 'doing theology', not mirroring it, will I hope become clear in the pages that follow.

[23] Muers and Zahl, eds, *The Vocation of Theology*, 178–90. For Bakhtin's development of dialogic modes of discourse, see his *Speech Genres and Other Late Essays*, trans. Vern W. McGee, ed. Caryl Emerson and Michael Holquist (Austin: University of Texas Press, 1986). For example, Bakhtin describes the character of discourses which seek to purge themselves of what he calls 'the other sacred word':

> Because of its sacrosanct, impenetrable boundaries, this word is inert, and it has limited possibilities of contacts and combinations. This is the word that retards and freezes thought. The word that demands reverent repetition and not further development, corrections, and additions. The word removed from dialogue: it can only be cited amid rejoinders; it cannot itself become a rejoinder among equally privileged rejoinders. This word had spread everywhere, limited, directing, and retarding both thought and lived experience of life. (Ibid., 133)

Cf. Williams's remarks also with Bakhtin's essay 'Toward a Methodology of the Human Sciences' in which he outlines this contrast between monologic and dialogic modes:

> The exact sciences constitute a monologic form of knowledge: the intellect contemplates a *thing* and expounds upon it. There is only one subject here – cognizing (contemplating) and

and text is construed as a binary relation of subject/object or 'active mind/passive object'.[24] This spatial rendering contributes to tendencies to read as though the goal were to silence all further readings, to have had the last word. 'It is a vision of leaving the object terminally voiceless and silencing whatever possibilities of common discourse are connected with its continuing life.'[25] Instead of these ultimately life-denying practices, Williams paints in broad but incisive strokes the character of theological practices that are dialogic. These, above all, take time as the relationship between self and other is understood to be fundamentally forged through conversation or dialogue; they are provisional and involve a willingness to be changed. In sum,

> the theologian practicing theology as an exploratory matter, not only as description, is entering a world in which dialogue is possible with an unbounded freedom: that freedom is shown in the constant rediscovery of the inadequacy of the concepts you began with and the constant discovery of the (already conversational and self-questioning) text's 'excess', its capacity to generate new meanings.[26]

It is my contention that engagement with Jones's artefacts trains or schools one in this kind of practice of theology that is life-sustaining, meaning generating and ultimately transforming.[27]

This book arises from the conviction that scholars, no less than poets, still long, as a matter of course, to make things possessing that quality we call beautiful. The point is not that we all need to become poets or whittle our own chairs (though time spent in either activity wouldn't be poorly spent!), but to recover our awareness of theology as a human practice, or in Jones's terminology, a gratuitous sign-making and so an inherently sacred practice. To recognize that which makes theology a human practice rather than a mechanical or merely descriptive one is to recognize that which makes theology more than human, a place of transforming relationship with the divine. Far from rendering theology merely human, remembering it as *ars* is the very condition of it becoming more than human, indeed as a graced human practice in which we

---

> speaking (expounding). In opposition to the subject there is only a *voiceless thing*. Any object of knowledge (including man) can be perceived and cognised as thing. But a subject as such cannot be perceived and studied as a thing, for as a subject it cannot, while remaining a subject, become voiceless, and, consequently, cognition of it can only be *dialogic*. (Ibid., 161)

[24] Ibid., 181.
[25] Ibid.
[26] Ibid., 185–6.
[27] Stephen Pattison, *Seeing Things: Deepening Relations with Visual Artefacts* (London: SCM Press, 2007) argues for and models a similar form of engagement, not just with literary texts or works of fine art but objects from the everyday as well. He thus points, with Williams and others, to the nature of this kind of 'reading' as a way of life or, as he writes, a 'quest … to develop friendship and fellowship with visible objects of all kinds' (19). It is also worth noting how much this form of reading has in common with the participatory and performative character of patristic and medieval literary practices which contemporary theologians are rediscovering. See, for example, Jason Byassee, *Praise Seeking Understanding: Reading the Psalms with Augustine* (Grand Rapids, MI: Eerdmans, 2007); Michael Cameron, *Christ Meets Me Everywhere* (Oxford: Oxford University Press, 2012); and Matthew Levering, *Participatory Biblical Exegesis: A Theology of Biblical Interpretation* (Notre Dame, IN: University of Notre Dame Press, 2008).

participate and become divine. Graham Ward, in reflecting on the kinds of practices involved in the art of icon writing (a form of sign-making that is not unrelated to Jones's own visual art), writes:

> The manifestation of beauty and its apprehension are part of an ongoing transformative activity. The analogical order of relations is apprehended by and fosters anagogical practice. At the heart of this practice is a *making*, a fashioning, a *poiesis*: The artist, the author, the reader, the patron, and commissioner have their part to play in this creativity, this cultivation of the thoughts of God. Anagogy is the development of a lifestyle, an aesthetics of living in which to apprehend the beautiful is to become beautiful. One practices beauty.[28]

The essence and end of all sign-making is this participation in and gradual ascent (the meaning of 'anagogy') towards the life of God. Jones's artworks offer just such places in which to 'practice beauty' and to become beauty along the way, remembering that this, like creation itself, is gift, grace.[29]

The art of David Jones: Three artefacts

Given his thesis that to be human is to be an artist, that is, a gratuitous sign-maker, it is fitting that Jones's self-portrait (he would only make one other) is simply titled, *Human Being*.[30] Jim Ede – once curator of Tate Modern London and creator of Kettle's Yard Cambridge – perceptively characterizes Jones's re-presentation thus:

> In this painting there remains the feeling of a personality; of someone sensitive to an outside world, material and spiritual; of someone with a strange force which comes, not out of the strength of his body, but from the strength of his intention. Eyes which collect things inwardly; a body still yet alert; and fingers which are sensitive instruments at his commanding. An ear too, it also is receptive, and David Jones's more than most.[31]

Not only did David Jones excel in a variety of the visual arts (including but not limited to watercolour, engraving and calligraphy), he is also one of the finest English poets of the twentieth century. Ede spoke of him in 1940 as 'not only the best water-colourist working in Great Britain today but by far the best engraver, a poet and writer of genius, in all a most imaginative artist'.[32] From Jones's rich and diverse works, I have chosen

---

[28] Graham Ward, 'The Beauty of God', in *Theological Perspectives on God and Beauty*, ed. John Milbank, Graham Ward and Edith Wyschogrod (Harrisburg, PA: Trinity Press International, 2003), 61.
[29] As Patrick Sherry writes, 'beauty, like grace, is given gratuitously and is transformative', in *Spirit and Beauty: An Introduction to Theological Aesthetics* (London: SCM Press, 2002), 136.
[30] The painting is reproduced as the frontispiece in Bankes and Hills, *Art of David Jones*; and in Dilworth, *David Jones*, 148, fig. 12.
[31] H. S. Ede, 'David Jones', *Horizon* VIII.44 (August 1943): 131.
[32] Ede, *A Way of Life*, 228.

three artefacts to study in detail in each of the three chapters that follow: a poem, a painted inscription and a wood engraving. This selection of three of Jones's artefacts gives us opportunity to cross the boundary between word and image, thus challenging overly rigid construals of this distinction and deepening our awareness of the porous and fecund relation between them.[33] My hope in handling each of these artefacts is to practice the mode of loving attention elicited by their nature as sacramental signs.

The poem, 'A, a, a, DOMINE DEUS', was published in 1974 in Jones's final book of poetry, *The Sleeping Lord and Other Fragments*.[34] The painted inscription was made in 1950 for the Feast of Epiphany and takes its text from the preface to the Christmas Mass.[35] The wood engraving, *Bride*, was made in 1930 and first printed as the frontispiece for a book of poems by his friend, Walter Shewring, titled, *Hermia and Other Poems*.[36] Though these dates help locate the works within certain periods, they are all artefacts which, in one manner or another, Jones revisited throughout his life. 'A, a, a, DOMINE DEUS', though by far the shortest of his poems (indeed the only single-page poem he would write), was reworked over a period spanning at least thirty years.[37] The inscription, though itself made in a relatively short period of time, uses a liturgical text that Jones would have heard repeated in the Mass throughout the entirety of every Christmas season (from 25 December to 6 January). It is the second inscription he made using this liturgical text, the first painted five years earlier in 1945.[38] Finally, Jones's *Bride*, though made relatively early in his life, remained his favourite engraving; he kept it in his room in Harrow, London, in his later years, and it has been argued *Bride* is a 'pictorial forerunner' of his later poetic works.[39] Jones himself thus lived with each of these artefacts. They were frequent objects of meditation, sometimes even prompting entirely new ventures or re-presentations under other forms.

---

[33] Though due to limitations of space, the absence of a close study here on one of Jones's watercolours is regrettable; it will, however, be the subject of future research projects in its own right. For an introduction to Jones's watercolour paintings, see Nicolete Gray, *The Paintings of David Jones* (Hatfield: John Taylor/Lund Humphries in association with The Tate Gallery, 1989); and Bankes and Hills, *Art of David Jones*.

[34] David Jones, *The Sleeping Lord and Other Fragments* (London: Faber & Faber, 1974), 9.

[35] The original inscription was given by Jones to Jim Ede and is part of the collection of Kettle's Yard, University of Cambridge, and on permanent display. A copy of the inscription is also included in Nicolete Gray, *The Painted Inscriptions of David Jones* (London: Gordon Fraser, 1981), 56, catalogue no. 22; and in Bankes and Hills, 154, fig. 140. Jones also used the inscription as an illustration in *The Anathemata*, 76.

[36] Walter Shewring, *Hermia and Other Poems* (Ditchling, Sussex: St. Dominic's Press, 1930). Subsequently printed in *Engravings of David Jones*, ed. Douglas Cleverdon (London: Clover Hill Editions, 1981), plate no. 88. Note that the print made from the wood block, reproduced as figure 3, was made in 1931.

[37] An early form of the poem is found in *The Roman Quarry and Other Sequences*, ed. Harman Grisewood and René Hague (London: Agenda Editions, 1981); a later, condensed version concludes his essay, 'Art and Sacrament', published first in 1955 in *Catholic Approaches*, ed. Elizabeth Pakenham (London: Weidenfeld & Nicolson), and later revised for inclusion in the collection, *Epoch and Artist*. This was a poem Jones continued to rework throughout his life. Cf. Romana Huk's account of the poem's development and where she comments, 'In a sense, one could say, Jones was *always* writing this poem', in 'Sacrament as *ars*', 190.

[38] The 1945 inscription is reproduced on the back cover of Bankes and Hills, *Art of David Jones*.

[39] Anne Price-Owen, *Fragments of an Attempted Painting: An Investigation of the Pictorial Concepts in David Jones's 'The Anathemata'* (PhD diss., University of Wales, Lampeter, 1992), 14.

These three works also realize the qualities by which Jones judged the worth of all art, namely, a unity of form and content, and a feeling of movement, of 'not being stuck still'.[40] They are remarkable for the unity between form and content at numerous levels as we will explore in the following chapters. At the outset, we may at least suggest how the material medium of each work is very much a part of its message. The painted inscription – an art concerned with the very material form of words themselves – re-presents a text that is itself about the Word being made Flesh; it unites his visual and verbal art and reminds us how 'words are material communication; things are material words'.[41] The wood engraving may be read, I suggest, as a re-presentation of the Church whose life is hidden in and springs from the wood of the cross. Lastly, though poetry has often been considered the least material of arts, the material aspects of Jones's poem are astonishing. The text itself – by making frequent use of peculiar capitalizations, rhythm, line breaks and so forth – is far more than a sequence of words. Beyond that though, there is the poem's own complicated, self-implicating and ambiguous relationship to the meaning of its own (re)production. The poet utilizes this medium to spur us on in the quest for sacrament among such objects 'projected from the Machine'.[42]

All of these works achieve this integrity without losing the feeling of movement which Jones says is his main criterion in judging a work. The furrowed lines of *Bride* have a remarkable degree of fluidity, evoking the substance of water and the play of light although engraved on the hard end-grain surface of a boxwood tree. The lettering of Jones's inscription in opaque watercolour conveys a similar liquid luminosity. Finally, though in a less obvious manner, even the typeset poem impels this sense of motion through the gradual evolution of its primary signifier: from the stolid 'A, a, a,' of its title line to the opening exhale as 'Ah!' to the incantatory, 'A, a, a,' and resolving in this final invocation, 'Eia.' This feeling of movement or fluidity is so essential to Jones because it is a quality of *living* works: not static, mere representations of other things, but as themselves things in the world with their own life and presence. This quality of movement draws in the reader, inviting him or her to participate in its sign-bearing presence and to 'make meaning' with it. Jones's works endlessly reward this kind of patient, extended engagement; there are ever more layers to be discovered and the more one looks at them, the more one sees. In this their sacramental character is most fully manifest. The realities to which the sacraments of the Church point and in which they participate cannot be exhausted with words. Art aspires to this – it seeks not a transactional relationship but this constantly renewing and generative practice. Jones's works – in both word and image – invite us to this kind of creative participation, an activity that by grace may also be a sanctifying or holy-making process.

---

[40] David Jones, 'David Jones the Artist: A Brief Autobiography', in *David Jones: Eight Essays on His Work as Writer and Artist*, ed. Roland Mathias (Llandysul: Gomer Press, 1976), 11.
[41] Williams, *Grace and Necessity*, 75.
[42] Jones, *The Sleeping Lord*, 9.

1

The quest for sacrament: 'A, a, a, DOMINE DEUS' poem

In the introduction, we raised questions about theology's vocation and practice, in particular the practice of theology as craft, including the craft of writing theology. Of course, there is something self-implicating about all of this: the very tools of our inquiry are themselves part of the inquiry. How, then, to proceed? I have proposed to address such questions indirectly by way of a close, attentive engagement with the art of David Jones. Fittingly, this first artefact not only is itself a writing – this poem, 'A a, a, DOMINE DEUS' – but also foregrounds questions about writing in the modern epoch. Though we have already been introduced to Jones's understanding of sign and sacrament, in this chapter I first explore further the tension Jones locates at the heart of all human beings and culture between sacrament and what he calls 'the utile' – the merely useful or functional. I then introduce Jones's short poem, 'A, a, a, DOMINE DEUS', in this context as dramatizing the search for the sacramental through the modern wasteland. Before engaging the poem directly, I pause to ask what kind of writer Jones himself is, how he started writing poetry and the kind of readers his work enjoins us to be. The main body of this chapter then is my own participation in the 'quest for sacrament' in the body of the poem itself. We will find that the very minimalism of this poem creates space for readers to ruminate, to imagine or 'fill up "what is lacking"'[1] and so to perform the quest for sacrament oneself. I conclude this reading with some early, gestational reflections on the kind of writers – and the kind of persons – this quest calls us to be.

Introduction: 'Asking the question' and the myth of Peredur

The language of quest is deeply rooted in the medieval romance tales of King Arthur and his court, which were dearly loved throughout his life by David Jones. In the Victorian period, the Welsh Arthurian cycle of stories (found in the treasure of tales

---

[1] David Jones, 'Art in Relation to War', in *The Dying Gaul and Other Writings*, ed. Harman Grisewood (London: Faber & Faber, 2008), 143.

known as *The Mabinogion*) were translated into English and thus re-integrated into this larger corporate imagination of the West.² One of these mythic figures to whom Jones repeatedly returned is the story of Peredur son of Efrawg, a kind of 'coming of age' story, recounting his journey from an innocent and sheltered youth, raised in the woods by his mother, to his becoming one of the revered knights of Arthur's Court. Along the way he encounters a multitude of unexpected challenges, battles and loves. His formation is by no means a straightforward path but full of pitfalls and human fallibility.

In his essay, 'Use and Sign', Jones recalls one of these failures in particular: 'You will recall how the hero in the ancient tale (Peredur, better known as Percival) was blamed, not only for not "asking the question" concerning the Waste Land, but for actually causing the land to be waste by failing to ask the question.'³ *The Mabinogion* recounts this failure as bearing the gravest of consequences, not just for Peredur but a whole kingdom:

> Peredur, I greet thee not, seeing that thou dost not merit it. Blind was fate in giving thee fame and favour. When thou wast in the Court of the Lame King, and didst see there the youth bearing the streaming spear, from the points of which were drops of blood flowing in streams, even to the hand of the youth, and many other wonders likewise, thou didst not inquire their meaning nor their cause. Hadst thou done so, the King would have been restored to health, and his dominions to peace. Whereas from henceforth, he will have to endure battles and conflicts, and his knights will perish, and wives will be widowed, and maidens will be left portionless, and all this is because of thee.⁴

The streaming spear and drops of blood about which Peredur fails to inquire are signs of something other, and not only signs but themselves full of efficacious, healing power. What Peredur does not know, but other stories in the Arthurian cycle suggest, is that this spear pierced the side of Christ and thus bears his salvific blood.⁵ It is a fundamentally

---

² The origin and meaning of the grail quest shaped the literary and cultural inheritance of the twentieth century not least through writers such as T. S. Eliot and Jones himself, influenced by writers such as Jessie Weston. For more on the history and development of the quest for the grail, see Juliette Wood, *The Holy Grail: History and Legend* (Cardiff: University of Wales Press, 2012).
³ Jones, *The Dying Gaul*, 184–5.
⁴ *The Mabinogion*, trans. Lady Charlotte Guest (London: Dent, 1906). I quote from this translation as it is the one with which Jones was familiar. For a more recent translation, see *The Mabinogion*, trans. Sioned Davies (Oxford: Oxford University Press, 2007). Jones also quotes this passage in his *In Parenthesis* (London: Faber & Faber, 1937), 210, n. M.
⁵ This identification of the spear with the lance of Longinus, the Roman soldier who is said to have pierced Christ's side from which blood and water flowed (Jn 19.34), is not yet in the Welsh version of the story of Peredur nor in Chrétien de Troyes's parallel Percival story written in 1180. The first explicit identification of this spear with that of Longinus is swiftly made, however, in the romance tale known as *The First Continuation*, completed before 1200, and in the subsequent continuations written in the early thirteenth century. As Juliette Wood in *The Holy Grail* writes, 'despite the vast antiquity attributed to the grail and later the Holy Grail, its appearance in literary form occurred within a single century. During this time, it developed from a mysterious jewelled object into a sacred relic of the Eucharist which could heal both physically and spiritually', 19. The Christianization of the grail quest story, as Wood emphasizes, was central to Jones's own inheritance of this tradition:

ambiguous artefact: like the Greek concept of *pharmakon* or indeterminacy, it may be both poison and cure.⁶ Because Peredur does not ask the question, however, this symbol remains solely an instrument perpetuating a cycle of violence and death. Its healing power is only realized, or so the lesson of Peredur implies, if there is one who inquires into 'meaning' and 'cause'.

Why did Jones consider the imperative to 'ask the question' so pressing for modern civilization? And just what, for that matter, *is* the question? Finding answers can be as allusive as the story of Peredur itself. For Jones, I suggest, to ask the question in modern civilization is an essential form of resisting an encroaching spirit of utility – or what Jones dubs 'the utile'. 'The utile' is his shorthand term for, as he writes, 'what is vulgarly and generally understood by "merely utilitarian" or "simply functional."'⁷ This view reduces the being of things to mere use; all things are instrumentalized, that is, valued purely for what they effect rather than what they are. To insist on the fundamental gratuity of creation is in clear tension with this kind of reductive or pragmatic utilitarianism: the gratuitous affirms the inherent value of all that is simply insofar as it is and is rooted in a theology of creation as gift.

We have already been introduced to the importance of Jones's formation by the modern recovery of a Thomistic metaphysics in which creation is a gift.⁸ 'Being' only 'is' at all because of the free act of the Creator who even now sustains it in its existence. Creation is fundamentally and thoroughly dependent – held in being by the divine Word which first speaks it into being. Creatures receive this gift of being through their own particular, finite forms: whether a blade of grass, a turtle, a human being or even an angel. The shape of each thing is the shape of the gift that it is. The primacy of the gratuitous or of the gift of existence means that the primary end or purpose of all creatures is to praise the Creator simply by being the kind of creature they have been made to be. The multiple uses, functions or finite ends which such creatures carry out are by no means nullified but ordered; they are gathered up towards this primary orientation or telos towards the Good, the Gift-Giver. So, for instance, the blade of grass pushes its way through the earth and provides food and nests for insects and soft ground for human beings; in simply being itself, it brings glory to its Maker.

This metaphysics of gift helps us articulate more clearly Jones's critique of the utile, which, as Jones claims, 'is ubiquitous in our civilization, yet the exact lie of it

---

Jones, like Eliot, turns to the ritual grail theories of writers like Jessie Weston to provide a means of understanding the meaning of the grail in the twentieth century. The grail quest was the supreme achievement of the Arthurian world, but it was for Jones a quintessentially Christian quest, expressed in the context of an ancient initiation ritual with the power to reunite the maimed king with the land through the actions of a hero. In the complex, multi-layered world of his poetry, the grail hero who heals the king merges with the Maimed King and with Christ as Redeemer of creation. (43–4)

⁶ Cf. Jacques Derrida, 'Plato's Pharmacy', in *Dissemination*, trans. Barbara Johnson (London: Bloomsbury, 2004), 71–9.
⁷ David Jones, 'The Utile', in *Epoch and Artist: Selected Writings*, ed. Harman Grisewood (London: Faber & Faber, 1959), 176.
⁸ For discussions of this metaphysics of the gift in philosophical theology, see John Milbank, *Being Reconciled: Ontology and Pardon* (London: Routledge, 2003); and Jean-Luc Marion, *The Reason of the Gift*, trans. Stephen E. Lewis (Charlottesville: University of Virginia Press, 2011).

is not easy to trace'.⁹ The utile is a particularly spiritual problem that manifests in the material forms of specific things or specific acts.¹⁰ The utile is a form of making and/or of using that has either forgotten or sets itself in outright opposition to the inherent sacredness of all that is. Examples are not hard to marshal – modern slavery is a stark instance, but subtler examples of the utile constantly besiege us in technology, in the banalities of consumerism and so forth. It would be wrong to imagine that the utile is something uniquely modern; it is rather a perennial, perhaps the original, human temptation. However, the ubiquity of the utile in the post-Industrial era is especially marked and is manifest in the kinds of artefacts we produce. The possibilities of mass production opened through a variety of inventions have seemed to reinforce this temptation towards instrumentalization and commodification and the eclipse of a horizon beyond, of the 'more than' or gratuitous heart of things.

If the utile is not a discrete object or an identifiable space, no wonder Jones writes that 'the exact lie of it is not easy to trace'. As John Hughes perceptively argues, for David Jones the utile is ultimately nothing in this ontological sense – that is, it is a slide away from the fullness of gift, of being, and so towards nothingness.¹¹ Jones gives a summary of this metaphysics in 'Art and Sacrament' thus:

> I understand [the philosophers] to say that for anything to be real it must have *esse*. … When philosophers tell us that 'bad' is a deprivation of some 'good' and is thus a negative quality only, we all can apprehend something of what is meant. We know that the 'bad' is real enough in the common speech sense of the word 'real', but that in a deeper sense the bad must be a deprivation of some reality. And in everyday speech we in fact employ this philosophical usage; as when a painter says of a painting which he does not like: 'It is so bad, it simply does not exist' or 'My dear, it just isn't there', or 'It's nothing'. These are but three examples from everyday jargon. We know what is meant just as we guess what is meant by those vivid and measured words: *Bonum et ens convertuntur*.¹²

Far from denying the reality of evil, to call the utile 'nothing' is to name it for what it is – a privation of Being, since to deny, to refuse or to corrupt the Good is ultimately to become less than what one truly is, a creature made to praise and glorify the Creator.

This clarification of the meaning of the utile enables us to see the expansiveness of his notion not only of the gratuitous but also of the sacrament. The sacramental is fundamentally anything that mediates the Good, which gestures through its concrete existence towards that which exceeds it. In light of this metaphysics of gift, we can see

---

⁹ Jones, 'The Utile', 183.
¹⁰ Robin D'Souza also identifies this fundamentally spiritual aspect of Jones's understanding of the utile and extra-utile, as embodied in his character, Private John Ball, in *In Parenthesis*: '"Extra-utile" is a term for Jones that describes humanity's God-like desire to create and to represent reality through sign and symbol but, in the world of *In Parenthesis*, the gratuitousness of art … serves to gesture quietly to the spiritual dimension of the human person that is the source of art and love' in 'From Egalitarian to Sacramental Community: Rewriting William Morris's Social Romance in David Jones's *In Parenthesis*', *Religion and Literature* 49.1 (2017): 107.
¹¹ John Hughes, *End of Work: Theological Critiques of Capitalism* (Oxford: Blackwell, 2007), 10.
¹² 'The Good and being are convertible'. Jones, 'Art and Sacrament', 157.

better how all things – insofar as they *are* – are capable of this sacramental mediation since nothing exists apart from some degree of participation in the gift of Being. The spider's web, the blade of grass, the entirety of creation is sacramental in this sense. But human beings particularly participate in the gift of Being through the mode of sacramental making, that is, *poiesis*. Jones's anthropology foregrounds the human being as *homo faber*, and yet, to be a poetic being is always also for Jones to be a participatory creature.[13] So Jones writes, 'Theologians say that the creation of the world was not a necessary, but a gratuitous, act. There is a sense in which this gratuitousness in the operations of the Creator is reflected in the art of the creature.'[14] Human making is our mode of response to the fundamental gratuity of all that is, and is a way of furthering this good. Human beings are richly creative creatures and, as material and spiritual, both embodied and rational, their mode of creativity is sacramental: 'Angels only: no sacrament. Beasts only: no sacrament. Man: sacrament at every turn and all levels of the "profane" and "sacred", in the trivial and in the profound, no escape from sacrament.'[15]

Sacrament mediates 'earth' – taken most broadly as the being or form of things – and 'heaven' – as the end towards which all beings are made and the gift by which all things are. Sign-making is this activity of relating through the work of our hands the material and the spiritual, earth and heaven, and ultimately beings and Being or creatures and the Creator. 'It is round about these deep questionings that artists contend when they work', writes Jones. 'Do they, in short, "fill up" in their arts "what is lacking" to the continuing processes of conjoining heaven and earth, or do they not? That is the question.'[16]

Sign-making is the mode of participation and furthering of this playfulness or gratuity of all things before the Maker. As he writes, 'A sign then must be significant

---

[13] For an excellent interpretation of Jones's participatory metaphysics, see Thomas R. Whitaker's essay, 'Homo Faber, Homo Sapiens', in *David Jones: Man and Poet*, ed. John Matthias (Maine, ME: National Poetry Foundation, 1989). For further exploration of the interpolation of *homo faber* and a participatory metaphysics within the Christian tradition, see Robert Miner, *Truth in the Making: Creative Knowledge in Theology and Philosophy* (New York: Routledge, 2004); and John Milbank, 'Christological Poetics', in *The Word Made Strange: Theology, Language, Culture* (Oxford: Blackwell, 1997), 123–44.

[14] Jones, 'Art and Sacrament', 153. See Rowan Williams's *Grace and Necessity: Reflections on Art and Love* (London: Continuum, 2005), 45–90 for an elegant exposition of Jones's work in light of this metaphysics of participation, particularly in relation to Jacques Maritain. Cf. also Aidan Nichols, O. P., who argues that '[Jones] embraced an entire theology, ultimately Thomist in inspiration, of the gratuitousness of creation and, by analogy, the gratuity of the work of artistic man' in *Redeeming Beauty: Soundings in Sacral Aesthetics* (Aldershot: Ashgate, 2007), 139. Jim Ede also writes that for Jones, 'most important of all was the Church's assertion against the moralists that God made and sustains everything GRATUITOUSLY. It is similarly this gratuitous quality, its lesser or greater presence that makes a painting good or bad', in *David Jones: A Memorial Exhibition* (Cambridge: Kettle's Yard Gallery, 1975), unpaginated.

[15] Jones, 'Art and Sacrament', 167. Jones is here trying to restore, as he puts it, the 'notion of sacrament with a small "s"' in Jones, 'Art and Sacrament', 178. In broadening our notion of sacrament, he does not thereby elide distinction between the sacraments of the Church such as baptism or the eucharist but instead understands these rites and those activities of the everyday, ordinary world as analogically related. This analogy means that he can speak of the activities of the everyday life as themselves being liturgical.

[16] Jones, 'Art in Relation to War', 143.

of something, hence of some "reality", so of something "good", so of something that is "sacred". That is why I think that the notion of sign implies the sacred.'[17] It is gratuitous in the same way that existence is itself gratuitous – brought into being freely and because of love, valued for simply being – the joy or delight that there is something rather than nothing. As he writes, 'There have been always frictions, estrangements and contradictions within man himself owing to the wedding within himself of the "utile" and the sacramental and … the fruit of this wedding was, to a less or greater degree, observable throughout the whole gamut of man's making.'[18] It is the negotiation of this tension that lends such creative dynamism and artfulness to human making. And yet, he continues, the problem with which he endlessly wrestles is this sense that the 'situational problem' of contemporary society is thus:

> Sometimes it looks as though a general separation had, by common consent, been made absolute and that the marriage contract certifying that man himself *is* this wedding had been nullified. Whereas we had supposed this union to be indissoluble and certainly had judged it to be consummated.[19]

The struggle so constitutive for Jones as a modern artist and for society more broadly is, 'How are we to reconcile man-the-artist, man the sign-maker or sacrament-maker with the world in which we live today? It would appear that there is a dichotomy which puts asunder that which our nature demands should be joined together.'[20]

How then are we to relate Jones's insistence on 'asking the question' in light of this understanding of the human being? Why might the question be important to this? Why is it that the question becomes the medium through which the gratuitous rather than 'simply functional'[21] arises? To stop and ask, 'Why, / what is this, / what's the meaning of this', interrupts our prosaic way of interacting with the world: it creates a kind of hiatus in us over against the tendency to bulldoze over things.[22] The question moves us from objectification to address; it creates a space for that which is close at hand to be something 'other' to us. To ask the question opens a space for a different kind of presence to manifest itself.

Furthermore, we might say that even to ask the question is itself a gratuitous act; it is not necessarily for an answer. As Jones writes, 'What little I have said is meant as a kind of question. A question to which I do not know the answer and which perturbs me all the day long.'[23] Rather than an instrument that can be merely manipulated for 'results', the question defines a continuing way of life. Jones's conviction that 'man remains, by definition, man-the-artist', despite all appearances does not solve the problem of the utile nor does it mean one no longer needs to 'ask the question'. On the contrary,

---

[17] Jones, 'Art and Sacrament', 157.
[18] Ibid., 176.
[19] Ibid., 176–7.
[20] Ibid., 178.
[21] Jones, 'The Utile', 176.
[22] Jones, *In Parenthesis*, 84.
[23] Jones, 'Use and Sign', 184.

his insistence on the need to continue asking the question arises precisely out of this conviction. As he writes in 'Art and Sacrament':

> That conviction will furnish no lorica or padding against the dilemmas and quandaries. Indeed, it is that conviction which strips off all defensive armour, so that the sharp contradictions and heavy incongruities may at least be felt. Vulnerability is essential, or we may not notice the dichotomy even if it exists.[24]

This interrogative stance imparts a way of being in the world, one characterized by vulnerability, even humility and loving attention. The point of the quest is not to delineate stark battle lines between the functional and the gratuitous, but to ask the way in which all things might be returned to their proper mode of participation in the Good. '[A] search for the sacred', as Rowan Williams discerns, 'is not looking for holy "territory" so much as searching for what lies beneath the surface'.[25]

Asking the question of 'A, a, a, DOMINE DEUS'

David Jones's poem, 'A, a, a, DOMINE DEUS', dramatizes this search for the sacramental amidst the artefacts that typify modern man and his epoch: 'perfected steel', 'automatic devices', 'glassy towers', 'nozzles and containers' – all products of that capitalized industrial beast, 'the Machine'. The poem provides no apparent resolution but remains ambivalent at best as to the endurance of sacrament in the era of the utile and its objects. Its minimalist, even utilitarian, language mirrors the sparse and barren landscape it paints. Perhaps this is a reflection of Jones's tutelage under the Maritainian principle to make art which 'by its subject and its roots, belongs to a time and a country'[26] – always a conflict for Jones to whom 'the present world-feeling is rather to be looked for, is better "illustrated", in a bomber plane, or an electric elevator'.[27] The apparent absence of 'His symbol' seems to define this poetic landscape as a desolate wasteland.

Most commentators on Jones's poem agree that it concludes in anguish and despair. So David Annwn writes of the final, '*Eia, Domine Deus*', 'There [is] no doubt at all that this line evokes an almost complete despair.'[28] And Colin Wilcockson similarly comments, 'not always does Jones see sense in everything; *A, a, a, Domine Deus* is an impassioned cry of despair.'[29] But, as Kathleen Henderson Staudt points out, Jones's comment on the title of this poem challenges us to question any unqualified conclusions. The poem, he

---

[24] Jones, 'Art and Sacrament', 178.
[25] Rowan Williams, *Silence and Honey Cakes: The Wisdom of the Desert* (Oxford: Lion Books, 2003), 112.
[26] Jacques Maritain, *Art and Scholasticism with Other Essays*, trans. J. F. Scanlan (London: Sheed & Ward, 1946), 61.
[27] Jones, 'Art in Relation to War', 137.
[28] David Annwn, *From A to Eia: A Small Book of David Jones' 'A, a, a DOMINE DEUS'* (Wakefield, West Yorkshire: Is Press, 1999), unpaginated.
[29] Colin Wilcockson, '"I Have Journeyed Among the Dead Forms": David Jones and the Wasteland Motif', *Flashpoints* (Spring 2010, Web Issue 13).

A, a, a, DOMINE DEUS

I said, Ah! what shall I write?
I enquired up and down.
                (He's tricked me before
with his manifold lurking-places.)
I looked for His symbol at the door.
I have looked for a long while
                at the textures and contours.
I have run a hand over the trivial intersections.
I have journeyed among the dead forms
causation projects from pillar to pylon.
I have tired the eyes of the mind
                regarding the colours and lights.
I have felt for His Wounds
                in nozzles and containers.
I have wondered for the automatic devices.
I have tested the inane patterns
                without prejudice.
I have been on my guard
                not to condemn the unfamiliar.
For it is easy to miss Him
                at the turn of a civilisation.

   I have watched the wheels go round in case I might see the living creatures like the appearance of lamps, in case I might see the Living God projected from the Machine. I have said to the perfected steel, be my sister and for the glassy towers I thought I felt some beginnings of His creature, but *A, a, a, Domine Deus*, my hands found the glazed work unrefined and the terrible crystal a stage-paste . . . *Eia, Domine Deus*.
                              c. *1938 and 1966.*

Figure 1 'A, a, a, DOMINE DEUS', in *The Sleeping Lord and Other Fragments*, London: Faber & Faber, 1974. Reproduced with permission of Faber & Faber

says, 'is really about how when you start saying in a kind of way how *bloody* everything is you end up in a kind of *praise-inevitably*'.[30] Can we see praise at the end of this poem? Certainly in no immediate way. And yet, for all its arid and desolate evocation of the modern wasteland, the poem offers itself as strangely habitable – a textual space that beckons return visits, luring the reader to mime its literary 'I': to look and look again at the poem's 'textures and contours', as though seeking 'His symbol at the door'; to fondle its disjuncted form as so many 'trivial intersections'; and to journey persistently from line to line as from 'pillar to pylon'. Contained on a single page (Jones's only poem of this length), the poem lends itself as an object to be turned over this way and that, akin to the artefacts the pilgrim-poet searchingly handles. And there are the many warnings within the poem itself that here need heeding: '(He's tricked me before/with his manifold lurking-places)'; and then again, just as the poem turns from verse to prose, one hears how 'it is easy to miss Him / at the turn of a civilization'. These injunctions turn the wheel of the poem itself, urging the reader to return once more in the hope of finding Him where He may yet lie hidden.

Remembering this poem is itself an artefact of the modern epoch, the question it then poses is whether it might itself yield the divine presence it so searchingly implores? Does it succumb to the modern malaise it despairs yet finally fails to transcend, or might the divine presence yet be discovered in the 'manifold lurking-places' of its lines? This is not a question easy to answer, but we might be encouraged to remember that Jones didn't particularly like supplying answers to questions. His responsibility, he felt, was to the question itself, to the interrogative stance. A. C. Everett characterizes this pattern in Jones's poetry as a 'dialectic of open question hidden answer, the quest itself being the answer'.[31] What might it mean then for us to ask the question of this poem? And what makes this poem and its readers' repeated returns more than another dutiful march through the gauntlet, more than the meaningless perpetuation of a cycle? In other words, what makes this perpetual turning momentous rather than monotonous?

In the following reading, I will suggest that Jones's artefact does not simply cast itself in despair amidst the rubble of the modern wilderness but that, precisely by asking the question of wasteland, it provides a way through it. To find this sacramental path through this wilderness, however, demands the cultivation of a different way of travel, perhaps even the turning of the 'I' of the poet himself. As Jacques Maritain in 'Frontiers of Poetry' warns, 'A revolution which does not effect a change of heart is a mere turning over of whitened sepulchres'.[32] I will trace this hidden path as it emerges through the gradual evolution of that most primary of vowels: from its opening exhale as 'Ah!' to the incantatory, '*A, a, a*', to its final invocation as '*Eia*'. For those who, like Mary of Bethany, take time to listen, this turning may be as momentous as it is subtle. It is these (r)evolutions of the capital 'A' which make this poem a hopeful performance rather than capitulation to despair.

---

[30] Letter to Jim and Helen Ede, 11 April 1939, quoted in Kathleen Henderson Staudt, 'The Decline of the West and the Optimism of the Saints: David Jones's Reading of Oswald Spengler', in *David Jones: Man and Poet*, ed. John Matthias (Orono, ME: National Poetry Foundation, 1989), 462.

[31] A. C. Everett, 'Doing and Making', in *David Jones: Diversity in Unity: Studies in His Literary and Visual Art*, ed. Belinda Humphrey and Anne Price-Owen (Cardiff: University of Wales Press, 2000), 72.

[32] Maritain, *Art and Scholasticism*, 80.

Before entering the poem itself, we might first want to know more about David Jones himself as a writer. In this next section, we'll briefly explore how Jones started writing poetry and how he negotiated some of these tensions posed by writing in, as Walter Benjamin aptly characterized it, 'the age of mechanical reproduction'.[33]

The art of writing in the age of mechanical reproduction

Jones is one of the few English artists to practice with such adeptness across both visual and verbal mediums. His first love was drawing, finding that as a young boy he struggled profoundly with his studies but always naturally picked up a pencil and paper with which to sketch.[34] At the very young age of 14 he went to Camberwell Art School where he studied until joining the Royal Welch Fusiliers for training as a soldier and crossing the channel to the war front in 1915. He returned to his studies in art at Westminster Art School in 1919. Following his new-found religious convictions through his experience at war and under the guidance of mentors like Father John O'Connor (the first translator of Jacques Maritain's *Art and Scholasticism* into English and, famously, the model for Chesterton's 'Father Brown' character), however, he eventually left these formal studies for the community of arts and craftsmen and women of Ditchling Commons, founded by Eric Gill and Hilary Pepler. Here Jones expanded his skill in the visual arts, trying his hand at wood carving and quickly excelling at wood engraving. Jones's obsession (as he himself described it) with drawing from a young age began to mature into a personal vocation. The intellectual stimulation and liturgical structure of the community's working rhythm seem to have offered him a platform from which he would go on to develop his unique voice as a working artist, integrating his many gifts into a way of life.[35]

It was not until the later 1920s that Jones began to experiment with writing poetry. He wanted, he says, to discover what it was like 'to make a shape with words'.[36] The broad and spacious concept of *ars*, learned through his time at Ditchling with Gill and his study there of Jacques Maritain's *Art and Scholasticism*,[37] facilitated such a move across mediums as it underlines the fundamental unity of this activity. Poetry consists no less than wood engraving or painting of 'a juxtaposing, of certain several parts with a view to establishing a certain whole'.[38] This venture across art forms, which Jones described as 'proceed[ing] from the known to the unknown',[39] produced one of the most loved and

---

[33] Walter Benjamin, *The Work of Art in the Age of Mechanical Reproduction* (London: Penguin Books, 2008).
[34] 'Autobiographical Talk', in *Epoch and Artist*, 26.
[35] For a detailed account of this period of formation in Jones's life, see Thomas Dilworth, *David Jones: Engraver, Soldier, Painter, Poet* (London: Jonathan Cape), especially chapters 3–5. Cf. also Thomas Dilworth, *David Jones and the Great War* (London: Enitharmon, 2012); and Keith Alldritt, *David Jones: Writer and Artist* (London: Constable & Robinson, 2003).
[36] Preface to *In Parenthesis*, x.
[37] Maritain, *Art and Scholasticism*, 74. The Ditchling community printed the first translation of this work into English by Rev. John O'Connor, published as *The Philosophy of Art: being 'Art et scholastique'* with an introduction by Eric Gill (Ditchling: St. Dominic's Press, 1923). Except in cases where it is particularly important for the sake of continuity to quote the translation by O'Connor which Jones himself used, I will be using this later, arguably better and more widely available, translation by J. F. Scanlan.
[38] Jones, 'Art and Sacrament', 159.
[39] 'Autobiographical Talk', in *Epoch and Artist*, 31.

profound long poems about the First World War, *In Parenthesis*. This incredible work is characterized by Jones's compassion and sense of humanity as well as its complex yet seemingly effortless layering of liturgical and mythical voices, interwoven with the rough and ready speech of the ordinary soldier.[40] 'As a result of meticulous adjustments during years of revision,' Dilworth reflects, 'dramatic voices operate like the unifying middle tone in a painting, their medial language allowing easy modulation between coarse lower-class eloquence and more formal "literary" expression.'[41]

His contemporaries and present-day critics still wonder at his ability to produce such a masterpiece without any previous experimentation in this art form. Ewan Clayton offers the fruitful suggestion that Jones's skill at intermingling voices, registers and tone should at least in part be seen as the fruit of his deep formation by the Roman liturgy:

> The Office is pieced together from many sources that span the centuries from Rome to the present day and draws on verse, song and scripture, invocation, litany, recapitulation and refrain. When Jones begins to write it could be argued that he instinctively relates to this way of 'making a writing' and taps in to the mind-set that anyone who has prayed in this way for an extended period of time develops. Texts are interwoven with reference to everyday experience and in the midst of everyday experience one comes to call on these timeless phrases, canticles and stories to give one's life shape and meaning.[42]

In his later epic poem, *The Anathemata*, this intimate connection between liturgical, cultural and literary form becomes more explicit as he enfolds the entire course of British history within the parentheses of the priest's consecration of the eucharistic elements. In its first lines, the scripted gestures and words of the priest are re-presented thus: 'We already and first of all discern him making this thing / other. His groping syntax, if we attend, already shapes: / ... the holy and venerable hands lift up an efficacious / sign.'[43] If the Mass is for Jones itself a work of art – indeed 'the work of art he loved the most'[44] – it is also the work from which he learned the most. As Francesca Brooks argues, 'Jones draws on the rubric of the Mass to provide a model for the performance of *The Anathemata* through visual and aural media. ... [He] is interested in what the enactment of the liturgy might teach the poet about the power of words and multi sensory media to make this material thing other.'[45] Further, rather than being at odds with Jones's own modernist context, the shape of the liturgy bears a certain likeness or kinship with modernist forms. As Thomas Dilworth reflects on the shape of the Mass: 'As art, it was essentially modernist: paratactic, without linear continuity, moving by juxtaposition and accumulation.'[46] Even as Jones adopts the

---

[40] For an account of Jones's character and development as a writer in relation to *In Parenthesis*, see Dilworth, *David Jones*, 128–30. Cf. also one of the most sensitive analyses of this subtle layering and interweaving of voices, Wilcockson, 'I Have Journeyed among the Dead Forms'.
[41] Dilworth, *David Jones*, 130.
[42] 'David Jones and the Guild of St. Joseph and St. Dominic', in *David Jones in Ditchling: 1921–1924*, ed. Derek Shiel (Ditchling: Ditchling Museum, 2003), 20.
[43] David Jones, *The Anathemata: Fragments of an Attempted Writing* (London: Faber & Faber, 1952), 49.
[44] Dilworth, *David Jones*, 69.
[45] Francesca Brooks, 'Liturgy, Performance, and Poetry of the Passion: David Jones and *The Dream of the Rood*', *Religion and Literature* 49.1 (2017): 91–101.
[46] Dilworth, *David Jones*, 69.

poetic techniques of his contemporaries, he also, in a manner akin to Chesterton and Tolkien (both influences upon Jones), transforms them.[47] As Alison Milbank argues, their shared metaphysics of the gift and participation, inherited through the writing of Jacques Maritain, means that such techniques do not merely reinforce a sense of the absurd or end in despair. Rather, they use such forms ultimately towards the end of a kind of re-gifting. We might say that he employs, even exploits, modernist techniques as different ways of 'asking the question'.

Milbank points us to this all-important text from Jacques Maritain's *Art and Scholasticism*: 'Our art does not derive from itself alone what it imports to things; it spreads over them a secret which it first discovered in them, in their invisible substance or in their endless exchanges and correspondences.'[48] This 'secret seed', according to Maritain's transcendental realism, is actually in the being of the object – this is, that divine spark, that participatory relation which all things have through their share in being. As 'secret', however, it needs to be rooted out, perceived, by an intelligent creature. There is thus an objective and subjective element at play. As Milbank summarizes:

> This form is both within the object (as recognised or divined by the artist/reader) and within the mind of the perceiver, forming the bridge between them. To detect this form is both to see the object as itself but also as *more* than itself: objects are both revelatory and hidden; they mean more than they seem or, as Maritain has it, there is a secret. The suspension of understanding in the defamiliarization effect stages and precipitates this sense of a hidden secret, of what Maritain calls an 'ontological secret' and David Jones calls gratuity.[49]

The technique of defamiliarization is especially important to the quest of 'A, a, a, DOMINE DEUS'. Milbank defines the technique thus:

> in the act of lingering over the words on the page or the problematic painting, the gap between the signifier – the word on the page or the painted form – and the signified – its meaning is stretched out as far as possible, so that in that mental space, the image is formed in the mind, and not immediately referred on to the referent: that is, the object signified as a phenomenon in the physical world.[50]

The end of the technique is to challenge the reader's assumed knowledge of a thing, to interrupt a too cosy sense of ownership and to instead focus on the 'process of perception' as a good in itself. However, as Milbank argues, Jones's understanding of the 'more than', of the gratuity in signification, supplements this modernist technique and the ends towards which it is used. We will see how Jones's poem, 'A, a, a, DOMINE

---

[47] See Alison Milbank, *Chesterton and Tolkien as Theologians: The Fantasy of the Real* (London: T&T Clark, 2008); and Alison Milbank, 'Make It New: Defamiliarization and Sacramentality in David Jones', in *David Jones: A Christian Modernist?*, ed. Jamie Callison, Paul S. Fiddes, Anna Johnson and Erik Tonning (Boston: Brill, 2018), 70.
[48] Milbank, 'Make It New', 74.
[49] Ibid., 71.
[50] Ibid., 64.

DEUS' dramatizes the gap between signifier and signified, thereby drawing the reader into the 'space between', this kind of suspended middle, in order to return the world back to us again, anew. 'Making strange' is ultimately a redemptive strategy. Or, as Alison Milbank puts it, 'the world is made strange in order to be re-enchanted'.[51]

Participating in this space between is a form of 'asking the question'. It is a kind of spiritual practice or discipline, requiring the development of the spiritual senses through which this form of things is perceived. The artist's work is to find the form of things wherever they occur and re-present them anew under another form. This process of re-presenting brings things back from this slide towards nothingness towards their fulfilment as participants in the Good. It is a practice in loving attention, a spiritual exercise, and also a way of 'asking the question'. Jones's poem then may be read as an exercise in making both the Incarnation and the world itself strange, or rather, as restoring our sense of its inherently radical newness.

The subtleties to which Jones's poem invites us may be discerned by way of comparison with the title of his epic poem, *The Anathemata* – a pun which turns on the difference one letter makes to the history of the word and its meaning. In the Greek New Testament, ανάθεμα or αναθήματα means the despised or rejected things, the same meaning carried forward by contemporary English. However, Jones recovers an alternate meaning of the word that, surprisingly, is nearly its antonym, meaning the 'devoted things' or 'something holy'.[52] This latter meaning was, in fact, the one more commonly used throughout the ancient world. Despite its foreignness, the meaning is not entirely lost to modern English, for this older 'beneficent meaning', as Jones calls it, is carried forward by the alternate plural form of 'anathemata'. The variant spellings in the Greek become a key for separating the English 'anathema' (presumably dependent on the *epsilon* [ε] variant) and 'anathemata', which draws on the *eta* [η] variant. Jones chooses this as his title not only in order to recover its 'ancient and beneficent meaning' but also precisely because the other meaning of 'despised, rejected things' is still taken up in it. In other words, he doesn't assert a blanket dichotomy between the despised and the devoted. Instead, the pun invites us to ask questions about this distinction and, more boldly, to question what things we consider despised and what things devoted, or, in more familiar terms, between the sacred and the profane. As he concludes, 'So I mean by my title as much as it can be made to mean, or can evoke or suggest, however obliquely: the blessed things that have taken on what is cursed and the profane things that somehow are redeemed.'[53]

But how do we engage with a text that seeks to perform 'the question'? What sort of readers does it require? Jones's answer is itself strikingly material. In his preface to *The Anathemata*, Jones directs his readers in the *way* he intends his poem to be read, principles which are applicable not just to this work but to all his poems (and paintings for that matter). Reading, for Jones, is a performative act, the text akin to a score, needing the ears and eyes and tongue – the physical body – of the reader as that

---

[51] Ibid., 71.
[52] The following exposition draws on Jones's own explanation of the term in his preface to *The Anathemata*, 28–9.
[53] Ibid., 28–9.

which moves her sensitive intelligence or a kind of 'feeling thought'. He writes, 'I intend what I have written to be said. ... You can't get the intended meaning unless you hear the sound and you can't get the sound unless you observe the score; and pause-marks on a score are of particular importance.'[54] This analogy with a musical score is worth unfolding as it goes to the heart of Jones's philosophy of art. The composer's work of art becomes the *materia* with which the musician or dancer will exercise her own art. Similarly, interpretation – or the skill of reading with understanding – is to play, with more or less degrees of sensitivity and acuity, the score of the text. For the artist-reader, her *materia* is the form and content of this written word, which passes through hidden 'transmogrifications' of the mind of the reader – this is that element which makes all art, even those considered most representationalist, abstract.[55] To read with understanding is itself to 're-present' and so to participate in this gratuitous activity of sign-making.

Above all, the significance of this analogy with the playing of a musical score is that it *takes time*. Jones is eager to emphasize this point: 'Lastly, it is meant to be said with deliberation – slowly as opposed to quickly – but "with deliberation" is the best rubric for each page, each sentence, each word.'[56] The practice of reading slowly is inimical to an age whose spirit is defined by efficiency and speed. 'Each word,' he insists, 'cannot do its work unless it is given due attention. It was written to be read in that way.'[57] Reading slowly cultivates virtue; it builds the habit of loving attention. Not only the words, but the pauses and spacings between words are meant to be inhabited by the reader; their function, too, is to mediate meaning. They slow the reader down and facilitate rumination. The true ornamentation of the page comes through its readership.

Jones's deep appreciation for the materiality of language and the medium of the printed page is clearly intrinsic to his understanding of the work of poetry itself. Even as a young boy, this physicality of the written word was impressed upon Jones, his father being a printer's overseer.[58] His analogy of the poem to a window casement is particularly remarkable:

> Thus a piece of turned iron pierced at intervals, and formed at one end to handle, by which we regulate the opening of a casement-window is neither less or more contrived by Ars than are those juxtaposings of concepts that take material expression under the shapes of arranged lines of words, spaces, commas, points, by which poets regulate the openings of casements for us to enjoy and suffer the sights they would show us.[59]

---

[54] Ibid., 35.
[55] See Jones's analysis of William Hogarth's 'Shrimp Girl' in 'Art and Sacrament', in *Epoch and Artist*, 174.
[56] Jones, *The Anathemata*, 35.
[57] Ibid., 36.
[58] As Jones tells us, 'At the time of my birth my father was a printer's overseer and that meant that I was brought up in a home that took the printed page and its illustration for granted' in Jones, 'Autobiographical Talk', in *Epoch and Artist*, 26.
[59] Jones, 'Art and Sacrament', 151.

For Jones, to write skilfully is to open a window for his readers: the dense physical space of the printed page is like a casement window waiting to be opened once more by the willing reader.

The spirit of Jones's embrace and use of the printed page as a poetic medium is illuminated by Robert Bringhurst in his essay, 'Typography without Typographers'. 'Typography,' he writes, 'is to literature as musical performance is to composition: an essential act of interpretation, full of endless opportunity for insight or obtuseness.'[60] Jones would have appreciated Bringhurst's understanding of typography as an essentially human craft. The roots of this modern-day craft reside in the art of the pre-modern scribe. Remembering these roots resists tendencies to reduce typography to 'nothing more than a colorless, tiresome, fiddly subdepartment of graphic design'.[61] Its fidelity is first to language, and so to meaning. 'A typographer,' Bringhurst insists, 'is a kind of scribe: one who has learned, through patient apprenticeship, how to work at second hand, replacing fingers, pen, and brush with a network of machines.'[62] As this network of machines becomes the very medium for the typographer's art, its craftsmanship resides in her capacity to create 'forms [which] still savour of the hands and minds that made them, not of machines that mimic the hands, nor of computers emulating the machines'.[63] He continues,

> It may seem that she works most of the time in the visual mode, but the typographer's first allegiance is not to anything graphic; her allegiance is to language and to something beyond language: to that quality in things – I like to call it poetry – which calls language into being. In simple terms, what drives the typographer is the existence of something to *say*. Or of something that *speaks*, if you like to put it that way. Typography is the sound of one hand speaking, vivid in the mind's eye, vivid in the mind's ear, silent as a prayer.[64]

As we will suggest, Jones's short poem is as much a carefully crafted work of typography as it is modernist verse, drawing the eyes and ears of its readers towards this 'something that speaks' even, or especially, in the silence.

The longer one dwells in the space of this wasteland poem, the more one sees. Hidden secrets are everywhere to be found. Indeed, Jones tells us by the peculiar dating of the poem that this has taken him twenty-eight years to write; it is saturated with meaning. How is one to read such a rich artefact? Rather than attempting to provide a purely literary or historical exegesis – who, after all, can know everything in the mind of the artist over the course of more than a quarter century? – in what follows, I engage in a kind of theological amusement catalysed by the poem but not contained

---

[60] Robert Bringhurst, *The Elements of Typographic Style*, 4th edn (Seattle, WA: Hartley and Marks, 2012), 19.
[61] Robert Bringhurst, 'Typography without Typographers', in *Everywhere Being Is Dancing: Twenty Pieces of Thinking* (Berkeley: Counterpoint Press, 2008), 218.
[62] Ibid., 219.
[63] Robert Bringhurst, *Tree of Meaning: Language, Mind and Ecology* (Berkeley: Counterpoint Press, 2008), 275.
[64] Bringhurst, 'Typography without Typographers', 219.

by it. I seek to show how a performative and participatory engagement with 'A, a, a, DOMINE DEUS' raises a series of extraordinary theological themes. Our reading explores how this poem which appears to be a desolate wasteland devoid of divine presence may yet be dripping with sacramental significance.

Performing the quest of 'A, a, a, DOMINE DEUS'

Jones's poem begins, on the title line, where written language begins, with the first letter of the alphabet, the capital and lowercase 'A' and 'a'. This letter, as David Annwn perceptively points out, is the first letter of not only the English or Latin alphabets but also the Greek Alpha and the Hebrew Aleph. But rather than forming this letter through syntactical relations into a word, that is, as the article 'a', as one might expect in the title of a poem, we encounter instead a series of stops and starts. This 'A, a, a,' has the character of infant babble more than articulate speech. How strange, then, that this most basic of sounds or half-speech is here a prelude for the pronouncement of the Divine Name itself: 'DOMINE DEUS'. The strong dental consonants of the 'D' and 'D' interrupt this rhythmic, pulsing, plucking sound. The all-capital letters of the Name in the erudite language of Latin seem to dominate or tower over the page. Even the spacing between each of these letters of the Name is doubled, contributing to its monumental, inscription-like character. It demands our attention, yet at the same time feels aloof, imposing and unyielding as letters carved in stone. What are we to make of this spatial rendering of the divine name?[65]

This all-capital DOMINE DEUS (or LORD GOD in English translations) is used in the Scriptures as a means of distinguishing this divine name from all other names. The LORD GOD or DOMINE DEUS translates the mysterious name given to Moses at the burning bush:

> But Moses said to God, 'If I come to the Israelites and say to them, "The God of your ancestors has sent me to you", and they ask me, "What is his name?" what shall I say to them?' God said to Moses, 'I AM WHO I AM.' He said further, 'Thus you shall say to the Israelites, "I AM has sent me to you."' God also said to Moses, 'Thus you shall say to the Israelites, "The LORD, the God of your ancestors, the God of Abraham, the God of Isaac, and the God of Jacob, has sent me to you."
> This is my name for ever,
> and this my title for all generations.'

This Name given to Moses paradoxically cannot be uttered or even written but only transcribed as 'I AM WHO I AM' [*EYHEH ASHER EYHEH*] or 'I WILL BE WHO

---

[65] Alison Milbank also notes this inscription-like character of the divine name in this poem in her 'Make It New', 75. She suggests this renders the name more like a 'thing' and so as a material object in the world that can mediate truth. I will develop this suggestion more extensively by attending to the inscription-like character of the poem as a whole and showing how the meaning of the name unfolds through time or the journey, that is, through the course of wasteland poem itself, returning to us in new, albeit even more hidden and subtle form, by means of these repetitions.

I WILL BE'.[66] These 'translations' are more like glosses on the Hebrew *YHWH*, the tetragrammaton, playing on its similarity in sound to the Hebrew word for being itself – *hayah* or 'to be'. The name signifies the God of Israel as the One God, the Creator of all times and places or the 'Maker of all that is, seen and unseen'.[67] By the power of this name, or by the power of the One who has given the name, the Israelites would be set free from their bondage to the Egyptians. However, the deeper meanings of the name would be learned through the Israelites' lonely yet perhaps more intimate space of the forty years wandering in the wilderness. Here they would learn the meaning of the name as a dependence upon YHWH for even daily food and drink. If the meaning of the name could only be learned from the journey through the wilderness, so too the journey of this poem invites us to a similar quest. From this point of entry into the wasteland of this literary landscape, the monumental character of the divine name seems only to hover in space, its meaning as yet unclear, as though the signifier of a presence remote and unyielding. Will the journey tell us something more? Something other?

Far from wooing us gradually into the wilderness, and 'speaking tenderly' to us (Hos. 2.14), the simple past declarative, 'I said', of the narrator's voice throws us into the middle: 'I said, Ah! what shall I write?' His voice is insistent and a repetition, as though he has told this tale before. His question immediately projects to the future: 'what shall I write?' The narrative begins in this suspended place, the time just before literary creation. However, this would-be author's pen remains hovering just above the page for the poem's duration. Its opening question acts as an interruptive gesture rather than the actual beginning of creative work. The latter has become a problem to itself, such a problem that it remains the focal point of the poem itself, like a scratch on a record when a needle skips, threatening to forestall the unfolding of the song.

However, the slight interjection, 'Ah!', inserted between the simple past and simple future, is not without consequence. This 'Ah!' is the first repetition of the capital 'A' since its titular announcement. But its repetition here is marked by a difference. The addition of that little 'h' – the sign of the aspirate in the English language – draws attention to the breath, the necessary, physical force which must be placed behind this 'A' enabling it to be audible, actual speech. This sighing 'Ah!' recalls the beginnings of human speech itself. *Webster Dictionary* describes the pronunciation of 'A' here as neither short nor long but 'low and back': 'ä as in *calm* and *father*.... It is formed with lax tongue muscles and with the lips more open than for any other vowel.'[68] It is that little 'h' which turns this opening of the lips and tongue around this most primal of vowels from a merely mute, gaping mouth towards the first creation of speech. As David Annwn reflects, 'this is the "low-back-wide" vowel formed with the widest opening of the jaws, pharynx and lips. It is often the baby's earliest sound in crying, both in inhalation and exhalation, and is a basic constituent in the universal proto-words of infancy: "Ma" and "Da".'[69]

---

[66] For an elegant and precise exposition of the doctrine of *creatio ex nihilo* in relation to the giving of the divine name to Moses in Exodus 3, see Janet Martin Soskice, '*Creatio ex nihilo*: Jewish and Christian foundations', in *Creation and the God of Abraham*, ed. David B. Burrell, Carlo Cogliati, Janet M. Soskice and William R. Stoeger (Cambridge: Cambridge University Press, 2010), 24–39.
[67] *The Nicene Creed*, http://anglicansonline.org/basics/nicene.html.
[68] *Webster's New Universal Unabridged Dictionary* (New York: Random House, 1996), xxi.
[69] Annwn, *From A to Eia*, unpaginated.

This widening of the jaw reveals not an empty hole, but an aspirate, the beginnings of human life and speech.

If this breath marks the beginning of human speech, so too might it recall the words spoken at the beginning of all creation itself: 'In the Beginning when God created the heavens and the earth, the earth was a formless void and darkness covered the face of the deep, while a wind from God swept over the face of the waters. Then God said' (Gen. 1.1). The Word of God issues forth from the Father through the power of the Spirit, bringing all things into being. But Jones's poem invites us to pause in the space of this '...', in this moment of creation just pending, the Spirit hovering over the pregnant waters.

The refrain 'what shall I write?' is also characteristic of so many of the spokespersons for God throughout the Hebrew Bible. We have heard Moses ask, 'what shall I say to them?' (Gen. 3.13). The prophet Jeremiah is especially echoed here: 'Then I said, Ah, Lord GOD! Truly I do not know how to speak, for I am only a boy' (1.6). Isaiah also: 'A voice says, "Cry out!" And I said, "What shall I cry?"' (40.6). Through its repetition of these prophet's cries, we might begin to hear something more in the opening question of this poem: Not only '*what* shall I write?' but, more piercingly, '*how* do I write at all'? What is the origin of human words, of human artefacts, their status, worth and purpose?

In this next line the pilgrim-poet turns outside himself to the world of creation around him for a reply to his question: 'I enquired up and down.' The 'up and down' indicates something of the cosmic dimensions of this search. This passage from Shakespeare's *Midsummer Night's Dream*, which Jones knew well, describes the poet's process of writing as also beginning in this enquiring 'from heaven to earth, from earth to heaven':

> The poet's eye, in a fine frenzy rolling,
> Doth glance from heaven to earth, from earth to heaven;
> And as imagination bodies forth
> The forms of things unknown, the poet's pen
> Turns them to shapes and gives to airy nothing
> A local habitation and a name.[70]

The 'I'/eye of Jones's poem itself enacts this journey, initiating this 'fine frenzy rolling' up and down the left-hand margin of the page. Will he thus find 'the forms of things unknown' and transform them into 'a local habitation and a name'?[71] The cosmic ascent and descent of this enquiry is immediately interrupted. The next line leads the eye not 'up and down' but sideways. The narrative voice breaks off with this parenthetical aside: '(He's tricked me before / with his manifold lurking places.)' This kind of parenthetical, bardic wink steps aside from the main narrative that has just begun. The

---

[70] Act V, Scene 1, lines 12–17 in *A Midsummer Night's Dream*, ed. R. A. Foakes (Cambridge: Cambridge University Press, 2003), 124.

[71] In his preface to *The Anathemata*, Jones queries the possibility of Shakespeare's vision of the poet's sacramental vocation in the modern world thus: 'To what degree, for instance, is it possible for the "name" to evoke the "local habitation" long since gone?', 25.

capitalized personal pronoun, 'He', points us back to the all-capital 'DOMINE DEUS' of the title line and the inset margin of this parentheses is aligned directly below it. This interruption to the narrative begins to inflect the opening question with new meaning. We are now inclined to ask not just 'what shall I write?' or even how shall I write? but for whom am I looking? Why do we need to find 'Him' in order to write? This 'who' becomes the prior question. More to the point here, where is He to be found? The language 'tricked' teases our interest further. Is this a cunning and deceptive rouse or a playful lover's game? The juxtaposition of 'manifold' and 'lurking-places' is itself strange, suggesting this crafty being could be hiding anywhere.

'Manifold' simply means 'many' or 'variety' and has diverse uses, from an engine manifold to the 'manifold mercies' of the Mass. Hopkins's great 'Kingfisher' poem resonates within this parenthesis: 'Christ plays in ten thousand places, / Lovely in limbs, and lovely in eyes not his / To the Father through the features of men's faces.'[72] Yet in contrast to the manifold beings of Hopkins's poem – kingfishers, dragonflies and the just man – this pilgrim-poet will be searching the 'dead forms', 'automatic devices' and 'perfected steel'. Can these also find 'tongue to fling out broad its name?' Can the pilgrim-poet himself 'act in God's eye what in God's eye he is'? Might Christ be manifest within the many folds of this poem too, even if they are only 'lurking-places', half-presences and traces? In his essay 'Art and Sacrament', Jones calls to mind the figure of Wisdom dancing playfully at the time of Creation:

> It is Holy Wisdom herself who says *ludo* [I play]. In the famous passage in the Book of Proverbs she is made to say *ludens in orbe terrarum*. She was with the Logos, when all things were formed, 'playing before him at all times' and as the Knox translation puts it: 'I made play in this world of dust, with the sons of Adam for my play-fellows.'[73]

So too may Wisdom Herself be dancing in the margins or the parentheses of this wasteland poem, luring us to play.

The pilgrim-poet resumes his narrative. His 'up and down' enquiry and sideways glance has led to another threshold place: 'I looked for His symbol at the door.' The definite article invites the question, what door and what is 'His symbol'? Might this imagery return us once more to the story of the Israelites on their Exodus from Egypt, just before they enter the wilderness? On the crucial night before being freed from their long exile in Egypt, the people are instructed to mark their doorposts with the blood of the sacrificed lamb so 'when he [the LORD] sees the blood on the lintel and on the two doorposts, the LORD will pass over that door and will not allow the destroyer to enter' (Exod. 12.23). The Jewish Passover points forward to the Christian Eucharistic feast and to Christ as the Passover Lamb whose blood is the covering or propitiation for sin. Is 'His symbol' the cross? If this is the symbol the pilgrim-poet seeks, we might at this stage at least ask, why? Why does the poet first look for the symbol of the blood

---

[72] Gerard Manley Hopkins, *A Critical Edition of the Major Works* (Oxford: Oxford University Press, 1986), 129.
[73] Jones, 'Art and Sacrament', 154.

of Christ in order to write? Is it mercy for himself that he seeks? We also might want to note here that if we read this line in the context of the Passover, it is actually the LORD Himself who stands outside the door and looks. Are we so confident we know the identity of this 'I'?

With the next line, time itself begins to feel distended: 'I have looked for a long while / at the textures and contours.' This repetition of 'looked' here with the auxiliary 'I have' increases our sense of the poet's labour, as though he has lingered so long outside the door, looking for these signs of ritual devotion, that the door has itself become the object of contemplation. His gaze becomes an intimate form of touch, tracing its 'textures and contours' and indeed the next line turns explicitly to touch: 'I have run a hand over the trivial intersections.' Despite his apparent loving intention, the pilgrim-poet is rebuffed by a seemingly non-intentional or 'trivial' world.[74] If one of the possible meanings of 'His symbol' is the cross, what makes these intersections 'trivial' or inconsequential rather than an efficacious sign?

That this playful hunt has morphed into a seemingly solitary descent becomes more apparent in the following line: 'I have journeyed among the dead forms.' The pilgrim-poet reached the depths of 'classical Hades … a place of no happiness'.[75] And yet, we still need to question the meaning of 'dead forms'. As David Annwn's reading reminds us, Jones is keen to insist that insofar as something has form it must be alive or real to some degree. We might recall his discussion of the definition of art in 'Art and Sacrament', broad enough to include even the strategy of war: 'insofar as form is brought into being there is reality', he writes. ' "Something" not "nothing", moreover a new "something", has come into existence.'[76] Can there really be such a thing as a 'dead form'? If there is form, there must be some 'being', some *esse*, however buried, fragmented or disenchanted.[77] Like the valley of dry bones in Ezekiel's vision, it may still be that, as Jones suggests in *In Parenthesis*, 'these raw bones live'.[78] The pilgrim-poet's journey among these dead forms may gesture once more to the person of Christ Himself as the One who descended into Hell, a journey that undoes the finality of death itself.

The upright and erect forms of 'pillar and pylon' of the next line counterbalance this circuit of the poet's eye from its downward descent to an upward climb, recalling once more Shakespeare's line, 'the poet's eye … doth glance from heaven to earth, from earth to heaven'. Pillars and pylons belong to the ancient and modern world alike as symbols of the achievements of human culture and civilization. In the journey through the wilderness, the presence of the LORD is symbolized by 'the pillar of cloud by day, to lead them along the way, and in a pillar of fire by night, to give them light' (Exod. 13.21). Yet the mechanical language 'causation projects' of this poem flattens any sense of genuine transcendence or divine presence here despite their ambitious vertical ascent. Furthermore, by the time we reach this point in the narrative, the multiple 'I's

---

[74] Cf. Song of Songs 2.4, 'and his intention toward me was love'.
[75] Thomas Dilworth, *The Shape of Meaning in the Poetry of David Jones* (Toronto: University of Toronto Press, 1988), 263.
[76] Jones, 'Art and Sacrament', 159.
[77] Ibid., 157. David Annwn makes this point in *From A to Eia*, unpaginated.
[78] Jones, *In Parenthesis*, 175.

of the pilgrim-poet have themselves begun to increasingly stack up along the margin of the page, imitating the monumental climb of these towers, except for their interruption by this jutting line – a suggestion perhaps of the breaking up of these pretences of human civilization and of the continuity of the bardic voice itself.

If the eye of the poet has swept along this 'rectilineal plane upwards',[79] he assures us in the next line that he too has sought to see within and through these forms, to the inner folds and spiritual depths of the material world: 'I have tired the eyes of the mind / regarding the colours and lights.' The 'eyes of the mind' recalls a text we know to have been salient to Jones, the Preface of the Christmas Mass, which reads, 'For by the mystery of the Word made Flesh, the Light of your brightness renews the eyes of our mind.'[80] For human creatures who are both intelligent and embodied, the spiritual ascent is dependent upon the mediation of the material world for drawing and expanding it upwards. Thus have the sun, moon and stars fuelled the imagination and metaphysical reflections of philosophers throughout human history. In his poem, 'The Sleeping Lord', Jones holds up the artefact of the candle as one of the fruits of the wedding of the utile and sacramental in human nature, its flame gently illuminating the present as well as leading the mind upward to the Invisible Light: 'for the quivering gleam of it / is of living light / and light /(so these *clerigwyr* [clerks, clerics] argue) / is, in itself, a good'.[81] In contrast to this gentle, quivering glow of candle flames, in the desolation of this poem's landscape, the functionalist, even ugly sounding preposition, 'regarding', casts its dim light forward and shapes how we imagine 'the colours and lights' as the 'bland megalopolitan light / where no shadow is by day or by night'.[82] In this urban wasteland, the poet's vision is dulled by overexposure, lacking genuine illumination.

If he has 'tired the eyes of the mind', the poet once more returns to the sense of touch with this intimation of bodily devotion to Christ: 'I have felt for His Wounds / in nozzles and containers.' Though the subject is the vulnerable, wounded body of the Lord, it is the vulnerability of the poet himself that comes to the fore in these lines, as though this quest is opening and wounding him. These lines fall at the midsection or navel of the poem (lines 13–14 of 28), and one feels drawn to the centre of something here in this quest's 'strange power of speech'.[83] Found at the end of pipes or tubes, nozzles are used to control or regulate the flow of liquid. Are we being invited to entertain the image of the wounds of Christ as nozzles through which flows the salvific blood? Might the containers not evoke – or rather, parody – the eucharistic chalice? The imagery recalls

---

[79] Cf. Jones's poem, 'The Wall', written from the perspective of a Roman soldier enquiring into the status, foundation and claims of the Roman Empire itself: 'did that wall contain a world / from the beginning / did they project the rectilineal plan upwards / to the floor of heaven', in *The Sleeping Lord and Other Fragments* (London: Faber & Faber, 1974), 12.

[80] *The Missal in Latin and English, Being the Text of the Misalle Romanum with English Rubrics and a New Translation* (London: Burns Oates and Washbourne, 1950). Jones's painted inscription of this text is the subject of our next chapter and is reproduced in Nicolete Gray, *Painted Inscriptions of David Jones* (London: Gordon Fraser, 1981), 56, catalogue no. 22.

[81] Jones, 'The Sleeping Lord', 77.

[82] Jones, 'The Tutelar of the Place', 63.

[83] Line 587 in Samuel Taylor Coleridge, *The Rime of the Ancient Mariner*, illustrated and introduced by David Jones, ed. with preface and afterword by Thomas Dilworth (London: Enitharmon Press, 2005), 78.

the motif of medieval paintings that picture saints or angels holding chalices before the cross to catch the blood which flows from the side of Christ, embraced in this graphic imagery as the very birthplace of the Church. Would the modern conceit, by contrast, be to control or perhaps even plug the flow of this healing blood, to 'contain' it? The deep irony of the juxtaposition is piercing in itself.

And yet, here at this deepest moment of painful – almost blasphemous – irony, one wonders if the imagination of the reader isn't unduly altered here. There is something irresistibly delightful, even joyous, about the word 'nozzles' in its resonance with noses, navels and novels. This jarring of expectations through the juxtaposition of the sacred and the profane might even draw an unexpected smile from the reader. Nozzles are things we don't think about much, let alone include in poems of epic descent and ascent. And yet, can one ever look at a nozzle the same? Could this functionalist tool be as important as the grand narrative of a novel? One starts to wonder about the ordinary as a possible place of enchantment after all. Furthermore, the wounds of Christ themselves, those 'objects' of religious devotion, are made strange and delivered to us entirely anew through association with this most 'secular' or utile of modern objects. Jones's 'anathemata' logic is put to great effect here as 'the blessed things ... have taken on what is cursed and the profane things ... somehow are redeemed'.[84] Both the secular and the sacred orders are unsettled, overturned; too cosy identifications are disrupted. This contemplation of the physical body of the Lord through the ordinary physical objects of the utile world enacts precisely the strange logic of the Gospels which Jones himself remarks on thus: 'The very incidents which may strike us as the most poetic and mythological ... are inextricably interwoven by the evangelists with down-to-earth existence at its most personal, its most prosaic and even squalid; and it is precisely in this that they see the saving mystery.'[85] It is this interweaving of the profound and the prosaic that distinguishes the Christian myth, writes Jones, 'transform[ing] the pattern completely'.[86] So too does the quest of this poem seek to partake in this 'saving mystery', weaving together the sacred and the profane and insisting on the possibility of finding Christ in these 'lurking-places'.

From this midsection of the poem the pilgrim-poet still journeys onward: 'I have wondered for the automatic devices.' Wonder, this stance of the philosopher, is directed here at the 'automatic devices' that dominate modern life in both the domestic and public spheres – alarm clocks, electric kettles but also, more darkly, automatic weapons and machinery. Jones himself has in fact frequently meditated on the significance of the latter, having been deeply formed by his time as a soldier in the Great War. These weapons may be seen, as he elsewhere argues, as the unconscious symbols of the age: 'For the gods of the power-age are best symbolised by those objects which are themselves power-devices. ... A severe, disinterested, unalloyed "functional-art", directed altogether toward action at its most characteristic and most intense.'[87] In his poem, *In Parenthesis*, the artefact of the gun takes on the character of a fetishized

---

[84] Preface to *The Anathemata*, 28–9.
[85] Quoted in Adam Schwartz, *The Third Spring: G. K. Chesterton, Graham Greene, Christopher Dawson, and David Jones* (Washington, DC: Catholic University Press, 2005), 358.
[86] Ibid.
[87] Jones, 'Religion and the Muses', 104, n. 2.

object with an agency of its own – the soldier's best friend, his only defence, his sister, even his lover. This biting speech is exemplary:

> and you
> men must really cultivate the habit of treating this weapon with
> the very greatest care and there should be a healthy rivalry
> among you – it should be a matter of very proper pride and
> Marry it man! Marry it!
> Cherish her, she's your very own.
> Coax it man coax it – it's delicately and ingeniously made
> – it's an instrument of precision – it costs us tax-payers,
> money – I want you men to remember that.
> Fondle it like a granny – talk to it – consider it as you would
> a friend[88]

In truth, it is the soldier who comes to be possessed by the gun and the marching soldier himself reduced to an automaton, a 'stiff marionette jerking on the uneven path'.[89] The poem itself concludes with the urgent call that the soldier leave his gun 'under the oak', thus rending open this relationship forged so tightly between the man and his weapon. The soldier thereby turns not only this weapon but his own identification with it, and even his own splintered self, into an offering, a sacrament. Once released, however, the gun itself becomes capable of reflecting light, a symbol of hope: 'Its dark barrel, where you leave it under the oak, reflects the solemn star that rises urgently from Cliff Trench.'[90] Even the gun of the modern soldier, like the spear of the Roman soldier that pierced the flesh of Christ Himself, is capable of becoming a redemptive sign. The search of this pilgrim-poet has begun to query not so much the artefacts themselves as his relationship to them. It may not be the objects which need saving but the poet himself, his relationship to these things that is in question. To be able to see beauty in the things that one has rejected as 'anathema' is essential to undoing the spell of the utile.

The disciplinary language of the next few lines is striking; the persona of the soldier, it seems, persists: 'I have tested the inane patterns / without prejudice. / I have been on my guard / not to condemn the unfamiliar. / For it is easy to miss Him / at the turn of a civilisation.' The phrase 'inane patterns' confronts the reader again with a frustrating oxymoron, akin to the 'dead forms'. A pattern should imply intelligent design and yet these are found senseless.[91] The patterns do not yield meaningful intent but seem empty and vain. So too does the structure of the poem test the reader as a pattern begins to emerge in the number of lines flush with the margin, beginning with two then breaking, then three lines before another break and finally building to four lines before another break. But then, instead of building to five, the pattern dissolves

---

[88] Jones, *In Parenthesis*, 183–4.
[89] Ibid., 37.
[90] Ibid., 186.
[91] As also noted by Annwn in *From A to Eia*, unpaginated.

at the midsection and the lines only fall or break more rapidly: 1 – break – 2 – break – 1 – break – 1 – break. The disintegration enacted here recalls this judgement also from *In Parenthesis*: 'it's like no-man's-land between yesterday and tomorrow and material things are but barely integrated and loosely tacked together.'[92]

The language of 'testing' is not only military but recalls the biblical language of testing and refining, just as the prophet Jeremiah is commanded, 'I have made you a tester and a refiner among my people so that you may know and test their ways' (6.27). And yet, as Jones elsewhere demurs,

> Not till 'pure intelligence' gives us the answer can we truly know how Chartres stands to the Parthenon, the *Primavera* to Picasso's bed; the light-fitting of 1942 to the chandelier of 1882, or how the strategy and tactic of Cannae stands to *Blitzkrieg*, that of Zama Valmy.[93]

The pilgrim-poet must guard against his own prejudice, his own temptation to 'condemn the unfamiliar' and to give up on the quest for 'sacrament with a small "s"'.[94] The struggle with the utile is not only without but within. Perhaps we might hear the meaning of this declaration, 'I have been on my guard / not to condemn the unfamiliar', by turning it inside out – something like 'I have let myself be vulnerable / so as to bless (and be blessed by) the unfamiliar'?

From fragment to flow

The poet's 'I' demarcates the body of the poem, mirroring in its upright fontal form those 'glassy towers' and 'perfected steel' structures that refuse to bend. Instead, they merely replicate, stacking up along the margin of the paper as though themselves attempting a monumental climb. But like the faltering 'A, a, a', these 'I's fail in their quest for continuity, broken up by trailing lines which thrust themselves between, like a glitch in the machine. By the time we reach his winding prose, it is as though the 'I' itself has been caught up in the vortex, as all these marginal 'I's sweep from the left to the right. Here they replicate ever more quickly, accumulating in a great heap. With this turn to prose, the pace and intensity of the search increase, steaming breathlessly forward until we meet once more that capital 'A' like a break on the line. The progressive pace of the poem enacts the turn of modern civilization itself as one bent on speed and efficiency above all else. The wheel is one of humanity's most revolutionary inventions, and modern culture is defined by wheels spinning at ever accelerating speeds. But the wheel has also been at the centre of the most profound moments of apocalyptic vision from Ezekiel to John's Revelation. The apparent dichotomy of the utile and the sacramental is thus intensified here with the 'dual anamnesis' of this line:[95] 'I have watched the wheels go round in case I might see the / living creatures like the appearance of lamps,

---

[92] Jones, *In Parenthesis*, 181.
[93] Jones, 'Art in Relation to War', 143.
[94] Jones, 'Art and Sacrament', 178.
[95] Ezek. 1; Rev. 4.6-8.

in case I might see / the Living God projected from the Machine.' The capital 'M' of the 'Machine' here is startling, like an inverse projection or mirrored reflection of the capital 'W' of 'His Wounds'. The pilgrim-poet still receives these images projected by the Machine in hopes that he might thereby perceive the Living God.

Many readers of Jones's poem find in the imagery of this line the modern artefact of the movie projector. So David Annwn writes, 'That cinema which seemed to offer so much has offered up mass-consumed icons of self-regard, has, in reality, become a very provisional and blinkered form of looking *without* seeing.'[96] In an essay titled, 'The Harp and the Camera', Owen Barfield attends to the way the artefacts we use foster different habits of vision. Though it is unlikely Jones was familiar with this particular essay of Barfield's, it aids in the exegesis or midrash of these condensed lines. Barfield describes the earliest form of the camera known as the *camera obscura* – a little box with an angled mirror inside on which an image of the outside world is reflected through the light of a small hole. Barfield reflects on the significance of the invention thus: 'There on the screen you had the complex three-dimensional real world, in which we walk about on legs, conveniently reduced to a little two-dimensional image which the pencil had only to trace. ... The art of imitating had been reduced to the technique of copying.'[97] Seeing 'in perspective', which the camera accomplishes with precision and efficiency, is not however the same craft as perception.

Barfield's account of the invention of the magic lantern moves us closer to the modern-day wheels of cinema and, later, the television. His description of this artefact resonates closely with the language of Jones's poem:

> That particular toy does not receive pictures into itself but, with the help of artificial light inside it, it projects (repeat, *projects*) them back onto the world outside itself, normally onto a blank screen, or a blank wall, or some kind of *tabula rasa*. But even if the wall is not blank, provided the artificial light is bright enough, the picture will be projected and it will either mix with or obliterate for the spectator whatever is actually on the wall.[98]

One need not stretch Barfield's description far to hear in it the turning of the modern viewer him or herself into the 'blank screen' or 'blank wall' onto which images continuously bounce off. Increasingly, the human person becomes shaped as that blank screen onto which endless images through artificial light are projected. Such practices form him or her as a 'viewer' but rarely 'one who sees'. There may increasingly be 'eyes all around' (Ezek. 10.9) as the modern world is increasingly dominated by the image, but less and less of those who truly see.

The question which Barfield presents and the quest Jones's poem poses is not whether or not there will be 'projection' in modern civilization. Rather, as Barfield writes, 'The question for the twentieth century is whether it is to be a projection of

---

[96] Annwn, *From A to Eia*, unpaginated.
[97] Owen Barfield, 'The Harp and the Camera', in *The Rediscovery of Meaning and Other Essays* (Middletown, CT: Wesleyan University Press, 1977), 69–70, 71.
[98] Ibid., 71.

nothingness or a projection of the sun-spirit, the spirit of light.'[99] The sacramental vision of the world is beautifully articulated precisely in terms of projection by Dionysius in *Divine Names*, one of Jones's favourite theological works: 'But we know [the Creator] from the arrangement of everything, because everything is, in a sense, projected out from him, and this order possesses certain images and semblances of his divine paradigms.'[100] Dionysius also, in his *Celestial Hierarchy*, interprets the 'iconography of the "winged wheels"' of Ezekiel's vision anagogically. These wheels, he writes, are both revolving *and* revealing because they turn not only around their own centre point but also around the Good. So Dionysius: 'Those Godlike wheels of fire "revolve" about themselves in their ceaseless movement around the Good, and they "reveal" since they expose hidden things, and lift up the mind from below and carry the most exalted enlightenments down to the lowliest.'[101]

Dionysius's exegesis thus provides the key question with which the poet is wrestling: Can the multiple images and semblances 'projected from the Machine' not only revolve but also reveal? Insofar as the wheels of civilization turn only around the immanent goods of power, efficiency and multiplication, they will fail to satisfy the human thirst for the 'more than', for symbols which truly reveal. So Jones declares in his essay, 'Religion and the Muses': 'But although we gaze like John the Divine and wonder with a great admiration, yet our natures are far from satisfied. The *numina* which preside over these forms are masters of illusion – this is a magician's world – the living God is not, after all, projected from the machine.'[102]

The King James translation of Prov. 29.18 brings out the importance of vision in stark terms: 'Where there is no vision, the people perish.' But the poet of Jones's poem thus far seems to lack vision – his subjunctive 'in case I might see … / … in case I might see' doubles our sense of his strenuous efforts and an increasing sense that he is trapped. We might remember here Jones's comparison of the craft of writing poetry

---

[99] Ibid., 77.
[100] Colm Lubheid and Paul Rorem, eds and trans., *Pseudo-Dionysius: The Complete Works* (Mahwah, NJ: Paulist Press, 1987), 869D/108.
[101] Ibid., 337D-340A/190.
[102] Jones, 'Religion and the Muses', in *Epoch and Artist*, 104, fn. 2. Cf. the patristic exegesis of the revelation of Ezekiel and the apocalypse of John as the vision of an entire cosmos that is held into being and ordered by the Word. The four living creatures are symbols of the four Gospels – a lion, a calf, a man and a flying eagle. As Irenaeus, another of Jones's theological companions, writes:

> From these things it is manifest that the Word, who is Artificer of all things and enthroned upon the Cherubim and holds together all things, and who was manifested to men, gave us the four-fold Gospel, which is held together by the one Spirit. … And as the living creatures are fourfold, so also the Gospel is fourfold; and fourfold also is the Lord's economy

in *Against the Heresies* (Book 3), trans. Dominic J. Unger (New York: Newman Press, 2012), III.11.8, 56–57. The living creatures are thus associated with the writings of the Gospels themselves – Matthew with the human, Mark with the lion, Luke with the ox and finally John with the eagle. They are sacred books not primarily on account of their historical accuracy or the individual perspectives they offer as witnesses, though these are important; they are sacred writings precisely because they *perceive* this singular man, Jesus of Nazareth, to be the Living God and invite others to see Him thus as well. Cf. Christopher Rowland, 'Ezekiel's *Merkavah* in the Work of William Blake and Christian Art', in *The Book of Ezekiel and Its Influence*, ed. Henk Jan de Jonge and Johannes Tromp (Aldershot: Ashgate, 2007); and Angela Russell Christman, '*What Did Ezekiel See?*': *Christian Exegesis of Ezekiel's Vision of the Chariot from Irenaeus to Gregory the Great* (Leiden: Brill, 2005).

to the opening of a casement window. But this pilgrim-poet is not able, at least through the strength or 'might' of his own pen, to effect the opening of this casement.

His narrative now nears its conclusion: 'I have said to the / perfected steel, be my sister and for the glassy towers I thought I / felt some beginnings of His creature.' This 'I have said' reiterates that first 'I said' with which the poem began. The pilgrim-poet imitates the prayer of Saint Francis of Assisi here, pleading that the 'perfected steel' and 'glassy towers' of the modern wasteland reveal their kindred and creaturely spirit. In Francis's 'Canticle of the Sun', the manifold creatures of earth mediate his praise to God:

> Praise be to you, my Lord, from Sister Water,
> Who is so useful and humble and precious and chaste.
> Praise be to you, my Lord, from Brother Fire,
> Through whom you lighten our night;
> And he is handsome and merry and vigorous and strong.[103]

These flowing and illuminating substances of Francis's prayer are both useful and beautiful. Are the materials of the industrial age any less capable than 'Sister Water' or 'Brother Fire' to mediate the praise of the Lord?

The vertical, straight-lined skyscrapers made of these materials are the icons of the modern city. The first almost prophetic sketch of this now ubiquitous structure was drawn by Mies van der Rohe in 1921 – an all glass and steel skyrise which became the standard through the inter-war period. Stephen Toulmin in *Cosmopolis* cites Mies van der Rohe as *the* figure of post–First World War architecture with its rejection of *art nouveau*'s lush curves, ornamentation and organic forms. 'Mies', Toulmin writes, 'abhorred local color. Instead, he looked for *universal* principles of design, equally appropriate to all geographical locations.'[104] According to Toulmin, Mies even rejects the principle of building to function, embracing an even more abstract structuralism 'like the universal abstract ideas at the base of Descartes' philosophy'.[105] Toulmin's analysis continues:

> [Rohe's] program for architecture produced buildings whose technical mark was mathematical clarity and precision, but which could be used for a dozen different purposes, and were equally at home (or out of place) in any city or country. An apartment block by Mies may thus be used to illustrate a text on Cartesian or 'coordinate' geometry, in which spatial locations are referred back to a given 'origin of coordinates' (O), and to the given 'axes of reference' (Ox, Oy and Oz). ... In Mies' principles, we see the man who dominated architectural design in Europe and North America right up to the 1950s rejecting the diversity of history and

---

[103] Translation by Brian Maloney in his *Francis of Assisi and His 'Canticle of Brother Sun' Reassessed* (New York: Palgrave Macmillan, 2013), xxiii.
[104] Stephen Toulmin, *Cosmopolis: The Hidden Agenda of Modernity* (Chicago, IL: University of Chicago Press, 1990), 155.
[105] Ibid.

geography, and the specific needs of particular human activities, in favour of universal, timeless principles.[106]

Such abstraction compromised the functionality of many of Rohe's buildings. His commitment to this abstract structuralism went even further than that of his contemporaries who maintained commitment to a principle of functionality, that is, that the ends to which it would be put by human beings should shape or even determine form. For Mies, it was the human who would need to adapt himself to the design, not the design to the human. The designs are unbending and unresponsive to both the particular surrounding environment as well as the needs and desires of its inhabitants.

One would be challenged to find a more apt figure of the 'Fact-Man' character of Jones's later poems in *The Sleeping Lord* collection than Mies. There is 'Brasso' of the 'The Dream of Private Clitus':

> There's always a Brasso to shout the odds, a fact-man to knock sideways and fragmentate these dreamed unities and blessed conjugations, why certainly old Brasso was up there – and, he was up the ladder, too, – the higher the casualties, the higher the climber.[107]

The 'fact-men' are visionaries of a type, but as Clitus remarks, 'only there's calculation in the very dreams of a Brasso'.[108] And yet, the poet of Jones's poem does seem to be drawing nearer to the form he seeks through these vertical straight-lined structures: 'I thought I felt the beginnings of his creature.' Perhaps we might hear these lines through Jones's comment in 'The Religion and the Muses': 'Beauty, however, of a certain order, undeniably adheres to these forms, the beauty of a mathematical formula "made flesh", given material projection. Awe-inspiring in its power-perfection.'[109] However, he ultimately finds that these, too, fail to satisfy his desire. We sense that he longs for these vertical steel structures to bend, to lean, to reciprocate his desire, 'but, *A, a, a, Domine Deus*', he exclaims, 'my hands found the glazed work unrefined and the terrible crystal a stage-paste ... *Eia, Domine Deus*.'

Like the 'chug', 'chug', 'chug' of a steam train coming to a grinding halt, so the punctuated breath of the poet pulls like a brake on the chain of his winding prose. The poet's own speech is knocked sideways, the confident and upright 'I', 'I', 'I', breaking up and fragmenting in the cry of '*A, a, a, Domine Deus*.' Is there a 'Brasso' here, too, to 'knock sideways and fragmentate these dreamed unities'? These breaks in syntax mark

---

[106] Ibid., 156.
[107] Jones, *The Sleeping Lord*, 21.
[108] Ibid., 22. Similarly, the 'Fact-Man' is incarnate in Jones's poem, 'The Tribune's Visitation' in *The Sleeping Lord* as the military leader who calls the men to leave behind '[o]ld rhyme' and 'older fantasies' (50–1):

> Suchlike bumpkin sacraments / and all the sweet remembered demarcations / are for the young-time for the dream-watches / now we serve contemporary fact. / Its the world-bounds we're /detailed to beat / to a common level / to discipline the world-floor / till everything presuming / difference / wither to the touch of us / and know the fact of empire.

[109] Jones, *The Sleeping Lord*, 104, n.2.

failure on one level but also entry into another form of speech. Its rhythmic pulsing, like plucks on a bow string, gather the disjuncted and fragmented lines, integrating them into the flow of prose and so also, perhaps, of grace. The stolid, stone-like capitals of the title line are transformed here into the liquid, leaning form of the italic. The letters themselves enact that bending and yielding which the 'glassy towers' and 'perfected steel' refuse.

Bending, leaning, inclining, stooping – this is always the movement of attentive desire and redemptive love in Jones's poetry, a movement recurring throughout *The Sleeping Lord* collection. Whether the bending of the priest to bless the elements,[110] marble statues-cum-divine mother,[111] to the living flame of candles, boughs of trees and even the deer 'whose desire is for these water-brooks'[112] – all these forms are inflected by the active, desiring lover of the Good.[113] In the poet's own (re)turn to prayer, his speech, too, becomes inflected with longing and is propelled forward not by mechanics but by desire. He now also leaves behind the incessantly repeated, 'I have', 'I have', 'I have' refrain of his narrative, as though divested of even his own powers of speech.

In the final images of the poem, the pilgrim-poet struggles to find the mediated presence of the Lord God not only in the utile objects of modern culture but in those manufactured as merely ornamental, too. Even these objects of gratuitous decoration fail to satisfy, perhaps most bitterly of all, as he concludes, 'my hands found the glazed work unrefined and the terrible crystal a stage-paste'. Akin to the priest whose 'holy and venerable hands lift up an efficacious sign' in the Mass, the poet's own 'groping syntax' is the very means by which 'we already and first of all discern him making this thing other'. He speaks not of 'a hand' as earlier, but now, of 'my hands', as though himself implicated in the failure of the quest, this final indictment as much confession as judgement.

The apocalyptic is here cleverly layered with the kitsch. Gems like the rhinestone began to be mass-produced in the nineteenth and twentieth centuries and are made from rock crystal, another word for which is 'paste'.[114] By contrast with such 'stage-paste',

---

[110] Cf., for instance, 'the Priest of the Household' of Jones's 'The Sleeping Lord' poem, who 'with a slight inclination of his body ... makes the life-sign over all the men'; and 'Does He Lean Low in His High Office', in *The Sleeping Lord*, 78, 79 and 73.

[111] Cf. these images of the 'Terra Mater': 'so at least she did *appear* to lean, detached as it were from / the relief work and more bodily perceived, yet still in her static / element of stone nor yet disturbing the balance of the masonry. / And so she herself gravely inclined herself'; and 'the proportioned limbs of Tellus Our Mother, lean- / ing living ... and all the world / seemed at peace deep within the folds of her stola as she leaned' in 'Dream of Private Clitus' in *The Sleeping Lord*, 19.

[112] Cf. this beautiful sequence of images in 'The Sleeping Lord', in *The Sleeping Lord*, 74–5.

[113] This is also the movement of Christ in the Gospel of John when he stoops down to write in the dust before the woman accused of adultery (8.1-11) – we are never told what he writes, but this mysterious writing seems to effect her unbinding from the judgement of the Law.

[114] 'paste' Def. 5 in *Oxford English Dictionary*, 2nd edn (Oxford: Clarendon Press, 1989): 'A hard vitreous composition (of fused silica, potash, white oxide of lead, borax, etc.), used in making imitations of precious stones; a factitious or artificial gem made of this.' The compound word 'stage-paste' is not in the *OED*. These last lines of the poem in which all is declared 'a stage-paste' might also be read in light of the infamous line in Act 2 Scene 7 of Shakespeare's play, *As You Like It*, ed. Michael Hattaway (Cambridge: Cambridge University Press, 2009): 'All the world's a stage / And all the men and women merely players' (Lines 142–4). The actor then recounts the seven stages of man as a microcosm of this bitingly cynical view of the passing of life to death and wryly describes

the last vision given to John the Divine in the book of Revelation is of the holy city, the new Jerusalem, coming down from heaven 'as a bride adorned for her husband' (21.2). This city is effulgent with 'the glory of God and [has] a radiance like a very rare jewel, like jasper, clear as crystal' (21.12); the walls of the city themselves are 'adorned with every jewel' (21.19); its streets are of 'pure gold, transparent as glass' (21.22). This city shines in all its opulence on account of the presence of the Lord God Himself. There is no temple, 'for its temple *is* the Lord God the Almighty and the Lamb' (21.22); no lamps are needed for 'the glory of God is its light, and its lamp is the Lamb' (21.23). With these visions of the heavenly Jerusalem, the pilgrim-poet of the urban wasteland asks whether this 'glazed work' and 'terrible crystal' yield such depths of beauty, yet he concludes it is only 'stage-paste', cheap, gaudy imitations. In these final moments, it is as though all has been thrown into the fire.

Were the poem to stop here we might safely conclude the journey has ended in failure. However, instead of another full stop punctuation, we meet these three punctuated points '...'. In his preface to *The Anathemata*, Jones emphasized that 'pause-marks on a score are of particular importance'.[115] What kind of pause-marks are these? What sort of crossing does this ellipsis signify? What kind of silence? One of despair, a final downward descent? Might these three piercing punctuations signify the pilgrim-poet's own compunction, confessing his failure to find the Lord God where he believes He somehow still must be?[116] Before this vortex of prose began, the breaking lines of the first part of the poem ended with the warning 'it is easy to miss Him / at the turn of a civilisation'. Is it possible this final piercing interval marks a turning of another kind? The kind of crossing only God accomplishes, the crossing of grace? It is after all, Jones tells us, 'under the shapes of arranged lines of words, spaces, commas, points, by which poets regulate the openings of casements for us to enjoy and suffer the sights they would show us'.[117] Like the 'turned iron pierced at intervals' by which we open a casement window, perhaps the journey of the pilgrim-poet in this place begins not only to incessantly turn but to open, too. Not merely another end, but a new beginning? Jacques Maritain in his 'Frontiers of Poetry' might encourage such hopeful anticipation: 'If the Spirit which floated over the waters must now hover above the ruins, what does it matter? It is sufficient if it comes.'[118]

The mysterious silence of the ellipsis, '...', gives way at last to one final exhale, '*Eia, Domine Deus*'. This final line returns us to the first 'A, a, a, DOMINE DEUS' yet with

---

these final sixth and seventh stages thus: 'and his big manly voice / Turning again toward childish treble, pipes / And whistles in his sound. Last scene of all, / That ends this strange eventful history, / Is second childishness and mere oblivion, / Sans teeth, sans eyes, sans taste, sans everything' (Lines 164-9).

[115] Jones, preface to *The Anathemata*, 35.

[116] I'm indebted to Mary Carruthers's work on the manuscripts of medieval monks and scribes for this connection between 'punctuation' and 'compunction': 'And the prickings, scorings, and "woundings" of the parchment which were necessary to draw the designs (and which are still visible on some of the pages) bring to mind – in the inventive way of all good composition – the com*punc*tion with which one should begin prayerfully to read the gospel text' in *Craft of Thought: Meditation, Rhetoric, and the Making of Images, 400–1200* (Cambridge: Cambridge University Press, 1998), 169. We will return to this insight in relation to Jones's practice of wood engraving in Chapter 3.

[117] Jones, 'Art and Sacrament', 151.

[118] Maritain, *Art and Scholasticism*, 83.

a difference. But what kind of difference? The Latin Dictionary only continues the bewildering ambiguity.[119] Used as an interjection, according to Lewis and Short, *eia* can mean, first, 'an expression of joy or pleased surprise' as when, for instance, 'in admiring an object, *Ah! ah ha! indeed!*'[120] Or, secondarily, it can be an interjection of impatient exhortation, as in '*ho! quick! come on!*'[121] Has he found what he has been looking for? Is this a moment of surprise? Or another intensification of the longing for that which has not yet arrived? Perhaps we might find it is something in between.

If this point in the poem is a kind of turning itself, I'd like to suggest the possibility that we read this final turn in light of Tolkien's literary technique, for which he coins the term, '*eucatastrophe*'. In his essay, 'On Fairy Stories', Tolkien describes a eucatastrophe as the final turn in the conclusion of a story that has the quality of joy, 'a sudden and miraculous grace: never to be counted on to recur'. Importantly, he explains, this joy does not deny 'dyscatastrophe, of sorrow and failure'. Rather, what it denies is 'universal final defeat and in so far is *evangelium*, giving a fleeting instance of Joy, Joy beyond the walls of the world, poignant as grief. ... It can give to child or man that hears it, when the "turn" comes, a catch of the breath, a beat and lifting of the heart, near to (or indeed accompanied by) tears.'[122] But Tolkien writes, effecting such a turn is

> not an easy thing to do. It depends on the whole story which is the setting of the turn, and yet it reflects glory backwards. ... In such stories when the sudden 'turn' comes we get a piercing glimpse of joy, and heart's desire, that for a moment pass outside the frame, rends indeed the very web of story, and lets a gleam come through.[123]

Tolkien's repeated description of this kind of ending as a 'turn' should draw the attention of readers of Jones's poem. If we tend more closely to this '*Eia*', might we catch some 'piercing glimpse of joy'?

What happens when we listen for the 'aural and oral intention' of this '*Eia*'? We have been prepared for the long 'A' sound of the diphthong 'ei' by the vowels of 'stage' and 'paste'. However, the pronunciation of this long 'A' is new to the refrain which resounds throughout the poem: from the stolid, upright, 'A, a, a, DOMINE DEUS' to the 'Ah!' of the first line and the liquid, leaning '*A, a, a, Domine Deus*'. The 'low-back-wide' vowel has now once more, yet more drastically, undergone another 'transmogrification'. We no longer see the 'A' though we hear it, in fact, pronounced for the first time *as* the capital letter 'A' – this signifier of the Lord God who says, 'I am the Alpha and Omega, the first and the last, the beginning and the end' (Rev. 22.13). But just as this 'A' is enunciated, it becomes hidden, veiled by the material form of the diphthong '*ei*'.

The hiddenness of the capital 'A' may be interpreted as a further withdrawal of the divine presence from this literary wasteland. However, perhaps something more

---

[119] As perceptively noted by Annwn in *From A to Eia*, unpaginated.
[120] 'eia' Def. Ia. in *A Latin Dictionary*, ed. Charlton T. Lewis and Charles Short (Oxford: Oxford University Press, 1879).
[121] 'eia' Def. II. in *A Latin Dictionary*.
[122] J. R. R. Tolkien, *Tree and Leaf* (London: Harper Collins, 2001), 69.
[123] Ibid., 70.

is going on here than meets the eye. After all, in the Eucharistic feast – the sign by which, for Jones, all signs are made whole – the LORD GOD is really present though veiled under the forms of bread and wine. In the Eucharist, Christ 'placed Himself in the order of signs'.[124] Jones directs his readers at the conclusion of his essay, 'Art and Sacrament', to this saying of De la Taille, just after his reciting of an early fragment of the poem which many years later would take the final printed form before us. De la Taille describes the Eucharistic sign thus: 'The Body of Christ is invisible; the outward shape he derives from the bread in order to give himself as food is visible but beneath that visible wrapping is concealed the hidden reality.'[125] In this same passage, he also draws attention to this beautiful hymn included in the Feast of Corpus Christi liturgy composed by Thomas Aquinas: 'Here, beneath these signs, are hidden / Priceless things, to sense forbidden; Signs, not things, are all we see, – / Flesh from bread, and Blood from wine, Yet is Christ in either sign.'[126]

It might be that this final '*Eia*' should also be counted among His 'manifold lurking-places'. After all, the very moment of Christ's apparent defeat on the cross, when His reign is most fully withdrawn and even openly mocked, is the very crux of salvation. When Christ gives up his spirit and breathes his last, he opens all creatures to the possibility of a new beginning. This beginning is not just another in an infinite series but is paradoxically the 'final beginning' by which all things, past, present and future, are made new. As Christ exhales on the cross, he also gives up his spirit. His human breath or spirit dies, but through this breath the divine Spirit is given anew. So too might this final diminutive 'a' of '*Ei-aaaah*' sink into the souls of its readers, resolving all the refrains that have come before and reviving the raw bones laid waste in the valley.[127]

This letter 'A', as we recalled in the outset of this journey, belongs not solely to the Roman alphabet but to the Greek and Hebrew as well. Perhaps not incidentally, we also find this '*eia*' hiding in the Greek word for worship itself, *latreia* (λατρεια). Its sound is echoed also in our English words for worship as 'praise' and 'pray'. To find this sacramental signifier at this journey's end one must listen 'silently, attentively & carefully / and with latreutic veneration / as did Mair Modlen / the eternally pierced feet of the Shepherd of Greekland'.[128]

---

[124] Maurice De la Taille, *The Mystery of Faith and Human Understanding Contrasted and Defined*. Trans. J. P. Schimpf (London: Sheed & Ward, 1930), 212.

[125] Ibid., 206.

[126] *The Roman Missal in Latin and English According to the Latest Roman Edition*, introduction and liturgical notes by Dom. F. Cabrol, O.S.B., 3rd edn (Tours: A. Mame, 1921), 579. As one of the missals which Jones used and studied frequently, he likely would not have missed this introductory note by Dom. Cabrol, highlighting the sequence for its artistry:

> With regard to the Prose *Lauda Sion*, it is impossible to say which is most to be admired – its dogmatic accuracy, its sublime ideas, the variety of its rhymes, or the perfection of its rhythm. Devotion to the Holy Eucharist could hardly be expressed with greater fervour or in a more exquisite form. It is one of the most beautiful Canticles in the Catholic Liturgy. (Ibid., 576)

[127] Cf. Catherine Pickstock's argument in 'What Does Othering Make? David Jones's "A, A, A, DOMINE DEUS"': '[T]he cry "*Eia*," of despairing lamentation, remains also, like the cry of dereliction on the cross, a cry of salutation, a recognition of a missing plenitude as the very meaning of total absence, the beginning of glorification', *Religion and Literature* 49.1 (2017): 175.

[128] Jones, 'The Sleeping Lord', 73.

But it is in returning to the Hebrew that this unsuspecting signifier unlocks the riddle of this quest. This 'A' may turn one final time in such a way that it 'reflects glory backwards', inflecting the entirety of the wasteland poem with this gleam of joy from 'beyond the walls of the world'.[129] '*Eia*' sounds also like the Hebrew word, *eyheh*, which means 'I am'. As we learned at the beginning of this poem, this is the part of the Hebrew gloss on the Divine Name of YHWH: EYHEH ASHER EYHEH or 'I AM WHO I AM'. Are we then to read this final line, '*Eia, Domine Deus*' as this final announcement, 'I AM, the Lord God'?

We began with that stolid, all-capital inscription-like writing of the divine name, 'DOMINE DEUS', and asked what to make of this spatial rendering of the name. The journey through the wilderness is itself the answer. For if we read this 'I' throughout as a signifier not of the solitary poet but also as the 'I AM' then the pilgrim-poet has never been alone. The meaning of the name is the promise of this presence no matter how far or long Israel may wander; there is One who will make the journey with them.[130]

The writing, and indeed the reading, of this poem has been a journey to which the ambiguous dual dating '*c. 1938 and 1966*' testifies. As we have seen throughout the poem, it is the space between figures that is the place of mystery and the most fecund beginnings. Even here, in the difference between the figures '*1938*' and '*1966*' is the distance of twenty-eight years. Is it coincidence, as David Annwn also asks, that this too is precisely the length of lines in the body of the poem itself? Are these dates only literal or do they yield a deeper meaning too? Perhaps they are the author's way of drawing attention back to the importance of taking time in the quest for sacrament; that through time, wayfaring, we sojourn towards Truth.

If we are right in hearing this echo of the divine name, the I AM, in this final '*Eia*', might it further illumine for us also the true character of the 'I' of the pilgrim-poet himself? The context of De la Taille's oft-quoted statement, 'He placed Himself in the order of signs' actually emphasizes precisely this identity of Christ with 'ourselves, you and I, the Christians of the whole world'. He goes on,

> ourselves, but assuredly not ourselves separated and isolated from Christ; ourselves united in Christ, aggregated to Christ, incorporated in Christ, one in Christ; there is the Christ living in us and we living in his life. This is why Christ in his own person wished to become a sacrament, in order to be the efficacious sign of all that. He placed himself in the order of signs, in the order of symbols, to have the joy of symbolising and, by symbolising it, of building up the mystical Body of which we are the members.

The truth of the pilgrim-poet's identity is hidden in Christ. In this reality lies hidden also the meaning of the quest. For the pilgrim-poet has enquired 'up and down', 'at the door' and even pleaded with 'perfected steel' and 'glassy towers'. But to answer, 'what shall I write'? he must turn within. It is this 'I AM' within each human being that

---

[129] Tolkien, 'On Fairy Stories', 69.
[130] Cf. Martin Buber and Franz Rosenzweig, *Scripture and Translation* (Bloomington: Indiana University Press, 1994).

Coleridge says is the spring of *poeisis*: the living power of the imagination is but 'the repetition in our finite minds of the eternal act of creation in the infinite I AM'.[131] It is the poet's participation in this infinite 'I AM' that makes the difference between 'dead forms' and living forms. As Malcolm Guite summarizes, 'It is as though the creative word that speaks the cosmos into being echoes back to God from minds made in his image. Where our echo meshes with his Word, we perceive the world.'[132]

The 'A' signifier throughout the poem has directed us to the breath of the poet, to that which makes written speech audible or living. The 'I' signifier in turn recalls the poet's sight or his 'eye'. Rather than a dualism or competition between sight and sound, however, we have found in our reading that the intermingling of these senses produces the richest meanings. We might thus conclude with one final interpretation of the 'I' and the 'A' by returning to Owen Barfield's essay, 'The Harp and the Camera'.[133] Barfield's critique of the camera and modern forms of vision does not resolve with a nostalgic return to the Romantic icon of the harp. Instead, he suggests the way forward is one in which the two are overlapping: 'Is it fanciful, I wonder, to think of a sort of mini-harp stretched across the window of the eye – an Apollo's harp if you will, as perhaps not a bad image for the joy of looking with imagination?'[134] The word 'window', he tells us, is in fact a corruption of the word 'wind-eye'.[135] Similarly, Jones's poem needs to be both seen *and* heard for its sacramental significance to be discerned. In this way it too becomes a kind of 'wind-eye' or, in Jones's own imagery, an open casement window by which we 'enjoy and suffer the sights [the poets] would show us'.[136]

Both the breath of the Spirit and the light of the Son are needed for this kind of seeing in the light of love. Perhaps it is finally this mystery of the Trinity which illumines the titular 'A, a, a, DOMINE DEUS' with which we began? As Annwn suggests, the small 'a's stemming from the capital 'A's are like the flowering of the Son and the Spirit from the Father. The Creator, like the Name itself, is not a thing, but a unity-in-relation.

The form of the cross

We've learned of Jones's deep appreciation for the materiality of language and the medium of the printed page as intrinsic to his understanding of the work of poetry itself. By exploring the arranged lines or 'textures and contours' of 'A, a, a, DOMINE DEUS', we can see how in this poem that appears to be a desolate wasteland devoid of divine presence, 'His symbol' may yet be discerned in its very shape. Let's turn one last time to the poem as a concrete whole and see if its form doesn't yield yet more meaning, especially in light of this redemptive turn we have discovered.

---

[131] Samuel Taylor Coleridge, *Biographia Literaria I*, ed. James Engell and W. Jackson Bate (Princeton: Princeton University Press, 1983), 304.
[132] Malcolm Guite, *Faith, Hope and Poetry: Theology and the Poetic Imagination* (Surrey: Ashgate, 2012), 176.
[133] Owen, *Rediscovery of Meaning*, 65–78.
[134] Ibid., 77.
[135] Ibid.
[136] Jones, 'Art and Sacrament', 151.

Merlin Jones observes that 'almost all Jones's work employs contrasts between static and dynamic elements'.[137] For instance, concerning his watercolour painting titled *The Maid at No. 37*, he observes how Jones 'counterpoints the hard angles and parallels of architecture with the curvaceous contours of the duster-waving maid and the boughs of the trees that wave around her. … [C]rucial for Jones', he suggests, 'is precisely that *contrast* between organic movement and architectonic stability'.[138] Attentive to Jones's typographic mind, Merlin Jones perceptively also asks whether the title of the painting itself doesn't also visualize this contrast: '(Is there another pun in the title here, juxtaposing curves and straight lines in the two numbers 3 and 7?).'[139] Might we apply this contrast of 'static and dynamic elements' to the forms of Jones's poem too?

We have seen this dynamic begin to emerge in tending to the poem's title line, 'A, a, a, DOMINE DEUS'. The stuttering stops and starts of 'A, a, a', with its intimations of human frailty and desire, is suggestive of the 'sequence and permutation' inherent to the creaturely realm, the little 'a' organically fluoridating from the big 'A'. This open, organic 'A, a, a' is, however, immediately halted by the hard dentals of the widely spaced 'DOMINE DEUS', its monumental lettering lending a kind of architectonic stability to the whole. Indeed, it is as though the poem itself were suspended from this Name for a vertical axis may be traced down the centre line of the poem, from the capital 'D' of the divine name to the first enjambed line, beginning with the capital 'H', straight down to the final '*Eia, Domine Deus*'. Each and every line of the poem intersects with this clearly defined axis, creating a sense of stability amidst the disjunction.[140]

If the stone-like, stolid 'DOMINE DEUS' or LORD GOD is a sign of the Eternal Word by whom and in whom all things have being, so we might imagine the 'sequence and permutation' of 'A, a, a' as a sign of the temporal flux and change inherent in creaturely existence. Interestingly, 'a' is the only vowel not in 'DOMINE DEUS'. We know Jones to be attentive to such things, having wrestled in his early years with basic reading and writing. As he says in a letter from 1964 of the struggle to spell his friend Bobbie Speaight's name: '(can *never* get the vowels in the right order in Bobbie's name. They are nearly all there – it reminds me of that thing one used to be told as a child, 'A, E, I, O, U, and sometimes W and Y)'. Perhaps then we might see this letter 'A', as the only vowel missing from 'DOMINE DEUS', as the signifier of the Incarnate Word, 'the Alpha and Omega, the beginning and the end (Rev. 22.13) and so in this sense supplementing the Holy Name of the Eternal Father. In being made flesh, he made himself subject to the fluxes of time, embracing the inevitable faltering stops and starts of human existence. Yet, as the primary signifier, the divine 'A', so to speak, Christ makes all these mutations and transformations in the creaturely realm possible at all: 'This

---

[137] Merlin Jones, *David Jones 1895–1974: A Map of the Artist's Mind* (London: Lund Humphries Publishers in association with National Museums & Galleries of Wales, 1995), 18.
[138] Ibid. (emphasis in original). For Jones's *Maid at No. 37* (1926), see Bankes and Hills, *The Art of David Jones*, 56, fig. 59.
[139] Jones, *David Jones 1895–1974*, 18.
[140] Alison Milbank describes the ambiguity of the form thus: 'The enjambed lines balance and stabilise the poem in the very same action by which their arrangement seems to break its flow and disjoint experience' in *Chesterton and Tolkien*, 163.

Master of Harlequinade, Himself not made, / maker of sequence and permutation in all things made.'[141]

The ultimate site of this consummation is the cross, 'His symbol', with which the quest of the poem began. As Andrew Davison writes, 'In every celebration of a sacrament, heaven and earth are brought close, mirroring that moment when Christ was suspended upon the cross between heaven and earth.'[142] Later in *The Sleeping Lord* collection, Jones asks us to see the symbol of the cross in the traditional form of the maypole. The figure of the cross itself is identified with 'the sawn-lode stake'. Like the ribbons entwined around the maypole, the liturgical dances of the people around this cross gather in many 'bruised stem[s]':

> Gathering all things in, twining each bruised stem to the swaying trellis of the dance, the dance about the sawn lode-stake on the hill where the hidden stillness is at the core of the struggle, the dance around the green lode-tree on far fair-height.[143]

The hidden stillness at the core of the struggle is the cross itself, that place and time of silence, of apparent absence. The 'sawn-lode pole' of the cross is the centre around which the cosmos orbits and civilizations turn. The liturgical offerings around the cross 'turn the season's syntax' and are the means by which the fragments of civilization, psyche and speech, like so many 'bruised stem[s]', are gathered back towards this life-giving centre.

In this sense, one can read the entire poem as a modern pilgrimage to Golgotha. Recall the key line: 'I have felt for His Wounds / in nozzles and containers.' We find these 'Wounds' in the very midsection or navel of the poem itself, at lines thirteen to fourteen of twenty-eight, and they are just left of centre, placed on the 'side' of the poem at the very same site that Christ's own body was pierced by the Roman soldier. In piercing the side of the Lord, the soldier looked only for proof of death, but the mixture of water and blood that streamed forth proved to be much more – a healing, salutary stream. This imaginative identification of the body of the poem with the body of the Lord further recalls the crucial question in Jones's poem, 'The Sleeping Lord': 'Is the configuration of the land / the furrowed body of the lord … / Does the land wait the sleeping lord / or is the wasted land that very lord who sleeps?'[144] So here we might ask, does the poet only wait for 'His symbol' to appear, or is his poem the very symbol he waits?

By means of this configuration of words on paper, this literary wasteland is itself visually transfigured in the form of the cross. For when we trace this horizontal line at 'His Wounds' together with the vertical line that forms the central axis of the poem, 'His Symbol' appears. Jones memorably concludes *The Anathemata* with this image of the cross as 'an Axile Tree' around which all time and places finally cohere.[145] Similarly, the fragmenting lines of Jones's wasteland poem are held together by this clearly

---

[141] Jones, *The Anathemata*, 63.
[142] Andrew Davison, *Why Sacraments?* (London: SPCK, 2013), 6–7.
[143] Jones, 'The Tutelar of the Place', 61.
[144] Jones, *The Sleeping Lord*, 96.
[145] Ibid., 243.

defined axis, the midsection or centre line to which all are joined. Even the final '*Eia*' is brought into careful alignment with this central axis. The fragmented lines stem outward from this centre line towards the left and the right and can be imaged to be like branches on a tree or ribbons turning around a maypole. This central axis is itself rooted 'on the hill' of prose below, resolving all in a final stream of healing prose. So too might we see in the many fragmented lines of this poem a participation in the liturgical dance around the cross itself, 'gathering all things in, twining each bruised stem to the swaying / trellis of the dance'. The pilgrim-poet offers his narrative up as anathemata, joining those

> who laud and magnify with made, mutable and beggarly elements the unmade immutable begettings and precessions of fair-height, with halting sequences and unresolved rhythms, search-ingly, with what's to hand, ... rifting the dark drifts for the wanderers that wind the world-meander, who seek hidden grammar to give back anathema its first benignity.[146]

Summarizing the spirit of *The Book of Balaam's Ass*, the work from which this poem was originally drawn, Jones writes, 'its about how when you start saying in a kind of way how *bloody* everything is you end up in a kind of *praise* – inevitably'. Discerning the cruciform shape in the poem gives us confidence to tread this doxological inevitability here as well, even, or perhaps especially, in the midst of the fragments of modernity. The juxtaposition of despair and doxology moves us in the direction of praise while that contrast of architectonic stability and organic movement meet in the form of the cross, anchoring all time yet without stopping its flow – the very movement of grace.[147]

That the work of our hands as writers be more than paper notes, monetary or administrative, but pleasing offerings and praises to and from the Lord God, a furtherance of the work of His hands, is humanity's dignity and glory. In the *Divine Names*, the first extended analogy given by Dionysius for the divine nature from things below is not a flower, a tree or even a worm, but rather an artefact, a work of human hands, namely, a lamp.[148] This lamp which projects light outwards becomes for him and his readers a way into the mystery of the Trinity: Bring several lamps together and their light mixes indivisibly in the air; separate one from the others and each burns no less truly. These lamps are paths to divine understanding. It is only because all things are, in their existence, projected out from the light of the Living God that they may become in return luminaries of the divine nature. So might all the works of our hands

---

[146] Jones, 'The Tutelar of the Place', 60.

[147] Cf. the Latin phrase, '*Stat Crux dum volvitur orbis*', 'The Cross stands while the world turns', which Jones quotes in his Introduction to the Ancient Mariner in Samuel Taylor Coleridge, *The Rime of the Ancient Mariner*, Illustrated and introduced by David Jones, ed. with preface and afterword by Thomas Dilworth (London: Enitharmon Press, 2005), 18. Cf. also Thomas Berenato's reading of time, history and 'forgiveness' in Jones's poetics, especially his wonderful phrasing of these dynamics here: 'The influence of the Cross irradiates history with Christ's forgiveness by introducing a flexibility in the structure of time' in 'David Jones and the Ancient Mariner: A History of Forgiveness', *Religion and Literature* 49.1 (2017): 147.

[148] Lubheid and Rorem, eds and trans., *The Divine Names* in *Pseudo-Dionysius*, 161–2.

be. This is the prayer that Jones's poem makes. It is the prayer also of the Secreta from Thursday in the Passion Week which reads,

> O Lord our God, who has commanded and preferred that these material things, created by thee for the support of our frail nature, should also be dedicated as offerings to thy name, grant that they may not only help us in this present life, but prove a pledge of immortality [*vitae aeternitatis efficient sacramentum*]: through our Lord.

It is only *through* the name '*Per Dominum*' that such return offerings become '*efficient sacramentum*'. And so with this prayer we return to the beginning and know as for the first time, something of the wisdom of this titular, 'A, a, a, DOMINE DEUS.'

Conclusion: Wounds that bless and defeats that revive

'There are victories that weigh heavily and overpower. There are also defeats that revive, where new, unlooked for strengths spring forth suddenly from the wounds received.'[149] So Jean-Louis Chrétien in *Hand to Hand: Listening to the Work of Art* describes the struggle of the painter Delacroix to paint the biblical story of Jacob's wrestling with the mysterious man beside the River Jabbok. He describes how, in order to paint this story it was necessary that Delacroix in some way *become* Jacob. He had to enter the riddles and paradoxes of that strange tale to such a degree that in the end the biblical story 'paints' Delacroix as much as Delacroix paints the mural. Such stories 'never finish taking place', Chrétien writes, 'if we offer them this place that is our life. Why does Jacob matter, if we cannot become him? Why does his angel matter, if he no longer has the force to assault us? What does this combat matter, if it cannot take place this very night?'[150] Such myths are forever arriving as events; they interrupt the prosaic and demand the rewriting of the personal narratives of their readers as much as the principal actors.

It is Jacob's apparent defeat, the blow to his hip socket by the angel that finally awakens him to the draw of the divine upon his life. His shedding of all defensive armour transfigures the adversarial combat to one of 'salutary intimacy', a means for 'communication of force' rather than annihilation.[151] The struggle with the mysterious angel requires all of himself and more. And yet, because the struggle is with this One who infinitely exceeds his measure it births a new identity, not only for Jacob but for a whole kingdom. Chrétien reflects on the significance of the central paradox of the story thus:

> There are wounds that one must not heal, for they are the source of our loving intimacy with our highest task, the one we have received, impossibly, without having sought it. … [T]he event of the intimate confrontation is also the advent of

[149] Jean-Louis Chrétien, *Hand to Hand: Listening to the Work of Art*, trans. Stephen E. Lewis (New York: Fordham University Press, 2003), 1.
[150] Ibid., 9.
[151] Ibid., 14; 4.

an unforeseen and new intimacy. Jacob needed a displaced hip, an uncertain gait from that point forward, in order to receive his most secure name, the one no man would ever have been able to give him.[152]

David Jones is a modern artist who also passed many hours of 'nocturnal solitude' in this 'intimacy of salutary combat'.[153] As we have seen, the paradox of wounds that bless and of defeats that revive are central to the quest for the sacrament in the era of the utile. As Jones himself reflects, with a nod to Chesterton, 'nothing succeeds like failure'.[154] His conviction that 'despite all appearances man is man-the-artist' and that all things exist only insofar as they participate in the Good is the irresistible goad that insists he must continue to write, to paint, to engrave and even, when the struggle is at its most intense, to live. He chooses to go on creating and speaking and so also chooses Life, again and again and again. Through the practice of art, the gratuitous sign-making proper to all human beings, that which is '*inanis et vacua* [becomes] radiant with form'.[155] Such struggles are innate to all acts of artistic labour that seek to be more than an assertion of will or self-image. To listen and respond to the call of the Name and the 'more than' in things is a costly venture, yet also the means of grace. Such is the enduring power of these narratives to write, and re-write, our very lives.

---

[152] Ibid., 3.
[153] Ibid., 4.
[154] David Jones, *Dai Greatcoat: A Self-Portrait of David Jones in His Letters*, ed. René Hague (London: Faber & Faber, 2008), 75.
[155] Jones, 'Art and Sacrament', 160.

2

The art of the incarnate word: *'Quia per Incarnati'* painted inscription

Introduction: Epiphany

On a cold, dark night in the year 1917, David Jones left the company of the trenches in search of dry firewood and came across a battered barn. Putting his eye against a crack in its wall, he discovered not 'the dim emptiness' he expected but rather the warm glow of candlelight, a makeshift altar and a few communicants celebrating the Mass. He writes of the event to a dear friend many years later thus:

> Just a little way back, that is between our support trench and the reserve line, I noticed what had been a farm-building, now a wreckage in the main owing to shell-fire. ... I thought Now that looks to be most likely the very place where there might be not only wooden objects of one sort or another, broken cart-wheels or other discarded bits of timber but, with a bit of luck, a wood-store perfectly dry and cut ready for use. So I went to investigate and when I came close to the wall and found there were signs of its having been a bit more knocked about than appeared from a few hundred yards away, but there was no door or opening of any sort on that side; but I found a crack against which I put my eye expecting to see either empty darkness or that I should have to go round to the other side of the little building to find an entrance. But what I saw through the small gap in the wall was not the dim emptiness I had expected, but the back of a sacerdos in a gilt-hued planeta, two points of flickering candle-light no doubt lent an extra sense of goldness to the vestment & a golden warmth seemed, by the same agency, to lend the white altar-cloths and the white linen of the celebrant's alb & amice & maniple ... You can imagine what a great marvel it was for me to see through that chink in the wall. And kneeling in the hay beneath the improvised *mensa* were a few huddled figures in khaki. ...I felt immediately that oneness between the Offerand and those toughs that clustered round him in the dim lit byre.[1]

---

[1] David Jones, *Dai Greatcoat: A Self-Portrait of David Jones in His Letters*, ed. René Hague (London: Faber & Faber, 2008), 248–9. Also reprinted in René Hague, *David Jones* (Cardiff: University of Wales Press, 1975), 57–8.

Jones's carefully crafted prose invites the reader to imagine what a marvel it was for him to see through that chink in the wall. The dilapidated barn bears the wounds of war and suggests the plight of the soldiers themselves: 'a wreckage in the main owing to shell-fire', more 'knocked about than appeared' and on the verge of collapse allowing for no apparent way in or out. That 'chink in the wall' recalls the 'chink' of a knight's armour, his vulnerable place through which the shaft of a sword may pierce him. By means of this chink, however, light pours through the wall and into Jones's solitary eye, transfiguring the shell of a structure to a place of communion. Here 'toughs' are found 'kneeling', 'huddled' and 'clustered round' – still wearing the costume of war yet no longer 'on their guard'. Wrapped in the robes of this peace-bearing ritual is the 'sacerdos' or 'offerand', the one who offers up, akin to the artist who offers up signs of things under other forms. It is the light, however, which remains the main agent of this scene, the two flickering points of candlelight 'lend[ing]' their 'golden warmth' to the white of the altar-cloths and magnifying the gilt-hued vestments and linens.

As Jones re-presents this scene, he recalls not only the event of 1917 which took place under the shadow of war but also the night in which, under the dark shadow of Herod, that other 'holy and consecrated' one was born in a 'dim-lit byre' with its improvised manger. The shepherds, those 'toughs' of the field, gathered round him as did also the mysterious magi, led by the light of a star. Akin to these night-travellers, Jones found few resources for physical comfort, but instead discovered within the kindling of a light that would illumine all the years to follow. This showing was a kind of personal epiphany for the 21-year-old Jones, the significance of which would decisively shape the course of his work and thought from this moment onward. To it he attributes his conversion to Catholicism after his return from the war. He writes to Hague, 'I was "inside" a Catholic in the trenches in 1917, but not so formally until 1921.'[2] Jones would later say that he somehow sensed the real presence of the Christ at this Mass and that this sense of the real presence necessitated his conversion. Moreover, it was this same sense that underpinned his conviction that not only the Eucharist but any work of art is 'a *thing* and not the impression of some thing'.[3] These early reflections would grow in depth and maturity through his discussions with friends, his lifelong devotion as a Tertiary Dominican and his reading of so many theological illuminaries such as Jacques Maritain and Maritain's many patristic and scholastic interlocutors.

If we want to see how Jones unfolds this strong connection between the real presence of the Eucharist and the conviction that a work of art is a thing in itself, we could do no better than turn to one of these works themselves, namely, a painted inscription made some thirty years later. Jones made this inscription for the Feast of Epiphany in 1950. His inspiration was the Preface of the Christmas Mass, recited daily from the Midnight Mass on Christmas Day (25 December) through to Epiphany (6 January). This work in watercolour and graphite on paper (500 × 380 mm) was photographed by Jones, and these photographs sent to friends and subsequently reproduced in *The Anathemata*.[4] The Preface which inspired it reads in full:

[2] Hague, *David Jones*, 56.
[3] Ibid.
[4] David Jones, *The Anathemata: Fragments of an Attempted Writing* (London: Faber & Faber, 1952), 76. It is also reproduced in Ariane Bankes and Paul Hills, *Art of David Jones: Vision and Memory*

> It is truly meet and just, right and availing unto salvation that we should at all times and in all places give thanks unto Thee, O holy Lord, Father almighty and everlasting God. Because by the mystery of the Word made flesh the light of Thy glory hath shone anew upon the eyes of our mind: that while we acknowledge Him to be God seen by men, we may be drawn by Him to the love of things unseen.[5]

In our exploration of Jones's inscription, we will see how he re-incarnates and glosses this text in subtle form, unfolding the depth of its theological meaning and facilitating for the reader a journey from the visible word to the invisible, that is, to the 'love of things unseen'. Here we are invited to leave behind the dilemmas of the wasteland for a time and to meditate on the primordial sacrament, of that of the Incarnate Word, by whose radiant beauty or eternal shining forth the eyes of the mind are renewed. This light in the darkness is not an exceptional shining through the interstices of an otherwise dim emptiness, but that light by which all things live and move and have their being; this is a world in which all things are gloriously 'cracked'.[6] The luminous grace of Christ pours through the being and wounds of all created things, healing and making new.

The inscription provides a place for exploration of the theological mysteries of the Trinity and Incarnation, and more particularly the analogy of Christ as the perfect form of the Father by whose radiance we are drawn to the love of Wisdom and ever fuller participation in the Triune life of God. The dynamic ascent towards the contemplation of Wisdom is facilitated and supported by it. Its luminous form provides a kind of visual icon or foothold by which we may venture into the depths of theological speculation; at the same time, the theological truths it re-presents illuminate the nature of the inscription itself – and indeed all art or *poiesis* – as a hopeful performance and participation in them. I have chosen to explore this inscription not least because of the density of theological reflection it guides and supports but also because of the way it illuminates the nature and purpose of the work of art more broadly for Jones, in particular, the grounding of *poiesis* in the theological.

However, in order to understand some of what's going on in Jones's artefact, we first have to understand something of this art of lettering in general and Jones's practice of it in particular. This background will inform our way of approaching the inscription in the next section as a unity of form and content. My reading will then open up more broadly to a theological discussion of the meaning of *claritas* and its relation to Christ

---

(Farnham: Lund Humphries, 2015), 154, fig. 140; and Nicolete Gray, *The Painted Inscriptions of David Jones* (London: Gordon Fraser, 1981), 56, catalogue no. 22. David Jones gave the original inscription to Jim Ede and is part of the collection of Kettle's Yard, University of Cambridge, and is on permanent display. See Thomas Dilworth, *David Jones: Engraver, Soldier, Painter, Poet* (London: Jonathan Cape, 2017), 294. Note that the date Jones later wrote in pencil on the original inscription '(c. 1953?)' was from memory and the correct date according to Nicolete Gray is 1950, and Bankes and Hills, *Art of David Jones*, as 1949–50.

[5] *The Missal in Latin and English, Being the Text of the Misalle Romanum with English Rubrics and a New Translation* (London: Burns Oates and Washbourne, 1950). This is one of the versions of the Missal which Jones personally owned and used; see Huw C. Jones, *The Library of David Jones, 1895–1974: A Catalogue* (Aberystwyth: National Library of Wales, 1995), 251.

[6] Cf. 'There is a crack, a crack in everything. That's how the light gets in' – lyrics from Leonard Cohen's song 'Anthem' on *The Future* album (Columbia Records, 1992).

as the Word of the Father. This detailed exposition will deepen our appreciation of the iconographic elegance of Jones's inscription as well as the metaphysical ground of *poiesis* more broadly.

'A living lettering': Painted inscriptions and the art of the incarnate word

Inscriptions are neglected as works of art generally, but specifically this has been so of Jones's until more recently, and still the most comprehensive study is Nicolete Gray's *The Painted Inscriptions of David Jones*, a contemporary who knew Jones.[7] The inscriptions are of interest to theologians not only because inscriptions frequently use religious texts but also because this form of art itself, as we will explore, fosters reflection on the relationship between words and the Word.[8]

There is an art to reading an inscription at least as much as there is in making one. Inscriptions are some of the most simple and most difficult works of art to approach. They seem to communicate directly to us but at the same time this apparent immediacy is a kind of Achilles heel. As Gray writes, 'People read instead of looking; paradoxically, because letters are so familiar people do not know what they really look like.'[9] We read for sense, for meaning, and inscriptions are composed of such meaning-bearing signs – letters, words and syntactical relations between words that make up sentences. On the one hand, inscriptions are meant to be read, to be meaning-bearing.[10] At the same time, this meaning is communicated differently from the way we usually expect language to communicate. Here the primary medium in the art of lettering is the physical bodies of the material signifiers themselves and their arrangement on the page.

As a work of art, an inscription may first be taken in simply as a beautiful object. The mind is able to rest from its usual labour of meaning making. One doesn't have to worry about the meaning of the words for a moment; the usual interpretive work of reading is suspended and one is free to delight in the sensible beauty of the forms themselves. Jacques Maritain in his *Art and Scholasticism* describes this aspect of the beautiful as a kind of intuitive knowing thus:

---

[7] For more recent works on Jones's inscriptions, see Bankes and Hills, *Art of David Jones*, especially chapter 'Word and Image', 150–64; Dilworth, *David Jones*, 284–7; Anne Price-Owen, 'From Medieval Manuscripts to Postmodern Hypertexts in the Art of David Jones', in *Writing and Seeing: Essays on Word and Image*, ed. Rui Carvalho Homem and Maria de Fátima Lambert (Amsterdam: Rodopi, 2006), 355–68; and Colin Wilcockson, 'Mythological References in Two Painted Inscriptions of David Jones', in *Journal of Modern Literature* 23.1 (1999): 173–82. Alison Milbank also gives a reading of Jones's inscription, 'The Tribune's Visitation', in her essay, 'Make It New: Defamiliarization and Sacramentality in David Jones', in *David Jones: Christian Modernist?*, ed. Jamie Callison, Paul S. Fiddes, Anna Johnson and Erik Tonning (Boston: Brill, 2018), 64–6.

[8] As Jones himself notes in his letter to Nicolete Gray, 29 December 1960, 'It's curious how relatively few people are moved by inscriptions' yet they integrate form and content as nothing else quite does' in Gray, *Painted Inscriptions of David Jones*, 107.

[9] Gray, *Painted Inscriptions of David Jones*, 11.

[10] One should say *usually* meaning-bearing for some modern letterers deliberately create nonsensical texts as discussed briefly, for example, by Gray in *Painted Inscriptions of David Jones*, 10–11. Of course, even this eschewal of meaning is itself meaning-bearing!

> The mind [is] spared the least effort of abstraction, rejoices without labour and without discussion. It is excused its customary task, it has not to extricate something intelligible from the matter in which it is buried and then step by step go through its various attributes; like the stag at the spring of running water, it has nothing to do but drink, and it drinks the clarity of being. Firmly fixed in the intuition of sense, it is irradiated by an intelligible light granted to it of a sudden in the very sensible in which it glitters; and it apprehends this light not *sub ratione veri*, but rather *sub ratione delectabilis*, by the happy exercise it procures for it and the succeeding joy in appetite, which leaps out to every good of the soul as its own peculiar object. Only afterwards will it more or less successfully analyse in reflection the causes of such joy.[11]

This moment of intuiting the beautiful through the senses is perhaps the first way in which inscribers desire their inscriptions to be received. What is remarkable about Jones's inscription of the Preface of the Christmas Mass is that it indeed delights and renews through the sheer beauty of its form and colours; yet the meaning of the words thus embodied are themselves precisely aids in the reflection of, as Maritain has it, the many 'causes of such joy'. On account of this profound wedding of form and content, the inscription becomes a place in which one dwells, experiencing the joy or delight of the beautiful and also exploring through it and by means of it the theological understanding of such experiences. It functions most akin to an icon – a kind of foothold or material signifier to which one continuously cleaves while journeying along the way of wisdom.

One of the gifts of the art of letterer then is, first, to return our attention to the beauty and significance of the materiality of language itself. The shape of the letter is to the calligrapher what the sculpted world of sound is to the poet. 'Letters', as Eric Gill reminds in his *An Essay on Typography*, 'are signs for sounds. ... They are more or less abstract forms. Hence their special and peculiar attraction for the "mystical mug" called man.'[12] Even as abstract forms, letters are deeply storied things. The settled forms of the English alphabet are the product of long histories of development from the pictorial hieroglyphs of the Egyptians through the Phoenicians and eventually to the Latin letters themselves. Yet if it is fair to say that these forms are settled, they are by no means static. 'Except for the classical purist,' writes Gray, 'the letter-forms are not immutable.'[13] She speaks instead of a rich 'quarry of abstract forms at the disposal of the lettering artist'.[14] The basic compositional elements of a given letter admit almost endless variation, gathering up all kinds of often unconscious connotations.

> [Letters] can be weighty or robust, as those used in English Regency posters, they can be dynamic and chaotic as in futurist typography, stammering as in Ben Shahn's testament for Sacco and Vanzetti, triumphant as in Filocalus' inscriptions

---

[11] Jacques Maritain, *Art and Scholasticism with Other Essays*, trans. J. F. Scanlan (London: Sheed & Ward, 1946), 21.
[12] Eric Gill, *An Essay on Typography* (London: Penguin Classics, 2013), 23.
[13] Gray, *Painted Inscriptions of David Jones*, 9.
[14] Ibid., 10.

for the Christian martyrs, full of swirling mystery as in the complex initials of the German Baroque writing masters.[15]

To tend to the body of the letter is to remember it is, in the full sense of the word, a character.

Jones first encountered lettering in art school, but it was not until meeting Eric Gill at Ditchling Commons that he felt he found in the modern day 'a living lettering'.[16] In his reflections upon Gill's death, he would write of his deep respect for Eric Gill as a letterer:

> One thing is certain: as a carver of inscriptions he stands supreme. There the workman scaled the heights of pure form, and some of his inscribed stones possess the anonymous and inevitable quality we associate with the works of the great civilizations, where an almost frightening technical skill, for a rare moment, is the free instrument of the highest sensitivity – and the Word is made Stone.[17]

Through Gill, Jones came to appreciate the significance of this profoundly incarnational medium, though he would not himself ever work in stone. Jones's comfortability in experimenting with lettering came only after he learned how to do wood engraving with Desmond Chute and soon he would render Gill's dynamic lettering his own.[18] René Hague insightfully describes his divergence from Gill thus:

> Eric would have been speechless had a pupil drawn those R's whose tails unblushingly thrust themselves from the junction of bow and stem, the slender S's that look to their neighbour, or to the margin, for support, the G's whose variety is an essay in calligraphic development, the E's that so craftily combine squareness with rotundity, the whole effect of an inscription – like a logan stone which the touch of a hand will rock and which yet stands solid and unmoving. ... The remarkable thing about David's inscriptional work is that there is in it nothing that is purely fanciful; every shape is determined by the particular evocation required

---

[15] Ibid.
[16] Ibid., 103.
[17] Jones, 'Eric Gill: An Appreciation', in *Epoch and Artist: Selected Writings*, ed. Harman Grisewood (London: Faber & Faber 1959), 300–1. Jones draws a contrast between his way of working and Gill's with reference to 'the Muse'. He classes himself and other artists like him as those who are driven by love of the Muse to undertake a risky journey to unknown shores, 'drifting on our experimental floats in search of the goddess on a chancy ocean'; by contrast, for Gill, 'the Muse of Sculpture must lump it until tomorrow at ten o'clock precisely – throw her a kiss till then – she would be in mind all the time, but she must be reasonable', in Jones, 'Eric Gill', in *Epoch and Artist*, 300–1; 298–9.
[18] Jones relates this in his letter to Nicolete Gray in *Painted Inscriptions of David Jones*, 103. For some of these early experiments incorporating lettering into his paintings, see his *Crucifixion* (c. 1922) in watercolour and pencil (Private Collection); and *Crucifixion with Inscription* (1924) painted in tempera on the wall at the chapel in Capel-y-ffin, reprinted in *David Jones in Ditchling*, ed. Derek Shiel (Ditchling: Ditchling Museum, 2003), 22. Cf. also Ewan Clayton's discussion of the Ditchling influence on Jones's painted inscriptions in 'David Jones and the Guild of St. Joseph and St. Dominic' in *David Jones in Ditchling*, ed. Derek Shiel, 20–2.

in *this* place for *this* thought. ... In David's case it produces a mine of allusion, suggestion, remembrance; in Eric's sheer purity of form.[19]

Gill's lettering conforms to the classical ideal – the search for the perfect form of a letter and its harmony with the whole. Jones's lettering seeks, as Hague reflects, not so much pure form as *this* particular form for *this* particular place and evocation. Bankes and Hills note the contrast thus: 'Gill, the brilliant designer of fonts, conceived each letter of the alphabet as a unit that could work in any combination. Jones, the painter and engraver, conceived each letter not as something that might stand alone but as an evocative form shaped in response to its neighbours.'[20] Jones's concern for the specificity and particularity did not require the invention of new letter forms, however. He made use of various palaeographical texts, perhaps above all Nicolete Gray's own *Palaeography of Latin Inscriptions in the Eighth, Ninth and Tenth Centuries in Italy* which she gave to him in October 1948.[21] Jones chose forms which, he states, '(1) I like the feel of for all sorts of inexplicable aesthetic (?) reasons' and '(2) Forms that evoke something of the meaning of the word in which the letter occurs (and the more undertones and overtones evoked the better) that evoke the content which the form should disclose and the more the content and form are one I take to be an advantage in any art – that I take as axiomatic.'[22]

These unique concerns contributed to the development of a much more playful, fluid style when compared to Gill's 'august elegance'.[23] If in Gill's hand, the Word is made Stone, so we might characterize the spirit of Jones's style through his own mutation of this phrase in his own poem, 'The Sleeping Lord': 'There's no resisting here: / the Word is made Fire.'[24] It is the gradual and sometimes volatile formation of the earth's stony crust that Jones's poem is here describing, highlighting the fluid processes of successive melting by molten lava and of slow moulding by water. The embrace of evolutionary process is a fitting analogue in many ways to Jones as an artist. The quality by which he judged all artwork was that it was moving, 'not being stuck still', and this judgement equally informs the kind of letterer he would become.[25] So Nicolete Gray, through her detailed analysis of Jones's inscriptions, concludes, 'In the abstract connotations of his lettering-forms David Jones was ... very much more interested in movement than in anything else.'[26]

---

[19] Hague, *David Jones*, 31.
[20] Bankes and Hills, *Art of David Jones*, 155.
[21] Dilworth, *David Jones*, 284: 'With Nicolete Gray, who had become an expert on the subject, he looked at photographs of inscriptions and manuscripts and discussed kinds of lettering. In October 1948, she had given him her *The Palaeography of Latin Inscriptions in the Eighth, Ninth and Tenth Centuries in Italy* (1948), which he frequently consulted.'
[22] Gray, *Painted Inscriptions of David Jones*, 107.
[23] Hague, *David Jones*, 31.
[24] Jones, *The Sleeping Lord*, 72. Note that in the Faber & Faber edition the passage reads, 'the Word if made Fire'; Thomas Dilworth flags the 'if' as a misprint and corrects as above in his *The Shape of Meaning in the Poetry of David Jones* (Toronto: University of Toronto Press, 1988), 211.
[25] Jones, 'David Jones the Artist: A Brief Autobiography', ed. Peter Orr in *David Jones: Eight Essays on His Work as Writer and Artist*, ed. Roland Mathias (Llandysul: Gomer Press, 1976), 11.
[26] Gray, *Painted Inscriptions of David Jones*, 12.

His primary medium of choice for his inscriptions – opaque watercolour on white paper – also supports this desire for movement and embrace of process, not only in the resulting letter forms but also in the artist's actual process of making them. But here Jones would not design an inscription at the outset but would plan and adjust as he went along. These many adjustments would then be painted over with Chinese White paint. The paint would embellish the work as a whole, giving further definition to the letters and making the paper itself have vitality. This respect for the givenness of the medium is characteristic of Jones. As he reflects, 'I accommodate the forms of the letters as I proceed until a kind of wholeness is achieved in *that* medium. … Such "idiosyncracies" as one may employ are occasioned by the requirements of the actual job in the process of doing it, and so are intimately bound up with the actual doing of it.'[27] In this manner, so-called 'mistakes' are so incorporated into the way of working as to be the very means of lending the work its glow or luminescence, that which gives the whole its 'sheen as a pearl' or *claritas* – the Latin term for the 'shining-out' aspect of the beautiful. This embrace of process with all its contingencies and adjustments is the best way Jones felt he could keep this sense of spontaneity or freedom in the overall feel of the inscription: 'I … want the thing to look "free" in some way – and to get a certain indefinable "feeling" perhaps no more than that I did not want it to look "set-out" and "spaced" but to run on.'[28] An essential ingredient in achieving this overall feel for Jones is thus attending not only to the bodies of individual letters but also to the relations and spaces between them, as Nicolete Gray argues in her reading of Jones's other Christmas inscriptions, the relation between individual letters is also central to his method, 'each letter … drawn in relation to that above and those beside'.[29]

Jones's characteristic sensitivity to the depth of meaning in any given sign, but especially those constituting human language, is immense and it is arguably this awareness and love for such associations which caused him greatest difficulty as an artist. The inscriptions, as Nicolete Gray points out, provide a certain solution to this struggle. As she explains, 'because the text itself contained for him both its immediate meaning and its trail of connotations, he was free to concentrate on the purely formal problems of each piece. These inscriptions are resolved, they have a unity, an apparent simplicity, a perfection which he found very difficult to achieve in his other work.'[30] Jones admired inscriptions because, he remarks, they 'integrate form and content as nothing else quite does'.[31]

This concern for the unity of form and content is also one of the primary reasons Jones prefers Latin for his inscriptions. As a declined language, it is much more economical than English and lends a 'monumental' quality to the language suitable to the inscriber's purposes. In this vein, Mary Carruthers, in her studies on premodern rhetoric, explains how the structure of Latin cast certain habits of the medieval monastic mind and how the practice of reading a Jones inscription may have a certain resonance with these ways of comporting oneself to Latin. According to Carruthers, 'In learning to read Latin the elementary procedure was to build up from the shortest

---

[27] Ibid., 16.
[28] Letter to Nicolete Gray, 4 April 1961 in Gray, *Painted Inscriptions of David Jones*, 104.
[29] Gray, *Painted Inscriptions of David Jones*, 19.
[30] Ibid., 14.
[31] Ibid.

units (letters and syllables) to longer and yet longer ones: words, and phrases, and then sentences.'[32] Furthermore, the lack of word divisions in the written page meant that the reader 'had to analyze the syllables first before they could be "glued" together in semantic units'.[33] A habit of mind is thus cultivated in which one 'discern[s] and then build[s] up meaningful patterns from sub-semantic elements of language, which [are] considered to have at the same time equally visual and oral resonance'.[34] Reading on this account is hardly passive; it is rather an activity, a practice of making meaning. As Carruthers explains, it functions

> less as a 'language' ... whose rational units are semantically whole and only referential or 'conceptual' in function, and more as involving recombinant sets of design elements, whose units are sub-semantic 'signs' of all sorts that *make* meanings (rather than necessarily 'having' them) in constantly varying combinations with others 'signs.' It encourages that ability to manipulate and calculate with letters which makes a few people even now extremely good at acrostics and anagrams.[35]

Pattern recognition is thus a key tool or skill in reading for meaning.

Still, Jones's preference for Latin is risky, potentially alienating a general modern readership for whom Latin is archaic and unfamiliar. Surprisingly, for Jones, this unfamiliarity is precisely its advantage. He writes, 'for blokes like me, who know very, very, little Latin, hardly any, Latin has the extra advantage of presenting one with a sort of pattern first and then only slowly (if at all!) the meaning of all (or some!) of the words.'[36] He imagines that if one did know Latin fluently, 'a good bit of the "magic" goes'. At this point (pre-Vatican II), the Mass is still said in Latin and Jones embraced this strangeness of tongue as contributing to the 'magic' of his participation in the rite. The Liturgy itself is not completely transparent, not so immediately or readily 'consumable'. But this delay in processing the words directs attention to the patterns of the liturgy and to its dramatic unfolding; it must be lived into. Similarly, not being able to immediately digest the painted inscription is an integral part of the way it acts as a formative space. It disrupts the usual ways in which one reads; it causes one to slow down and stay within the signs themselves for a time, to recognize it as a mediatory space. The purpose is not to deflect understanding but rather to defer it. As made up of signs, language is meant to point beyond itself, but when this process and the usual routes or habits of mind are slowed down or even halted, it makes you conscious of passing through. It fosters a kind of *use* that seeks a form of *union*. By slowing down the process of interpretation, the reader may be more fully inducted into its meaning: she is *performed* by it as much as she is performing it.

Jones's inscriptions form some of the most beautiful of his oeuvre as is increasingly recognized. One of the reasons for delay in the critical appreciation of Jones's inscriptions is their often personal, particular and occasional character. Yet, it is

---

[32] Mary Carruthers, *The Craft of Thought: Meditation, Rhetoric, and the Making of Images, 400–1200* (Cambridge: Cambridge University Press, 1998), 136.
[33] Ibid.
[34] Ibid., 137.
[35] Ibid.
[36] Letter to Helen Sutherland, 8 March 1961 in Gray, *Painted Inscriptions of David Jones*, 106–7.

precisely these traits that make them such wonderful embodiments of the sacramental. Furthermore, Jones's inscriptions frequently marked the sacramental high points in the life of the church and of an individual – Christmas, Easter and Good Friday, or the christening of a friend's child and even the passing of a loved one.[37] As a priest marks these moments through the rites of the church – the Eucharist, baptism, unction and so forth – so we may see Jones's inscriptions as his own participation in these sacramental moments as an artist. Creating these inscriptions became a prolonged ritual practice for him. From 1948 through the early 1960s, he made such inscriptions annually at Christmas time, photographed them and then sent them to friends as Christmas cards, each personalized with writing on the back. Acclaimed increasingly as works of art in their own right, they do not lose the savour of these personal and liturgical contexts. Indeed, it is these contextual elements that give them so much of their richness and personality. They are deeply liturgical works themselves, marking the events of life and the passing of time, a form of meditation, celebration and participation. It is this context as much as any formal factor which lends them their unique substance and something of the quality of hymns, blessings or prayers.

In sum, there are many elements of an inscription which are used to convey meaning and to which the reader is to be sensitive: the overall feel of the inscription as a whole; attention to the details of the letters as shapes and their relations to one another; the use of colour; and of course the context for which the inscription is made and from which its texts are drawn. All of this loving attention is oriented towards the end of understanding with greater depth or new insight the meaning of the text that is thus embodied. Reading an inscription is, then, more like a form of meditation, a 'craft of making thoughts about God', as Carruthers aptly characterizes monastic rhetoric.[38] As such, it is itself a work of mediation and participation, facilitating this ascent of the mind from the visible word to the 'love of things unseen'.

Journeying through the inscription of the preface to the Christmas Mass

Given this nature of inscription making as an art of the word incarnated, it is fitting that Jones would often make inscriptions for the Christmas season.[39] Jones's inscription

---

[37] For instance, see the inscription made in 1956 for the confirmation of Harman Grisewood's daughter, Sabina, in Gray, *Painted Inscriptions of David Jones*, 70, catalogue no. 40; the festive inscription for the marriage of Hugh and Antonia Fraser [1957] (Gray, *Painted Inscriptions of David Jones*, 71, catalogue no. 42). Another particularly moving inscription, made in the same year as the inscription of the Preface of the Christmas Mass, commemorates the death of his friend, Lucile Grisewood, by framing his beautiful poetic-like 'rifts' on her name, birthplace and burial site with this monumental Latin text: 'VITA MUTATUR N[ON] TOLLIT[U]R' ('Life is changed not taken away') in Gray, *Painted Inscriptions of David Jones*, 58, catalogue no. 25. Cf. Colin Wilcockson's exposition of the former inscription in his 'Mythological References in Two Painted Inscriptions of David Jones', 173–82.

[38] See her *The Craft of Thought*, especially, 1–6.

[39] He made nine Christmas inscriptions in total between the years 1948 and 1961. See Gray, *Painted Inscriptions of David Jones*, 17.

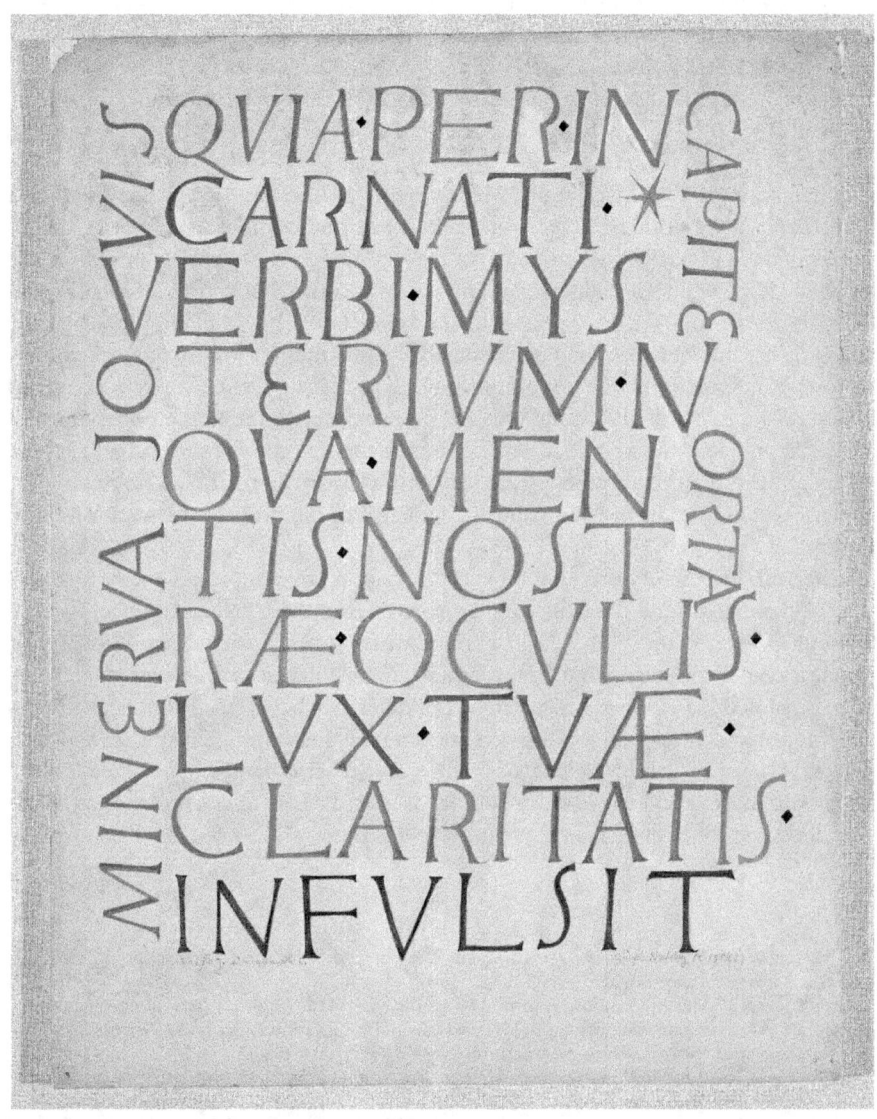

Figure 2 *Quia per Incarnati*, 1950, watercolour and graphite on paper, 500 × 380 mm, Kettle's Yard, University of Cambridge. Estate of David Jones (Bridgeman Copyright). Used with permission. For an image of this inscription in colour, see https://www.kettlesyard.co.uk/collection-item/quia-per-incarnati/ (accessed 5 June 2020)

retains the Latin of the Roman Missal and selects the central line of the Preface, framed with a border text drawn from Greek mythology:

QUIA ♦ PER ♦ INCARNATI ♦ VERBI ♦ MYSTERIUM (For by the mystery of the Word made flesh) ♦ NOVA ♦ MENTIS ♦ NOSTRAE ♦ OCULIS ♦ LUX ♦ TUAE ♦ CLARITATIS ♦ INFULSIT (the light of thy brightness has shone anew into the eye of our mind) MINERVA JOVIS CAPITE ORTA (Minerva has sprung from the head of Jove)[40]

On the back of this inscription, Jones orients his readers by giving them this translation along with a few personal notes, not unlike the notes he offers in his long poems. He writes that prior to Vatican II, this Preface was also used on the Feast of Corpus Christi, a change he laments on account that it 'provided a liturgical link between the Word made Flesh in the stable and what is made present at the Mass'.[41] That link between the Eucharist and the Incarnation was forged indissolubly in Jones's imagination by that illumined and illuminating scene which he marvelled to see through 'that chink in the wall'. Of the reference to the Roman mythology of Minerva and Jove, he adds, 'The words round the margin were proposed (I think by one of the Pontiffs in perhaps the sixteenth century, not sure) as expressing the Eternal Generation of the Son from the Father, but the proposition was not found acceptable.'[42]

Even this briefest of introductions to the inscription reminds its recipients of Jones's love of juxtaposing and drawing together material from such diverse times and places, of forging 'eclectic links'.[43] It is a cast of mind which Jones himself describes as having 'made a heap of all I could find'.[44] However, as Colin Wilcockson in his essay on two of Jones's painted inscriptions insists, 'there is a difference between a heterogeneous and a homogeneous heap' and Jones forges such connections with deliberation and care. There is always an 'informing purpose' which the reader is invited to trace out for him or herself and so also engage in the process as a kind of learning along the way.[45] The few directives Jones gives his recipients with regard to this inscription suggest it is to

---

[40] The translation is Jones's own, written on the back of one of the original inscription; see Gray, *Painted Inscriptions of David Jones*, 30–1.
[41] This quote is also taken from Jones's own notes on the back of the original inscription when given to Jim Ede of Kettle's Yard, Cambridge, in 1969; for the quote in its entirety, see https://www.kettlesyard.co.uk/collection-item/quia-per-incarnati/ (accessed 12 February 2020).
[42] Ibid., 30–1. This proposed insertion of 'Minerva Jovis capite orta' for the Begetting of the Son into the liturgy was one of the proposals made by Florentine humanists to translate the liturgy into Ciceronian Latin and was rejected under Urban VIII. See F. Cabrol, 'Breviary', in *The Catholic Encyclopedia*, 15 vols, ed. Charles Herbermann (New York: Appleton, 1913), vol. II, s.v., which may have been Jones's source. Cf. Gabriel Diaz Patri, 'Poetry in the Latin Liturgy', in *The Genius of the Roman Rite: Historical, Theological, and Pastoral Perspectives on Catholic Liturgy*, ed. Uwe Michael Lang (ChicagoIL: HillenbrandBooks, 2010), 69. Many thanks to Rev. Thomas S. Drobena for this reference.
[43] Wilcockson, 'Mythological References in Two Painted Inscriptions of David Jones', 174.
[44] Preface to *The Anathemata*, 9.
[45] Wilcockson, 'Mythological References in Two Painted Inscriptions of David Jones', 30–1.

be read theologically and in the context of Christmas. Our reading here is a journey through some of what this inscription might be prompting.

Jones's inscription of the Preface of the Christmas Mass is the second he made in that liturgical year, and the only one he would make specifically for Epiphany. As had become his custom, it was likely made with the intention of sending smaller photographed copies to friends as gifts.[46] This liturgical context would have immediately unfolded its intelligibility for its recipients in many directions. The star in the upper right-hand corner – notably the only sign that isn't a letter – might appear as the star of Bethlehem which guided the wise men through the night of the Eastern sky to the child born of Mary and Joseph.[47] Epiphany, the 6th of January, is the first major feast day of the church calendar following Christmas and marks the manifestation of Christ to the Gentiles as represented by the wise men who knelt down and paid him homage with their gifts of gold, frankincense and myrrh. The scandalous claim of this gospel story is that the very Maker of the star which led the wise men to Bethlehem is here made visible, in-fleshed, in the child over whom the star came to rest. '[I]nfinity / Dwindled to infancy', in the words of Gerard Manley Hopkins.[48] The finite, visible body of Jesus of Nazareth is seen to be the very embodiment of Wisdom itself as Christ, the God-Man, the One by whom the visible stars and all creatures, even his own fleshly body, are made and have their being. The illumination of this 'LUX TUAE CLARITATIS' is by way of this leading from the visible to the invisible, an arc of revelation embodied in the second half of the Preface: 'that while we acknowledge Him to be God seen by men' – the descent of the divine to be manifest in human form – 'we may be drawn by Him to the love of things unseen' – is paradoxically the way of our ascent towards the divine.

The New Testament lectionary reading in the Roman Missal for the Feast of Epiphany is drawn from Paul's letter to the Ephesians and gestures towards the cosmic and universal dimensions of this revelation:

> Although I am the very least of all the saints, this grace was given to me to bring to the Gentiles the news of the boundless riches of Christ, and to make everyone see what is the plan of the mystery hidden for ages in God who created all things; so that through the church the wisdom of God in its rich variety might now be made known to the rulers and authorities in the heavenly places.[49]

---

[46] Gray, *Painted Inscriptions of David Jones*, 17. We might note again that this use is by no means inimical to the 'status' of the inscriptions as works of art, as Gray comments:

> It is, I think, a mistake to think of the original inscriptions as just Christmas cards. They are substantial works, over which the artist spent much time and effort, and which he guarded jealously and exhibited with his paintings on the few occasions when he had exhibitions. Christmas was a reason for making an inscription for its own sake; the photographs were a bonus. (Ibid.)

[47] See Mt. 2.1-12.

[48] 'The Blessed Virgin compared to the Air We Breathe' (1918), in *A Critical Edition of the Major Works* (Oxford: Oxford University Press, 1986), 158–61.

[49] Eph. 3.8-10.

Jones's incorporation of a pagan myth as an analogue for Christian revelation is particularly apt in a work made for a feast day that celebrates Christ as the light of all people, a claim that in Jones's hands is not triumphalist but demands humility, tuning one's ear for wisdom across the rich variety of time and place – those manifold 'lurking places' of the divine light. Minerva in particular is fitting as she is the Roman goddess (her Greek equivalent is Athena) of wisdom. For Jones, the world of culture as much as the world of nature is capable of bearing patterns or imprints of divine revelation.

The liturgical context of Epiphany already unveils in many directions the meaning of this inscription. But it is necessary to take time to enjoy its appearance – its visible form an invitation to dwell at length with it as the way 'toward the love of things unseen'. There is in this inscription a great sense of openness, space and movement, as well as clarity and simplicity. He carefully balances the white or negative space with the lines and curves of the letters, holding the gaze in the space between them, or almost encouraging the eye to dance back and forth. The letters are lightly and delicately held on the surface of the canvas as though floating on water. The gaze is invited to roam, resting lightly or only temporarily on a single part. Even the brightly painted 'VERBI', while continually drawing the eye back to itself, also deflects a final settling of the gaze through its offset position. The lettering is some of the most classical of his inscriptions, though he still avoids uniformity (note the variation of capital 'E's) and retains a lilting quality in his letters, especially in those deviant 'S's lurching towards the right. The letter forms of this inscription conform closely with those from the second half of the ninth century found in Nicolete Gray's palaeography book which Jones frequently consulted. She describes this period during the reign of Pope Formosus as a classical renaissance with an 'experimental revivalist atmosphere'.[50] Her characterization of the inscriptions from this period are apt summaries of this inscription of Jones's too, 'cut with classic regularity in fine broad strokes and beautifully moulded curves … the letters are delicate as well as dignified'.[51]

The sea-green and red-ochre colours of the 'INCARNATI VERBI' add a mood of gaiety and festivity, while the 'goldish-yellowy-greyish colour' is often used by Jones to recall 'the thing oblated or set aside' – that which is offered up.[52] The similarly coloured golden star ties all this to Epiphany and to the star of Bethlehem that led the wisemen to the Christ child – that very Maker of the stars himself offered up, here *in materia*, as star-dust. The Chinese White highlights these forms throughout and this luminous environ in turn is punctuated by the dark black diamonds, binding and delineating the words as the mortar of syntax. The base, foundational line of the more widely spaced 'INFULSIT', painted in sharp black, adds contrast and mystery. Even the grey of the central text lends the appearance of each letter as a carefully crafted stone. Altogether, the whole suggests something like the facade of a loosely structured wall, each letter delicately painted in watercolour and carefully placed as an individual stone through which the eyes are led to the lightness of the paper on which they rest. If the left-hand

---

[50] Nicolete Gray, *Palaeography of Latin Inscriptions in the Eighth, Ninth and Tenth Centuries in Italy* (reprinted from the Papers of the British School at Rome Vol. XVI [New Series Vol. III], 1948), 97–8.
[51] Ibid., 97.
[52] Gray, *Painted Inscriptions of David Jones*, 109.

marginal text evokes the pillar of classical culture, the diagonal line perhaps looks forward once more to the Gothic arch of medieval architecture.

The overall feel of the inscription recalls this poetic imagery in Maritain's *Art and Scholasticism*, evoking these glorious cathedrals of the High Middle Ages: 'The architect, by the disposition he knows, / Buildeth the structure of stone / like a filter in the waters of the Radiance of God, / And giveth the whole building its sheen as to a pearl.'[53] In these buildings, even the dense solidity of stone is made a conduit for this liquid luminosity. These tall stone towers are built not to block but to shelter and channel light. The form reflects a vision of the whole world as 'filled with the glory of God', where even the most opaque substances are not obstructions but 'filters' for the rays of this visible and invisible Light. The artist of this 'disposition' inhabits and creates a world in which all things are porous. Though on a less grand scale than the medieval cathedral, Jones creates on the matrix of paper this 'dreamlike feeling of passing through glass'[54] and inducts his readers into a world in which what is most true or real is this radiance shining from eternity through all creation.

The marginal text rises vertically, contributing to the sense of solidity of the left-hand margin, not unlike one of the classical Greek or Roman pillars. Here the two planes intersect, however, at the 'V' of the brightly coloured offset 'VERBI', interposed between the 'O' and 'V' of the golden-hued 'JOVIS', as though opening and stretching it from its centre. A horizontal–vertical axis is thus constructed through the juxtaposition of the marginal and primary texts. But so too is each letter related to that above and those beside. Between the letters of the primary text, especially those painted in grey, a strong diagonal pattern emerges. So one may follow an almost continuous sloping line from the 'M' of 'MYS' to the 'V' of 'TERIVM' to the 'M' of 'MEN' to the 'N' of 'NOST'. Or, starting from the same 'M' of the third line and crossing down towards the right to the 'M' of 'TERIVM' to the 'N' of 'MEN'. This diagonal relation between letters is reinforced by the strong diagonals of certain individual letters as well – the centrality of the red 'V' sets precedence here, its strongly pointed descent the most simple form or basis of all letters with a diagonal (N, Y, X, A, M). The intensity and energy of this shape are reinforced throughout the inscription.

This careful and beautiful arrangement of the letters on paper is meant to prompt and support the search for meaning, to elicit the desire to know and understand. Mindful of Jones's desire to 'evoke the meaning of word in which the letter occurs (and the more undertones and overtones the better)', how might these shapes, colours and relations perform the meaning of this text? Without compromising the feeling of the inscription as 'free' and 'running on', there seems to be a striking intentionality in the overall structure of this work. He had used this same Preface for an inscription made for Christmas in 1945. Revisiting the Preface five years later, Jones not only introduces

---

[53] Unattributed quote in Jacques Maritain, 'Essay on Art', in *Art and Scholasticism*, 96. Bankes and Hills also find architectural analogies fitting in their description of Jones's inscriptions: 'The inscriptions, particularly the Latin or Roman ones, are constructed with rows of letters that stand like columns or lean like buttresses. *EXIIT EDICTUM* ... an inscription sent out for Christmas 1949, which tells of the birth of the firstborn Son of God within the empire of Augustus, might be imaged in this way as a living temple' in *Art of David Jones*, 155.

[54] Bankes and Hills describe this as the 'oceanic quality of his visual art' in *Art of David Jones*, 155.

this marginal text but also relates the two through this meeting point at 'V' of the 'VERBI'. When this form is set in play with the content of these two texts, one may discern in this axis a re-presenting of the meeting of the eternal and the temporal in the mystery of the Incarnation.[55] Fittingly, many of Jones's Christmas inscriptions play with ways of re-presenting this meeting of the eternal and the temporal. For instance, the other inscription which he made earlier in this same liturgical year – for Christmas rather than Epiphany – re-presents the wedding of the temporal and eternal by wrapping the marginal text around the central text; the whole evokes an image of a womb, re-enforced by the round and open shapes of the letters. Once again, Jones's attention to the unity of form and content is evident here as the central text reads (in translation), 'Virgin mother of God, he whom all the world cannot contain enclosed himself in thy womb, being made man.' The marginal text which wraps around this comes from the heavens, mediated by the voice of the angel Gabriel to Mary: 'Behold I bring good news to you of great joy.'

Rather than this enclosed, circular structure, our Epiphany inscription relates the temporal and eternal as two interlocking planes. The vertical text, 'MINERVA JOVIS', is about the relations within God's eternal being – this classical analogue of the Son, as Wisdom, eternally Unbegotten of the Father – while the horizontal text concerns the revelation of this mystery to time-bound creatures through the Son's becoming Incarnate as the Word. The particular point of 'conjunction' is, fittingly, this red 'V' of the 'VERBI'. This 'overlap' or union of the horizontal/temporal and the vertical/eternal in the minimalist form of the 'V' signifies with elegant economy the mystery of the Incarnate Word in whom the eternal and temporal are perfectly united. Within the horizontal text, too, the wedding of these two realms in Christ is bodied forth. On this plane, the red 'VERBI' is layered or sandwiched between the syllables 'CARN' – the Latin root meaning 'flesh' – and 'TER' – the Latin root meaning 'three' or 'having three', and thus perhaps a gesture towards the Trinity. This suggestion that 'TER' might be a recalling of the Trinity is further supported by the fact that he chooses a round shape for the letter 'E' here, a form which he otherwise restricts to the vertical text which relates explicitly to the eternal divine life. Through these relations among the letters of the horizontal plane then, too, we find this re-presenting of the Word as participating in both the Triune nature of God and the material flesh of creation.

Might the diagonal lines of the 'V' and the relation of the letters to one another in the horizontal text bear further interpretive weight? In his decorations for *The Four Gospels*, Eric Gill embellished the diagonals of letters such as the 'A' as ladders or mediating lines between heaven and earth.[56] The diagonal line of the Gothic archways as we've seen was also dear to the arts and crafts tradition and incorporated by Jones in his own poetry.[57] Within this inscription, the diagonal line inflects the stability of the

---

[55] Reprinted in Gray, *Painted Inscriptions of David Jones*, 55, catalogue no. 20.

[56] See, for instance, the letter 'N' at Jn 1.1, 'In the beginning was the Word'; and the letter 'A' at Mk 15.42, 'And now when the even was come' in *The Four Gospels of the Lord Jesus Christ according to the Authorised version of King James I* / with decorations by Eric Gill (Waltham St. Lawrence: Golden Cockerel Press, 1931), unpaginated.

[57] 'The Dream of Private Clitus', in *The Sleeping Lord* and the seminal work by John Ruskin, 'The Nature of Gothic', in *The Stones of Venice*, vol. 2 (London: Dent, 1907).

horizontal/vertical structure with a sense of flexibility and movement. It also interrupts the severe ascent of the vertical. Perhaps more than the direct vertical of the pillar of classical forms, the diagonal trajectory is fitting to Christian doctrine of the relations of the eternal and the temporal: if the direct pillar of classical forms suggests a perfect, straight ascent from the earth to the heavens, the diagonal suggests a more gradual ascent of finite creatures, one which does not leave behind the particular forms of creatures as they rise but rather are perfected along the way.[58]

We can gain further understanding by looking at the Inscription in the context of the 'Rite and Fore-time' section of *The Anathemata* in which he later included it as an illustration. In his commentary on *The Anathemata*, René Hague declares that the Preface of the Christmas Mass 'summed-up the theme of "Rite and Fore-time"', namely, 'that this New Light shone upon all from all time'.[59] Jones artfully re-works the Preface into this section of *The Anathemata* thus:

> From before all time
>   the New Light beams for them
> and with eternal clarities
>   *infulsit* and athwart
> the fore-times:
>   era, period, epoch, hermera.
> Through all orogeny:
>   group, system, series, zone.
> Brighting at the five life-layers
>   species, sub-species, genera, families, order.
> Piercing the eskered silt, discovering every stria, each score
>   and macula, lighting all the fragile laminae of the shales.[60]

Jones imagines this shining of the Light across all time and place through this recitation of scientific categories that would ring in the ear of any biologist or archaeologist. As he follows this New Light down through the layers of the earth's crust, this diagonal line reasserts itself once more:

> Through all the unconformities and the sills without sequence,
> glorying all the under-dapple. ...
> Oblique through the fire-wrought cold rock dyked from
> convulsions under.
> Through the slow sedimentations laid by his patient creature
> of water.

---

[58] For a contemporary theological articulation of 'the diagonal' as characterizing the Christian understandings of perfection or deification, see Anthony D. Baker, *The Diagonal Advance: Perfection in Christian Theology* (Eugene, OR: Cascade Books, 2011).
[59] René Hague, *Commentary on* The Anathemata *of David Jones* (Toronto: University of Toronto Press, 1977), 70.
[60] Jones, *The Anathemata*, 73.

Which ever the direction of the strike, whether the hade is
to the up-throw or the fault normal.[61]

This New Light traces an 'oblique' line through all the contortions, inversions and convulsions by which the earth's varied strata are formed, or as his reference to Hopkins has it, 'glorying all the under-dapple'. One might find resonances between the diagonal of the Gothic arch not only by 'looking up at those gusty vaults of the faded green'[62] but by digging down deep in the layered 'stone' of the earth's crust itself.

A 'hade' is a geological term meaning an 'inclination of a mineral vein, fault, etc., from the vertical'.[63] Jones may be playing here on the meaning of 'hade' as a fault line, recalling our fallen nature as a tendency to incline away from the vertical or from the Good. Jones was familiar with the theological tradition which views human sin as a 'happy fault', as he writes in his 'Art and Sacrament' essay: 'To speak in theological terms, the Tree of the Cross presupposes the other Tree, and stretches back to the 'truly necessary sin of Adam' and the 'happy fault', so that St. Thomas in the Good Friday hymn could write: '*Ars ut artem falleret*'.[64] The Art of the Cross follows the 'fault line' of human nature, thereby outdoing the 'art' or schemes of the Fall. Reading the inscription in this light deepens the significance of the red and green colours of the 'INCARNATI VERBI' too. These traditionally festive colours marking the Christmas season and the nativity of Christ also recall God's 'art' or 'scheme' of salvation as the sacramental blood of Christ and the Tree on which it was shed, the '*Crux fidelis*' and '*dulce lignum*' of the Good Friday hymn.[65]

In *The Anathemata*, Jones places the inscription directly facing a passage in which we learn of 'The Red Lady', the name given by archaeologists to the bones of a skeleton uncovered in an ancient Palaeolithic burial site contemporaneous with the Cave of Lascaux drawings. The poem presents 'The Red Lady' as 'the *egregious* [illustrious] young, toward the prime, / wearing the amulets of ivory and signed with the life-giving ochre'.[66] In his footnote to the passage, Jones draws attention to the ivory as the 'incorruptible substance' and to the ochre colour as a 'cerement of powdered red oxide of iron, signifying life'.[67] This association of the ivory with the 'incorruptible' and the red with 'life', when taken together, alludes to the 'life incorruptible' – these ornaments and markings of early burial rites themselves signs that her 'natural end' too 'is eternal felicity'.[68] The 'red ochre' shade with which Jones paints the 'VERBI' thus gathers in all those who lived and died in this 'fore-time' and the whole sign-world, particularly here the Palaeolithic art which he so admired. The red 'VERBI' is thus properly the sign of not only the Christic sacrifice and spilling of life-giving blood but also of this

---

[61] Ibid., 74.
[62] Jones, 'The Dream of Private Clitus', in *The Sleeping Lord*, 16.
[63] See 'hade' in *Shorter Oxford English Dictionary*, 5th edn (Oxford: Oxford University Press, 2002).
[64] Jones, 'Art and Sacrament', 168. This line from the hymn *Pange lingua* is translated in the Missal as 'a scheme deeper than the schemes of the serpent' in *The Roman Missal in Latin and English According to the Latest Roman Edition*, Introduction and Liturgical Notes by Dom. F. Cabrol, O. S. B., 3rd edn (Tours: A. Mame and Sons, 1921), 385.
[65] Jones, *The Roman Missal*, 384.
[66] Jones, *The Anathemata*, 77.
[67] Ibid., 76, n. 1.
[68] Jones, 'Art and Sacrament', 148.

ancient 'South Wallian'. As he writes, 'For what was accomplished on the Tree of the Cross presupposes the sign-world and looks back to foreshadowing rites and arts of mediation and conjugation stretching back for tens of thousands of years in actual pre-history.'[69] This symbol is thus both properly human and divine, and a sign of the consummate union of the two. A passage from the *Dialogues* of the Dominican Saint, Catherine of Siena, beautifully conveys its portent, as she writes in the voice of the divine of 'My Eternal Wisdom, My Only-begotten Son' thus:

> This is that Light, which has the color of your humanity, color and light being closely united. Thus was the light of My Divinity united to the color of your humanity, which color shone brightly when it became perfect through its union with the Divine nature, and, by means of the Incarnate Word mixed with the Light of My Divine nature and the fiery heat of the Holy Spirit, have you received the Light.[70]

Human nature shines brightly and fully in the person of Jesus Christ, yet his Light refracts through all humankind and, as microcosm, all creation. In his divinity, He is Light and the source of all light (and so too of our ability to perceive colour) in creation; and in his humanity, he with us becomes 'incarnadined'[71] – coloured in this crimson red, the colour of blood and so of kinship, life and life-giving sacrifice.

For Jones and this tradition of theological aesthetics in which he stands, seeing is never reducible solely to the physical mechanics of sight but is, as the twentieth-century Catholic philosopher Josef Pieper insists, irreducibly spiritual: 'We are talking here about man's essential inner richness – or, should the threat prevail, man's most abject inner poverty. And why so? To *see* things is the first step toward that primordial and basic mental grasping of reality, which constitutes the essence of man as a spiritual being.'[72] Seeing is the integral work of body, imagination, will and intellect together, yet ever dependent on the illuming rays of the divine *claritas*. In his commentary on Pseudo-Dionysius's *The Divine Names*, Thomas Aquinas elaborates these luminescent metaphors in this ontological direction:

> God sends out upon each creature, together with a certain flashing (*quodam fulgore*), a distribution of His luminous 'raying' (*radii*) which is the font of all light; which flashing distributions (*traditiones*) are to be understood as a participation of likeness; and these distributions are 'beautifying,' that is to say, are the makers of the beauty that is in things.[73]

---

[69] Ibid., 168.
[70] Catherine of Siena, *The Dialogues of St. Catherine of Siena, Seraphic Virgin and Doctor of Unity*, trans. Algar Thorold (Vancouver: Eremitical Press, 2009), 114.
[71] Jones, *The Anathemata*, 240.
[72] Josef Pieper, 'Learning How to See Again', in *Only the Lover Sings: Art and Contemplation*, trans. Lothar Krauth (San Francisco, CA: Ignatius Press, 1990), 34. On the Augustinian inheritance of this co-inherence of physical and spiritual sight, see Margaret Miles 'Vision: The Eyes of the Body and the Eye of the Mind in St Augustine's *De Trinitate* and *Confessions*', *Journal of Religion* 63 (1983): 125–42.
[73] Trans. Ananda Coomaraswamy in 'The Mediaeval Theory of Art' in *Figures of Speech or Figures of Thought: The Traditional View of Art* (Bloomington, IN: World Wisdom, 2007), 54.

This striking imagery of Aquinas's commentary further illumines the forms of Jones's inscription. The seventh horizontal line of the inscription: 'RAE ♦ OCULIS' forms a kind of word-picture of illumination. Jones isolates the final syllable of 'NOSTRAE' and pairs it on the same line with the Latin word for 'eyes', 'OCULIS'. 'RAE' may thus be read as it sounds phonetically, like the English 'ray', recalling the 'divine ray of light'. One might then further notice also how the long, extended legs of the 'E' jut outward from the 'A' and reach, even lean, towards the 'OCULIS'. The 'A' or 'Alpha' is frequently in Jones's works a sign of the divine Artist, 'the font of all light'. The union of the 'A' with the 'E' here, the latter form defined by its three extended legs, may be a kind of signifier of the Trinity itself – the mystery of the One-in-Three and Three-in-One. On even this minute and particular level, then, the form of the Æ bodies forth the 'luminous raying (*radii*)' or, as another translation puts it, 'lightning-like communications' that pour into the eyes of the mind.[74]

Intriguingly, the very verb in the Preface used for this act of illumination – 'INFULSIT' – is paradoxically painted in a dark, albeit lively, black rather than a luminous gold as we might expect. This black is further emphasized by the extensive painting of Chinese White around the letter forms. Might this striking choice of colour have theological resonances, recalling the Johannine Prologue announcing the Incarnate Word as 'the light [which] shines in the darkness, and the darkness did not overcome it' (Jn 1.5)? Or perhaps a reminder that the light of Christ descends even as far as the 'underworld', illuminating even the darkest of minds, as the Psalmist declares: 'If I say, "Surely the darkness shall cover me, and the light around me become night, even the darkness is not dark to you; the night is as bright as the day, for darkness is as light to you"' (139.11-12). This is not a light which shines through the interstices of an otherwise dim emptiness, but is the Uncreated Light who has made both night and day. So Dionysius writes in the first chapter of his *Mystical Theology* of 'him who has made the shadows his hiding place'.[75] Invoking the Trinity to lead 'where the mysteries of God's Word / lie simple, absolute and unchangeable / in the brilliant darkness of a hidden silence', he evokes this experience of suddenly seeing such bright light that is so overwhelming it makes everything go dark.[76] Although we are 'like the owl dazzled by the light of the sun', the divine Light adapts itself to us gently and slowly, renewing, strengthening, enlarging.[77]

Jones translates *claritas* simply as 'brightness' and as a reader of Jacques Maritain, Aquinas and others, he was aware of the weighty significance this word carried in this

---

[74] Cf. the translation by James F. Anderson *An Introduction to the Metaphysics of St. Thomas Aquinas* (Washington, DC: Regnery, 1953), 90–1:

> Dionysius shows how God is the cause of splendour of form, saying that He transmits to all creatures, with a certain lightning-like brightness, a ray of His own brilliant light, which is the source of all illumination. And these lightning-like communications of the divine ray of light are to be understood according to analogical participation; and as Dionysius says, they are 'beautifying', that is, productive of beauty in things.

[75] Lubheid and Paul, *Pseudo-Dionysius: The Complete Works*, trans. Colm Luibheid (Mahwah, NJ: Paulist Press, 1987), 136.

[76] Ibid., 135.

[77] Aristotle, *Metaphysics* ii, lect. 1 quoted in Thomas Aquinas, *Summa Theologiae* I.1 q. 5, a. 1. (Volume 1 [1a.1]: Christian Theology, trans. Thomas Gilby O. P. [London: Blackfriars, 1964]).

tradition of theological aesthetics. Alongside integrity or wholeness and harmony, *claritas* is one of the three 'pillars' or classical conditions defining the beautiful. These three conditions of the beautiful became in the hands of patristic and medieval theologians a way for exploring the beauty of the Triune persons, and the Son as 'VERBI' or Word in particular. That Jones has coloured 'LUX TUAE CLARITATIS' in the same golden colour as the marginal text, which, as we've seen, has to do with the eternal begetting of the Son from the Father, may intimate something of this close connection between the *claritas* of beauty and the Trinity. As Jacques Maritain reflects in *Art and Scholasticism*, 'To establish fully the dignity and nobility of art, we have found it necessary to go back as far as the mystery of the Trinity.'[78]

Deeply rooted in the Christian Platonist tradition, Maritain's aesthetics went against the grain of modern aesthetics in his insistence on the objectivity of beauty. This is not to eliminate the subjectivity of the viewer but to insist that this subjective response is just that – a *response* to 'the real', to that which is given. This is because, as we have seen, the beauty of all created things is a participation in transcendental Beauty, that is, the Beauty of God's own self, which Maritain and Aquinas gloss as existence itself (*esse ipsum*).[79] Thus while there is a subjectivity in the experience of the beautiful – the beautiful is 'that which pleases the eye when seen' (*id quod visum placet*)[80] – such objects really are beautiful whether perceived by the viewer or not. As we have seen, discerning the beautiful of the real involves this ongoing process of formation.

The three classical objective conditions of the beautiful are cornerstones in Maritain's philosophy. He summarizes them in his *Philosophy of Art*: first, 'integrity, because the understanding loves proportion'; second, 'proportion, because the understanding loves order and unity'; and third, 'splendour or clarity, because the understanding loves light and intelligibility'.[81] Concerning this third, Maritain expands thus:

> A certain shining quality is in fact according to all the ancients the essential character of beauty – *claritas est de ratione pulchritudinis* [Aquinas Comm DN, ch. 6], *lux pulchritificat, quia sine luce omnia sunt turpia* – but it is a sunburst of intelligibility: *splendor veri* said the Platonists, *splendor ordinis* said St. Augustine, who adds that 'unity is the form of all beauty,' *splendor formae*, said St. Thomas in his precise metaphysical language.[82]

---

[78] Maritain, *Art and Scholasticism*, 97.
[79] For more on Maritain's aesthetics, see John G. Trapani Jr., *Poetry, Beauty, & Contemplation: The Complete Aesthetics of Jacques Maritain* (Washington, DC: Catholic University Press, 2011); John W. Hanke, Maritain's *Ontology of the Work of Art* (The Hague: Martinus Nijhoff, 1973).
[80] *Summa Theologiae* I-II q. 27, a. 1. (Volume 19 [1a2ae. 22–30]: The Emotions, trans. Eric D'Arcy [London: Blackfriars, 1967].) John Milbank explores this foundational text and its relevance to modern aesthetics in 'Beauty and the Soul', in *Theological Perspectives on God and Beauty*, ed. John Milbank, Graham Ward and Edith Wyschogrod (Harrisburg, PA: Trinity Press, Int'l, 2003), 1–34. Particularly noteworthy is Milbank's exposition of the sense of sight as a form of touch.
[81] *A Philosophy of Art*, trans. Rev. John O'Conor S. T. P. with an introduction by Eric Gill O. S. D. (Ditchling: St. Dominic's Press, 1923), 34. This is the translation with which Jones was most familiar and by which he was deeply formed during his time at Ditchling.
[82] Ibid., 34–5.

Claritas, this 'certain shining quality', is, according to Maritain, 'the essential character of beauty'.[83] In the Ditchling Press edition of the text, he cites this most beloved remark of Aquinas from his *Commentary on Divine Names*: 'He is Beauty itself, because he gives beauty to all created beings, according to the property of each, and because He is the cause of all unison and all clarity. Indeed every form, that is to say every light, is "a certain irradiation coming out of the primal clarity", "a sharing in the divine clarity."'[84]

Keeping in mind the rich colours and shapes of Jones's inscription – especially those in gold and that brightly coloured VERBI – we may turn now to the way these three conditions of the beautiful are put to work in Aquinas's theology of the intra-triune relations. In moving our focus to this written artefact from the thirteenth century, it is worth remembering that Aquinas's *Summa Theologiae* is itself a work of art, using *materia* at hand to make a kind of dwelling place, not unlike those great Gothic cathedrals of the High Middle Ages, that may shelter and disclose a mystery, and even invites imaginative play.[85] Aquinas's *Summa*, we might say, like the poet and priest who 'set up' the things they have received, gathers together Scripture, teachings of the Fathers, ancient philosophers and so on, to disclose a mystery, not to dissolve it; its goal too is to give delight through contemplation, a *preparatio* of the joy of that 'final' sight that has no end.

Claritas, Caritas and the analogy of the *Verbum Cordis*

Aquinas's enumeration of the three conditions of the beautiful comes fairly late in the first book or *Prima Pars* of the *Summa* at question thirty-nine. His broader concern in this question is with how we are to speak of a God who is both simple and triune. By joining Aquinas at this point in the discussion, we thus find ourselves lodged already in the depths of his theological inquiry into the mystery of the Triune God. Having already explored questions pertaining to the nature of the Trinity more generally and the divine persons in particular, Aquinas begins here, in question thirty-nine, to inquire how we might speak of the divine persons as they are *in relation* to the divine essence or being. He has already done the hard chiselling and ground-breaking work in defining the divine persons precisely *as* relations, finding this delicate balancing point between modalism and tritheism.[86] His focus in question thirty-nine becomes even more refined within this mystery of divine being as he seeks to understand each of the divine persons in turn, asking how we are to speak of or name each person in relation to the one divine substance (which has itself, remember, already been said to be constituted *just as* these persons-in-relation). If the Trinity is somewhat like a

---

[83] Ibid., 35.
[84] Ibid., 45.
[85] Cf. Jones's explication of the purpose of his own artwork by returning to the Latin roots of the English word, 'edify', namely, *aedificare*, from *aedis*, meaning 'dwelling' and *facere*, 'to make'; literally, to build or to make a dwelling in preface to *The Anathemata*, 33.
[86] *Summa Theologiae* I q. 29, a. 4 (Volume 6 [Ia. 27–32]: The Trinity, trans. Ceslaus Velecky O. P. [London: Blackfriars, 2006]).

multi-faceted crystal, he seeks now to see the whole more clearly by attending to these different facets in turn.

Aquinas finds his way of approach through the tradition of associating or 'appropriating' certain attributes of the divine being held in common by all to one of the three persons in particular. One feels acutely in this exercise the tension inherent in such 'God-speak': for God to be simple means that all essential attributes must be truly and fully said of each and all the divine persons. Nonetheless, he defends the tradition of appropriating essential attributes to persons precisely on account of its fruitfulness in helping our meagre minds grow in understanding this divine mystery. In other words, although there is a risk that such speech will lead to misunderstanding, it is allowed or rather gifted as a way of 'clarify[ing] through things we do understand'.[87] Theological inquiry can only proceed by thus accommodating the divine mystery to finite minds.

He begins to explore at length this tradition of naming divine persons by way of appropriating essential attributes to particular persons with this question in article eight, 'whether the holy doctors have correctly assigned essential attributes to the persons'.[88] By the time of his writing, a long tradition of appropriation had already developed and he goes about ordering this mass of material in as natural or 'human' a way as possible. He flags once more the principle of accommodation at work: 'Since our mind is led along from creatures to a knowledge of God, its way of thinking about him has to follow a pattern deriving from them.'[89] The principle of accommodation by which he organizes this material is itself, notably, a profoundly incarnational principle. He structures his inquiry in a manner exemplified by the Incarnation itself: God leads into ever-greater layers of beauty and mystery through the creaturely. It is this principle which the second half of the Preface to the Christmas Mass articulates as the movement of revelation in the person of Christ: 'That while we acknowledge Him to be God seen by men, we may be drawn by Him to the love of things unseen.'

Aquinas thus organizes his theological inquiry by using Aristotle's 'four orderly stages' of inquiry into the nature of any creature: 'We examine it first in itself, as it is a certain being; next, as it is one; thirdly as it has in it a power to act and to cause; fourthly, as it stands in its relationship to its effects.'[90] It is with this first stage of orderly inquiry that Aquinas begins. The first set of appropriations to be considered are, therefore, those seeking to perceive the divine persons in light of their relation to the divine being or existence itself: How does the Father relate to or stand in relation to the divine existence? Is his relation different from that of the Son and the Spirit? And what about the Son and the Spirit in turn? What terms might be helpful to bring out these distinctions? So Aquinas: 'the first level, namely about God in himself in terms of his own being, appears in Hilary's appropriation – of eternity to the Father, beauty to the Son, joy to the Holy Spirit.'[91] Eternity signifies one who has no beginning or end in

---

[87] *Summa Theologiae* I q. 39, a. 7 (Volume 7 [1a. 33–43]: Father, Son and Holy Ghost, trans. T. C. O'Brien [London: Blackfriars, 1976]).
[88] *Summa Theologiae* I q. 39, a. 8.
[89] Ibid.
[90] Ibid.
[91] Ibid.

time, who is dependent on no created thing but is the source of all creatures. It is thus established as an essential attribute of the one true God and so also must properly be said of the Father, Son and Spirit if one is to hold that each and all are truly and fully God. However, appropriating eternity here to the Father as a heuristic tool helps clarify the uniqueness of the Father's being in relation to the other persons: the Father alone is Unbegotten, 'a principle not from a principle',[92] while the Son and the Spirit are both, in some sense yet to be defined, said to be from the Father. The Son and Spirit are not 'from' the Father in the same sense that creatures are 'from' the Father because they too share in the essential attribute of eternity. By this careful balance of thought, Aquinas guards against a monarchical concept of the Father while at the same time defining distinction.

If eternity is in this attenuated sense appropriated to the Father, so, according to Hilary, it is fitting to speak of the Son in particular as beautiful. To explore why, Aquinas turns to the three classical attributes of beauty – integrity, harmony and clarity – as aids to our squinting eye, aligning each attribute in turn with a dimension of the Son's relation to the Father.

> Comeliness [*species*] or beauty [*pulchritudo*] bears a resemblance to the properties of the Son. Beauty must include three qualities: integrity or completeness [*integritas, sive perfectio*] – since things that lack something are thereby ugly; right proportion or harmony [*debita proportio sive consonantia*]; and brightness [*claritas*] – we call things bright in colour beautiful. Integrity is like the Son's property, because he is a Son who in himself has the Father's nature truly and fully. To suggest this Augustine, commenting on Hilary, says, *In whom*, namely the Son, *there is life, primal and supreme* etc. Right proportion is consonant with what is proper to the Son inasmuch as he is the express Image of the Father; thus we notice that any image is called beautiful if it represents a thing, even an ugly thing, faithfully. Augustine touches on our point saying, *In whom there is so complete a reflection and such absolute equality*, etc. Brightness coincides with what is proper to the Son as he is the Word [*Verbum*], *the light and splendour of the mind* [*lux est splendor intellectus*], in Damascene's description. Augustine alludes to this in the same text, as *complete Word* [verbum perfectum], *from whom nothing is wanting, and the Art* [Ars], *as it were, of the Almighty*, etc.[93]

Beauty is properly appropriated to the Son with regard to his very being as this is constituted by his relation to the Father. Because the Son has perfectly in Himself the being of the Father without lack or any change, he is said to be beautiful in the sense of having full 'integrity or completeness'. Furthermore, because the Son 'is the express Image of the Father', that is, he faithfully and perfectly 'copies' the Father's being, the Son is said to be beautiful according to the second condition of 'right proportion or harmony'. It is important to pause here and relate in what sense Aquinas means the

---

[92] Ibid.
[93] Ibid.

Son copies the Father's being, not least because of its relevance to Maritain's and Jones's aesthetics. A faithful copy is not replication or duplication but a re-embodiment of Form. The flexibility in this concept is at the heart of Maritain's and Jones's thesis that all art is in some sense abstract as Jones pointedly illustrates this in his *Blackfriars* essay of how a skilled blacksmith's rendering of a statue of Mary, though on the surface not necessarily obviously 'Mary' or even a woman, may nonetheless be a more true image of her than a painting that seeks to produce exactly like to like. *Mimesis* in this sense is not 'mere' imitation but a participation.[94]

Finally, we reach Aquinas's reflection that the Son in his being is said to be beautiful according to its third condition, namely, brightness or *claritas*. Aquinas gives only this hint of what *claritas* means when he simply says, 'We call things bright in colour beautiful.' For a fuller understanding of the meaning of *claritas*, Aquinas gestures here to the analogy of the Son as the Word or VERBI – that shining word at the heart of Jones's inscription: 'Brightness [*claritas*] coincides with what is proper to the Son as he is the Word.' How fitting that in the context of our journey through an art form entirely taken with the material forms of words themselves our inquiry into nature of the beautiful has led us back to the Son as Word, even the 'art' of the Father.

The personal name of the Son as Word (as given in Jn 1.1: 'In the beginning was the Word and the Word was with God and the Word was God') plays a key role in Aquinas's earlier discussion in the *Summa* of the nature of the processions of the divine persons.[95] The analogy of the Word with human words is put to work towards understanding the nature of the procession of the Son from the Father. Aquinas draws on the distinction made in human speech and thought between a spoken word and an inner word. The spoken word is a sensible or material procession which makes manifest an invisible or internal process of thought. The inner word is the mind's concept of which the spoken word or utterance makes manifest in the form of a sign. It is this inward generativity or immaterial procession of the inner word that serves as a fitting analogue for the eternal procession of the Son as Word of the Father. In his discussion, Aquinas argues the Arian and Sabellian heresies fail to think of procession as an inward activity; they instead conceive it only as 'a going forth to something outside'.[96] The analogue of the inward procession of the word is essential in helping us perceive these intra-Trinitarian processions. He writes,

> the best example of [inward procession] appears in the intellect where the action of understanding remains in him who understands. Whenever anyone understands because of his very act of understanding, something comes forth within him, which is the concept of the known thing proceeding from his awareness of it. It is this concept which an utterance signifies; we call it 'the word in the heart' [*verbum cordis*], signified by the spoken word.[97]

---

[94] Jones, 'Beauty in Catholic Churches', *Blackfriars: A Monthly Review* (July 1926): 438-41.
[95] *Summa Theologiae* I q. 27, aa. 1–4. Cf. also q. 34, aa. 1–3 in which Aquinas inquires into the meaning of the name 'Word'.
[96] *Summa Theologiae* I q. 27, a. 1.
[97] Ibid.

The analogy of the 'verbum cordis' or inner word emphasizes the unity and personal nature of the relation between the thing known and its knower: 'For clearly the better a thinker understands something, the more personal is the idea he conceives and the more a part of himself it is; since in its act of understanding the mind becomes one with what it understands.' This intimacy or union at the heart of the inner word in the human realm is perfected in the divine. As Aquinas writes, 'therefore since God's understanding is the very peak of perfection ... God's word of necessity is perfectly one with its source and in no way diverse from it'.[98] As Velecky further clarifies, 'it is as if in thinking of himself that God begets God, He is pure intelligibility, and his act of understanding issuing in his Word is identical with his very being'.[99]

Aquinas's discussion of the begetting of the Son further illuminates the nature of this inner word.[100] The usual use of begetting or generating language is in the physical realm as in 'biological development' which involves change. However, through a more careful attunement to the meaning of 'generation', he aligns the word not essentially to change but to life: 'In its proper sense [generation] refers to living things [*viventibus*], and then it means that a living thing originates from a principle which is alive and conjoined to it; and this is properly called "birth" [*nativitas*].'[101] Furthermore, birth is properly applied only in cases where 'the thing which comes forth reproduces the likeness of its originator'.[102] Thus to proceed from another by way of generation is not exclusively applied to biological development nor is it a kind of wooden repetition but is the activity proper to a living thing, a vital activity and a conjoining between that living thing from which one proceeds and with whose being one shares a likeness. So Aquinas can conclude:

> in that last sense the notion of generation does apply to the procession of the Word in God. For the coming forth is like that in the mind's action, which is a vital activity, and is from a conjoined source, as already said; it reproduces specific resemblance, since what the intellect conceives is the likeness of what is understood; and it exists in the same nature because to be and to understand are identical in God.... Hence the procession of the Word in God is called 'generation', and the Word itself proceeding is called 'Son'.[103]

Aquinas's analogical work here not only illuminates the mystery of the Trinity but also returns us to a renewed appreciation of the everyday processes of human thought in all its dynamism, as a 'vital activity' and generative.

This understanding of human thought – and by analogy the relation of the Father and Son – however, is incomplete, corrupt even, without its expansion into its properly Trinitarian shape. And for this Aquinas turns to an exploration of inner procession of

---

[98] Ibid.
[99] Ceslaus Velecky O. P. (ed), Appendix 5, 'Divine Processions' in Volume 6 [Ia. 27–32]: *The Trinity*, trans. Ceslaus Velecky O. P. (London: Blackfriars, 2006), 138.
[100] *Summa Theologiae* I q. 27, a. 2: 'is there in God a procession which can be called "generation"?'
[101] Ibid.
[102] Ibid.
[103] Ibid.

the Spirit. Still working with this analogy of inward processions in the human being, he pushes further through recognition that the spiritual nature of humankind resides not solely in these movements of the intellect but is indissolubly bound with movement of the will, with freedom. If we are creatures who know, we are equally creatures who love. So Aquinas:

> Now in us there is another spiritual process following the action of the will, namely, the coming forth of love, whereby what is loved is in the lover, just as the thing expressed or actually understood in the conceiving of an idea is in the knower. For this reason besides the procession of the Word another procession is posited in God namely the procession of Love.[104]

In God, what is perfectly known – namely, the Son by the Father and the Father by the Son – is also perfectly loved. The relation of Father and Son is this Love itself. This Love is the Spirit, the third person of the Trinity. The procession of love is understood not as a 'begetting' but a kind of breathing or 'spirating'. The Spirit proceeds not as a kind of likeness to the Father or the Son but, akin to the human will, as an 'urge and motion towards something'; it signifies a 'living motion and impulse'.[105] Elsewhere Aquinas more clearly describes this unique inward dynamism of the will thus:

> Loving takes place because the lover is moved in a certain way by what he loves. For what is loved draws the lover to itself. Hence love, unlike understanding which is made perfect by the likeness of what is understood, reaches its perfection when the lover is drawn to the very thing he loves, not to some likeness of it.[106]

Following this long route through scholastic discussions of procession, generation and spiration, we may return finally to Aquinas's exploration of Hilary's appropriations of eternity to the Father, beauty to the Son and, at last, of joy to the Spirit. So Aquinas:

> 'To use' [uti] *means to put something at the disposal of the will and 'to enjoy'* [frui] *is a use with delight.* That use whereby the Father and Son rest joyfully in each other accords with the Holy Spirit's proper name, 'Love'. ... That use by which we rest joyfully in God also has a connection with what is proper to the Holy Spirit as he is Gift.[107]

To stumble here, at the height of a scholastic discussion on the nature of the triune relations, upon the language of 'use' – '*uti*' – is jarring, perhaps even more so than our discovery of the language of the beautiful. Function is found no less worthy than beauty for illuminating the mystery of God in Godself. Aquinas is drawing here on Augustine's distinction made in his *De Doctrina Christiana* between *uti* and *frui* – to

---

[104] *Summa Theologiae* I q. 27, a. 3: 'is there in God another procession besides the generation of the Word?'
[105] *Summa Theologiae* I q. 27, a. 4: 'is the procession of love in God generation?'
[106] From the *Compendium theologiae* 46 as quoted in Appendix 5, 'Divine Processions', 139.
[107] *Summa Theologiae* I q. 39, a. 8.

use and to enjoy.[108] The point of the distinction is to orient and guide the '*uti*' of any creature in light of and as a foreshadowing of the *frui* or rest in the divine: 'Because you have made us and drawn us to yourself, and our heart is unquiet until it rests in you.'[109] This enjoyment is the telos of all creatures towards which they move; always already realized, eternally, in the triune life of God.

This human passion of joy – this 'use with delight' – is thus closely related to love and desire. In his discussion of the human passions, Aquinas defines love as the 'feeling of a thing's attractiveness', while desire is 'the movement toward' that object and, finally, pleasure or enjoyment is rest in that object. The eventual union signified by this joy is 'a result of love'.[110] Joy arises as a result of union. In the Godhead, this love is perfectly realized as the resting of the Father in the Son and the Son in the Father. The beautiful relation of the Father and the Son is thus also a joyful relation. This is no stony static imaging but one of ongoing effulgence.

Finally, we have arrived at the apex of this theological tradition of the inner Trinitarian shape of the human person as a fitting analogue of God's very own being. This is perhaps nowhere more beautifully spoken than by Augustine in *On the Trinity*, the fontal text for Aquinas's reflections:

> The kind of word then that we are now wishing to distinguish and propose is 'knowledge with love.' So when the mind knows and loves itself, its word is joined to it with love. And since it loves knowledge and knows love, the word is in the love and the love in the word and both in the lover and the utterer.[111]

'And so', Augustine concludes, 'you have a certain image of the trinity, the mind itself and its knowledge, which is its offspring and its word about itself, and love as the third element, *and these three are one* (1 Jn 5.8) and are one substance'.[112] So Aquinas himself reiterates: 'the Son is the Word; not, however, just any word, but the Word breathing Love; *The Word as I want the meaning understood is a knowledge accompanied by love* [amor notitia est]'.[113] It is this unity of knowledge and love that constitutes the very being of God.

Having explored this understanding of Christ as beauty or *claritas* in the context of the doctrine of the Trinity, one final return to Jones's inscription is salient. In particular, our foregoing theological exploration may deepen our appreciation of that odd, nonconformist red 'V' which juts from the horizontal plane to the vertical plane. That which is so remarkable about this singular 'V' is how much Jones is able to signify through the particularities of its simple form and through its elegant placing in relation

---

[108] Saint Augustine, *De Doctrina Christiana*, ed. and trans. R. P. H. Green (Oxford: Clarendon Press, 1995), I.7–10. For more on this distinction see Rowan Williams, 'Language, Reality and Desire in Augustine's *De Doctrina*', in *On Augustine* (London: Bloomsbury, 2016), 41–59.

[109] Augustine, *Confessions*, trans. Maria Boulding (London: Hodder & Stoughton, 1997), 39.

[110] *Summa Theologiae* I.II q. 26, a. 2.

[111] Augustine, *The Trinity (De Trinitate)*, trans. Edmund Hill, O. P. (Hyde Park, NY: New City, 1991), IX.2.15/279.

[112] Ibid., IX.3.18/282.

[113] *Summa Theologiae* I q. 43, a. 5, ad. 2.

to the whole. Arguably, in these two descending diagonal lines joined at their point the theological meaning of the inscription finds summary.

In relation to the vertical line 'MINERVA JOVIS', it acts as a visual icon of the eternal relations of Father, Son and Spirit. As the 'V' of the horizontal 'VERBI' opens the word 'JOVIS' at its centre, so in the person of the Father there is already this 'more than' that is the person of the Son. The juxtaposition of 'V's – the red 'V' and the golden 'V' of the 'JOVIS' – might itself be glossed through these three conditions of the beautiful – integrity, harmony and claritas – which Aquinas 'sets up' to disclose something of the mystery of this eternal relation of the Father and the Son. As the Son has in himself the Father's nature truly and fully and so is said to be beautiful in having this full integrity or completeness of being in Himself, so too does the red 'V' have in itself, with its own integrity and completeness, the form of golden 'V' of 'JOVIS'. Or seen from another angle in light of the second condition of the beautiful as right proportion or harmony, the red 'V' 'represents faithfully' the form of the golden 'V' from which it stems, just as the Son is said to be the express image of the Father. Finally, Jones's use of colour takes on theological significance as we remember that we call things bright in colour beautiful, and so the third condition of the beautiful, *claritas*, is drawn in. Thus we may see in this singular 'V' form the beauty of Christ as the integrity, proportion and splendour of the Father.

In light of the mystery of the Trinity, the choice of red for the colour of this brightness or shining forth here leads to another layer of meaning, suggesting also the Love of the Spirit. 'Brightness coincides with what is proper to the Son as he is the Word,' Aquinas writes, but this is 'not, however, just any word, but the Word breathing Love'.[114] Might we also see in this 'V' the shape of a descending arrow and so too a suggestion of the movement of God towards His creatures, a sign of the missions of the Son and the Spirit as the two hands of the Father? A sign of the sending out of the Son as one who, though equal with God, took the form of a servant (Philippians 2)? And might its bright red colour remind us further of the descent of the Spirit in the form of flaming tongues at Pentecost?

In the simple form of this singular red 'V' and its relation to the whole of which it is but a part, we find shining forth this mystery of the Trinity as eternal, beautiful and joyful. Dwelling at length among its multivalent forms and colours, with the glossing of Augustine, Aquinas and others, the light of the revelation of the Son as *claritas* and the Spirit as *caritas* 'has shone anew into the eye of our mind'. It is by the agency of this loving Word of the Father – the *Verbum Cordis* – that the eternal circling of the Triune life of God opens out to a radical otherness in the act of creation, bringing into being those creatures which are not God but receive their being as a gift. 'By his Word or Son,' Aquinas states with great economy, 'the Father is uttering himself or creatures; and equally that by the Holy Spirit or Love proceeding Father and Son are loving both each other and us.'[115] All creatures are words of the Father spoken and redeemed in love.

---

[114] *Summa Theologiae* I q. 43, a. 5.
[115] *Summa Theologiae* I q. 37, a. 2.

Conclusion: *Poiesis* as christological participation

Imitation and participation in Trinitarian unity constitute the full dignity of art for Maritain and Jones. For Maritain the beautiful work of art is 'a work resplendent with the glitter or the brilliance, the mystery of a *form*, in the metaphysical sense of the word, a radiance of intelligibility and truth, an irradiation of the primal effulgence'.[116] This 'glitter' or 'the mystery of *form*' is not drawn *ex nihilo* from the artist's mind but is perceived by him in the heart of things already made:

> It is his eye and his mind that have perceived and disengaged it, and it must itself be alive within him, have assumed human life in him, live in his intelligence with an intellectual life and in his heart and flesh with a sensitive life, for him to be able to impart it to matter in the work he is doing.[117]

The mind desires union with that which it knows, a relation which requires not only knowledge but also love, and results in joy. The maker brings this knowledge to birth under material form, just as this desirous knowing is in turn helped along through the very process of making. Artefacts are the fruit of this inner Word breathed in Love.

Maritain is quick, however, to show how this generativity is perfectly realized within God alone:

> The Mind, the subsisting Mind, can fully realise in God alone, in the pure Act alone, the fundamental exigencies of its nature and give birth to *another self* at once substantial and personal, to a Word which shall be truly a Son. In the Holy Trinity alone do we see the coincidence of two functions which everywhere else are separate, the utterance of the Word and the generation of the Son, the Mind ending in a subsisting goal, in which the integrity of its own nature becomes substantially merged.[118]

As spiritual and material creatures, human beings desire to bring forth or realize this inner word in a medium which is itself both material and spiritual. 'The mind, despite the manifold defects peculiar to our species, strives to engender in us, is anxious to produce, not only the inner Word, the idea remaining inside us, but a work at once material and spiritual, like ourselves, with something of our soul over and above.'[119] The work of art overflows from and replenishes this inner love and knowledge and so is profoundly personal. So Maritain again, 'art's most fundamental demand is that the work make apparent not something else already made, but the spirit from which it proceeds. As God makes created participations of His being exist outside Himself, so the artist puts himself – not what he sees, but what he is – into what he makes.'[120]

---

[116] Maritain, *Art and Scholasticism*, 96.
[117] Ibid.
[118] Ibid., 97.
[119] Ibid.
[120] Ibid.

In other words, art reveals the world anew through, not despite, the particularity of the artist. Rowan Williams wonderfully summarizes this philosophy thus: 'Though divine creation cannot be imitated, what it does is to define the nature of a love that is involved in making. It is both the *gift* of self and the gift of *self*.'[121]

Jones's inscription is thus a sign of this divine gift of illumination upon which its very own possibility of creation rests. Such illumination is the source of all human art insofar as this re-presents or embodies and points towards the good, true and beautiful. It is itself a performance of that mystery of the Incarnate Word to which it points. The very act of *poiesis* is a real sharing in these divine mysteries, dependent on the infusing of that Light which is from before all time. The vocation to art is ultimately, from this theological perspective, a call to Christological participation.[122] That this is not just a Christological but more fully a Trinitarian participation is crucial. It is not only the beauty of form that is the aim but the sharing of this in love. There is great danger and potential for abuse when quest for truth becomes separated from love, and so also when love is separated from truth. It seems to be this kind of Trinitarian logic that is the source of Rowan Williams's gloss on Gill's famous line, 'Look after goodness and truth, and beauty will take care of herself.'[123] Williams emphasizes, 'It is not so much that if you look after truth, beauty will look after itself as it is that if you work with this sort of *love*, beauty will look after itself.'[124] Not just the Word made Stone, we might say with Jones, but the Word made Fire.[125]

---

[121] Rowan Williams, *Grace and Necessity: Reflections on Art and Love* (London: Continuum, 2005), 164.
[122] Cf. John Milbank, 'Christological Poetics', in *The Word Made Strange: Theology, Language and Culture* (Oxford: Blackwell, 1997), 123–44; and Hanke, *Maritain's Ontology of the Work of Art*.
[123] Eric Gill, *Beauty Looks after Herself: Essays by Eric Gill* (Tacoma, WA: Angelico Press, 2012), 245.
[124] Williams, *Grace and Necessity*, 168.
[125] Jones, 'The Sleeping Lord', 72.

3

'The Vessel of the *Ecclesia*': '*Bride*' wood engraving

Introduction: Wedding guests

Shelter, protection, guidance – though not always explicitly named, these have been underlying values in all of Jones's work studied thus far and are central to his poetic, cultural and theological vision.[1] In 'A, a, a, DOMINE DEUS', it is their felt absence which distresses the pilgrim-poet as he wanders in the wasteland as one exposed on 'an open plain'.[2] And yet we found that the cry of despair itself opens beyond itself to the saving presence of the Lord God, the I AM, who makes the journey with us. In our reading of the inscription of the Preface to the Christmas Mass, we heard of Jones's personal experience of wandering in the open plain of war where he stumbled – incredibly – upon a Mass unfolding under the shelter of a tattered wooden barn. This revelation ignited an internal fire that would guide his life and work from that moment on. That night, however, Jones still felt himself to be as one on the outside looking in: 'As I looked through that squint hole … I didn't think I ought to stay long as it seemed rather like an uninitiated bloke prying on the Mysteries of a Cult.'[3] What Jones perceived in that glimpse is a whole world: all times and all places gathered into one unity under the species of those 'quasi-artefacts', bread and wine.[4] Under the shelter and protection of that 'dim-lit byre', all the world is contained because, in the elegantly condensed words of the liturgy, 'He whom all the world cannot contain enclosed himself in thy womb, being made man.'[5] For Jones, as his friend Kathleen Raine writes,

---

[1] David Jones, 'Introduction', in *The Rime of the Ancient Mariner*, Samuel Taylor Coleridge, illustrated and introduced by David Jones, ed. with preface and afterword by Thomas Dilworth (London: Enitharmon Press, 2005), 35.
[2] This phrase resounds like a repeated mantra throughout Jones's poem, 'The Book of Balaam's Ass', in *The Sleeping Lord* (London: Faber & Faber, 1974), 104, 107 and 111.
[3] René Hague, *David Jones* (Cardiff: University of Wales Press, 1975), 58; David Jones, *Dai Greatcoat: A Self-Portrait of David Jones in His Letters*, ed. René Hague (London: Faber & Faber, 2008), 249.
[4] David Jones, 'Art and Sacrament', in *Epoch and Artist* (London: Faber & Faber, 1959), 162.
[5] Cf. Jones's painted inscription in Nicolete Gray, *Painted Inscriptions of David Jones* (London: Gordon Fraser, 1981), 55, catalogue no. 20.

While so many moderns re-dissolve man into the cosmos, with David Jones it is quite the contrary; for him the whole cosmos is 'made man' when God puts on our human flesh, which is of one substance with the bear and the 'thick-felled cave fauna' and the older and less creaturely dinosaur and 'unabiding rock' and the 'terra-marl' from all which we are made. 'Incarnational' was perhaps for David the most significant word of all. What is 'capable of being loved and known' is God incarnate.[6]

In other words, the serendipity of this discovered Mass pointed to an enduring importance for Jones: the ubiquity and profligacy of incarnation and sacrament. In each and every created thing there is a star – the *claritas* or 'secret seed' – that guides us, with the Magi, to Wisdom.

In 1930, more than a decade following this epiphany, Jones made a wood engraving that he named *Bride*.[7] Although it was the last completed engraving he was to make, according to Thomas Dilworth, 'he liked *The Bride* more than any other wood engraving he had done. ... At the end of his life, he would consider it his "favourite".'[8] Within the space of its diminutive frame (8 × 11 cm), Jones re-presents the mysteries of the Church as one deeply initiated into its liturgical rhythms and ceaseless symbolism.[9] To view the *Bride* is something of an initiation itself. No longer knocking as strangers to be let in, we are ushered in as wedding guests, brought close to the bride herself and this intimate communion of creatures gathered at the foot of the cross.

---

[6] Kathleen Raine, *David Jones and the Actually Loved and Known* (Ipswich: Golgonooza Press, 1978), 25.

[7] When Jones signed this print of the engraving, he did not use the definite article but simply wrote, '*Bride*', which, notably, functions as both a proper and a common noun; I will in turn refer to the engraving as *Bride*. We might note that 'Bride' is also the name of the matron saint of Ireland (also called Saint Brigit or Mary of the Gauls). I am not thus suggesting her identity be fixed as *this* Bride; to the contrary, as we will see in the course of the chapter, Jones insists that one always best proceeds to knowledge of the common or universal through the personal and specific. For more on the history and legends surrounding Bride or Bridget of Kildare, see *Celtic Christianity*, ed. Christopher Bamford and William Parker Marsh (Hudson, NY: Lindisfarne Press, 1982), 63–9; and Edward C. Sellner, *Wisdom of the Celtic Saints* (Notre Dame, IN: Ave Maria Press, 1993), 68–75.

[8] Afterword to Samuel Taylor Coleridge, *The Rime of the Ancient Mariner*, ed. Thomas Dilworth, 107. William Blissett also notes that in his visit on 8 July 1959, 'Mr Jones signed and gave me his wood engraving, *The Bride*, which he said was perhaps his best' in *The Long Conversation: A Memoir of David Jones* (Oxford: Oxford University Press, 1981), 24. Jones soon stopped engraving at this relatively early age apparently because of the strain it put on his eyes, as recounted in Thomas Dilworth, *David Jones: Engraver, Soldier, Painter, Poet* (London: Jonathan Cape, 2017), 113, 132, 147. *He Frees the Waters in Helyon* (1932) was his last attempt at wood engraving in Dilworth, *David Jones*, 147, fig. 11.

[9] Capitalization of 'Church' here and throughout is to intimate the mystery of the Body of Christ whose boundaries are, as we'll see, more fluid than the institutional church. As Dilworth emphasizes,

> Jones did not become a Catholic to save his soul. He regarded the conciliar statement that 'there is no salvation outside of the Church' as nonsense. ... Experience of the 'numinous', of 'Mystery', of 'incomprehensible otherness' fed in Jones deep liturgical devotion that would last the rest of his life. ... Even now the Mass was for him the paradigm of symbols, capable of containing and interpreting legend, myth, and pagan religion.

in *David Jones*, 68–9. In this sense, there is no contradiction between this interpretation of *Bride* through the liturgy of the Church and Dilworth's summation that 'her archetype is Mother Earth' in Dilworth, *David Jones*, 118.

Though first published in 1930 as the frontispiece to a collection of poems by his friend, Walter Shewring, titled, *Hermia and Some Other Poems*,[10] Jones's inspiration for the engraving is much more likely to have been the series of copper engravings, commissioned by Douglas Cleverdon in 1927, that he had just completed for Samuel Taylor Coleridge's poem, *The Rime of the Ancient Mariner*.[11] In his study of these engravings, Thomas Dilworth recovered a cancelled engraving which Jones originally intended as the frontispiece of the poem that bears remarkable thematic and structural parallels to *Bride*: A veiled female figure in a chapel kneels before a candelabra in prayer with rosary beads and a bouquet of flowers in hand; behind her is a crucifix around which is inscribed '*hoc sacramentum magnum est*'.[12] This cancelled engraving was Jones's first attempt at the illustrations, working in a medium in which he was relatively inexperienced. He did not intend his engravings to be straightforwardly illustrational; rather, he wanted 'to get in copper the general fluctuations of the poem'.[13] This unsuccessful engraving was conceived as a frontispiece both because *The Ancient Mariner* begins with a wedding feast and because the culmination of the poem, for Jones, is the Eucharistic feast.

On any account, Jones's return in 1930 to these themes in the medium of wood was extraordinarily successful, creating one of the most beautiful and profound of his engravings. Jones's *Bride* achieves the quality which, for him, made Coleridge's poem 'unique and set apart', conveying depths of meaning in a form that 'almost anybody can enjoy, from the most sophisticated and critical to the least'.[14] As he would write a year later in his Introduction for the 1964 edition of the illustrated poem:

> Behind the fluent artistry and the popular ballad form, it conceals or discloses deeps and strata of meaning where, in the words of the Psalmist, *Abyssus abyssum*

---

[10] Walter Shewring, *Hermia and Some Other Poems* (Ditchling: St. Dominic's Press, 1930). The engraving was subsequently printed in *Engravings of David Jones*, ed. Douglas Cleverdon (London: Clover Hill Editions, 1981), plate no. 88. My reading is based on the print from the original wood block which I received as the gracious gift from the parents of the Reverend Doctor John Hughes, 1978–2014: ET LUX PERPETUA LUCEAT EI.

[11] Originally published as Samuel Taylor Coleridge, *The Rime of the Ancient Mariner*, with ten engravings on copper by David Jones (Bristol: Douglas Cleverdon, 1929). Later reprinted in a limited edition of copies as Samuel Taylor Coleridge, *The Rime of the Ancient Mariner*, with ten engravings on copper and foreword by David Jones, Clover Hill Editions (New York: Chilmark Press, 1964). Throughout this chapter, I will be citing from this most recent edition: Samuel Taylor Coleridge, *The Rime of the Ancient Mariner*, illustrated and introduced by David Jones, ed. with preface and afterword by Thomas Dilworth (London: Enitharmon Press, 2005).

[12] Afterword to *The Rime of the Ancient Mariner*, ed. Thomas Dilworth, 85. Anne Price-Owen, writing even before the discovery of this cancelled engraving, agrees that the engraving is not substantially related to Shewring's book of poems: 'The [*Bride*] engraving does not relate to any particular theme or poem in [Shewring's book], but its decorative quality makes it an enhancing accompaniment to this volume of rather banal poetry' in *Fragments of an Attempted Painting: An Investigation of the Pictorial Concepts in David Jones's 'The Anathemata'* (PhD diss., University of Wales, Lampeter, 1992), 14.

[13] David Jones to Douglas Cleverdon, 22 June 1927, University of Indiana Library quoted in *The Rime of the Ancient Mariner*, ed. Thomas Dilworth, 85.

[14] Introduction to *The Rime of the Ancient Mariner*, ed. Thomas Dilworth, 15. This introduction is also reprinted in David Jones, *The Dying Gaul and Other Writings*, ed. Harman Grisewood (London: Faber & Faber, 2008), 186–225.

Figure 3 *Bride*, 1931, wood engraving on paper, 140 × 110 mm, Kettle's Yard, University of Cambridge. Estate of David Jones (Bridgeman Copyright). Used with permission.

invocat. In a figurative sense deep calls to deep in all great works, but here owing to the subject-matter of the poem, the remaining words of the verse of the psalm, *in voce cataractarum tuarum*, are equally applicable.[15]

In like manner, Jones's *Bride* charms and enchants the viewer with its luscious and suggestive figures – both 'elusive' and 'allusive' in form and content.[16] Jones's analogy for his experience of reading Coleridge's poem aptly fits that of his wood engraving as well: 'I suppose one of the commonest echoes of childhood is the remembrance of hearing enclosed, in little space, the sea-shell's muffled echo of the limitless ocean's ceaseless surf-break.'[17] This ceaselessly resounding subject-matter is ultimately, for Jones, a complex re-telling of redemption as enacted principally in the Mass. As Jones wrote in his Introduction to Coleridge's poem,

> What is pleaded in the Mass is precisely the argosy or voyage of the Redeemer, his entire sufferings, death, resurrection and ascension. It is this that is offered on behalf of us argonauts and the whole argosy of mankind and indeed in some sense of all earthly creation, which, as Paul says, suffers a common travail.[18]

This reading is by no means reductive for Jones. Rather, because this Redeemer is the Creator and Sustainer of all creation in all times and all places, this particular story carries all stories in its wake as their fulfilment and perfection. The Church's story is for him this universal story, drawing within itself the 'whole argosy of mankind' – not only Noah but Odysseus, too, and 'those nearer far of our own Celtic West':[19]

> [The early Greek and Latin Fathers] saw that the ship, the mast, the voyagings, the odysseys and argosies, the perils and ordeals that were part and parcel of classical tradition, could and should be taken as typic of the Church's voyaging. They had a perception of the vessel of the ecclesia, her heavy scene in the troughs of the world-waters, drenched with inboard seas, to starboard Scylla, to larboard Charybdis, lured by persistent Siren calls, but secure because to the transomed stauros of the mast was made fast the Incarnate Word.[20]

Coleridge's poem was clearly an inspiration to *The Anathemata*, which begins and ends in the few moments in which the priest consecrates the elements. In between, all history unfolds. In her passing through the waters of time, the Church is frequently imagined as a great ship, a metaphor also for Mary and the Bride of Christ.[21] According to Price-Owen, '*The Bride* is perhaps the earliest, most complete pictorial forerunner

---

[15] Ibid., 15.
[16] Ibid.
[17] Ibid.
[18] Ibid., 16.
[19] Ibid.
[20] Ibid., 35.
[21] Anne Price-Owen explores these images in relation to *Bride* in detail in *Fragments of an Attempted Painting*, 11–50.

of *The Anathemata*. Jones evokes it many times when personifying the Church as the bride of Christ.²²

Again, Jones's description of Coleridge's poem illumines the quality of his engraving as well:

> its imagery has a metamorphic quality. With swift artistry, with something akin to the conjuror's sleight of hand, the images seem now this, now that, a little like the shape-shifting figures in Celtic mythology. ... [I]t has its own *hud a lledrith* [magic and fantasy], that is to say, it spellbinds. It is not only the Wedding Guest who 'cannot chuse but hear', but you and I.²³

Jones writes that this 'feeling of movement', of 'not being stuck still', is for him a central aesthetic principle; as he boldly states, a work of art 'must be fluid in some way or other. That is, perhaps, my criterion in assessing the worth of any picture.'²⁴ This 'metamorphic' quality is not only like those characters of Celtic mythology but also very much like the biblical mythology of the Song of Songs, that beautiful love song or poem of Scripture which has long been read in some sense as a love song between God and his people and has nurtured the nuptial metaphor of the Church as the bride of Christ throughout its history. As Paul Ricoeur in his reading of its literary texture argues, there is a wonderful indeterminacy characterizing the song throughout, holding open this space for a 'plurality of interpretations'.²⁵ The identities of lover and beloved are not fixed but are continuously shifting, exchanging places, melding and receding. That which characterizes the poem then is not any singular identity or narrative but these continuous movements of love, the play between absence and presence, dreaming and waking, embracing and admiring. The space that opens between the lover and beloved is the place of fecundity, of meaning, and ultimately of love. As Ricoeur beautifully summarizes, 'Is it not from the end of the world and depth of time that love arises? But then no name corresponds to or answers the question "who?"'²⁶

This continual exchanging of places is not only a mark of the Celtic and Scriptural texts which Jones loved but embodied in the movements of the liturgy which also so deeply formed him. For Jones the reality of the Church cannot be separated from

---

²² Ibid., 14.
²³ Introduction to *The Rime of the Ancient Mariner*, ed. Thomas Dilworth, 16.
²⁴ Peter Orr (ed.), 'David Jones the Artist: A Brief Autobiography', in *David Jones: Eight Essays on His Work as Writer and Artist*, ed. Roland Mathias (Llandysul: Gomer Press, 1976), 11, 12.
²⁵ 'The Nuptial Metaphor', in *Thinking Biblically: Exegetical and Hermeneutical Studies*, Paul Ricoeur and André LaCocque, trans. David Pellauer (Chicago, IL: University of Chicago Press, 1998), 267.
²⁶ Ibid., 270. Rowan Williams makes this observation regarding the paradoxical nature of Augustine's hermeneutics in particular, though applicable more generally to patristic and medieval tradition of allegorical or figurative reading:

> Where literalism is to be rejected, it is because it proposes to us a static object of knowledge capable of possession and thereby fails to stir us to longing for the greater fullness of God. So there is a paradoxical dimension to [Augustine's] hermeneutics: what most locates us in our earthly experience in all its reality is what most opens up the fuller sense because it most prompts desire.

in 'Augustine and the Psalms' in *Interpretation* (2004), 23.

its performance of the liturgy. The practice of singing the Psalms is one particular way in which the melding of Christ's voice and the human voice takes place and the sacraments are marked by this exchange of identities between Christ and the Church.[27] David Torevell argues, in his *Liturgy and the Beauty of the Unknown*, that the liturgy is chiefly characterized, like the Song of Songs, by these movements of desire. He writes, 'any understanding of worship is best served by locating it within the trajectory of divine and human desire, a movement which begins with the "ecstatic" procession of God's love, made visible in the incarnate Word, encouraging a return movement towards that which is endlessly beautiful'.[28] By orienting its participants towards the beatific vision, the ordinary present existence is thus re-enchanted. Such a vision 'lifts participants away from seeing life as a mere lump of existence and ... reinstates them on a trajectory of desire towards the infinitely unknowable and beautiful'.[29] Ultimately, the liturgy conducts the wedding between heaven and earth, carving a path between this world and the next, between seeing through a veil darkly and seeing face to face.

Given the character of these liturgical, Scriptural and Celtic influences upon Jones, it is no wonder that, in turning to his engraving, *Bride*, there is no singular answer to the question, 'who is she?' The identities of the prime characters are endlessly shifting and the 'time, places, and even the emotions and actions' are wonderfully ambiguous.[30] The central figure of the bride emerges like a tower from a bed of flowers, her bodice as a fruitful vineyard. She is paradoxically both within and without. The windows behind her suggest that she is indoors, enclosed, and yet this 'within' seems also to contain the whole world. The tresses of her hair mingle with the translucent veil across her shoulder and long neck while her head is crowned with a garland of roses and celestial stars. To her right a stag presses his eager chest towards her as though leaping into the foreground of the frame while on her left a singing bird is perched, its subtle form almost melding with the background. Her crooked right arm reaches to light a votive candle from a black candelabra in the lower right corner. This black circle seems to open an almost vertiginous descent but for the strong ascent of the straight-lined candles that point towards a surrealist-styled crucifix: the grotesquely wounded feet of Christ pinned to an almost gothic skull by a protruding iron nail. Lines evoking smoke and incense stream upward from the candles, while blood flows down like sun rays from the knee of the crucified limb just as it exits the frame. This hardly begins to do the engraving justice: its thick profusion of image, symbol, texture, frame, balance and so forth seems to open worlds of meaning and interpretation without end. How are we to approach this?

In what follows, I first introduce the tradition of wood engraving in Britain of which Jones is a part. As we have seen throughout this study, the medium is essential

---

[27] Jason Byassee explores in depth this practice of reading the Psalms as performing our unity with Christ in *Praise Seeking Understanding: Reading the Psalms with Augustine* (Grand Rapids, MI: Eerdmans, 2007); cf. Williams, 'Augustine and the Psalms', 17–27. See also Catherine Pickstock, *After Writing: On the Liturgical Consummation of Philosophy* (Oxford: Blackwells, 1998), particularly the chapter, 'Seraphic Voices: The Space of Doxology', 220–52 for an extended reading of the intermingling and exchange of voices characterizing the Roman rite as a whole.

[28] David Torevell, *Liturgy and the Beauty of the Unknown* (Aldershot, Hampshire: Ashgate, 2007), 2.

[29] Ibid.

[30] As Paul Ricoeur characterizes the Song of Songs in 'The Nuptial Metaphor', in *Thinking Biblically*, 268.

to the meaning of the work and wood engraving is particularly rewarding in this regard. I then explore the liturgical and aesthetic character of Jones's engraving as a whole before engaging in a more detailed reading of its richly symbolic figures. These readings will unfold in dialogue with Jones's prose poetic works, especially poems from *The Sleeping Lord* collection, which help convey this continuity between liturgy, church and cosmos.

Following the furrowed line: The craft of wood engraving

Wood engraving has been described as 'the velvet of media. With deeper blacks and purer whites than in any other graphic medium, it can express a vast range of tone and texture from powerful masses to delicate tendrils.'[31] Though Jones began his formal training as an artist from the young age of 14, it was not until his time at Ditchling Commons that he began to work in the medium of wood. Jones did some wood carving – from small figurines and crucifixes to door locks and a salad spoon and fork – but it was in wood engraving that his gifts as a visual artist would shine.[32] He learned not from Eric Gill but Jones's peer and comrade, Desmond Chute.[33] Jones quickly excelled, soon making illustrations for books printed on the Ditchling Press. His first complete series of illustrations was for *A Child's Rosary Book*, published in 1924.[34] Though Jones had not yet started writing poetry, he already showed great facility in crossing the boundary between word and image. Akin to Blake, his visualizations are creative re-tellings, forging a generative rather than merely reproductive relationship with the narrative.[35] But in order to appreciate the kind of engraver Jones became, we must first understand the distinctive tradition of British wood engraving into which he was grafted.

In any introduction to the craft of wood engraving, the first essential thing to grasp is its fundamental difference from wood cuts, a distinction which all but practitioners frequently confuse.[36] While the prints they produce, to the untrained eye, often appear indistinguishable, wood cuts and wood engraving are different from one another in nearly every aspect including tools, technique and even the kind of wood they require. First, wood cuts use the long grain of wood – like the plank of a board – and a variety of trees suffice, though pear is common. Wood cuts are made using a tool akin to a

---

[31] Dorothea Braby, *British Wood Engravings of the 20th Century: A Personal View*, ed. Albert Garrett (London: Scolar Press, 1980), 5.
[32] See Jonathan Miles and Derek Shiel, *The Maker Unmade* (Brigend, Wales: Seren Press, 1995), 45–7 and 79–84.
[33] Keith Alldritt, *David Jones: Writer and Artist* (London: Constable & Robinson, 2003), 50. Cf. also *Inner Necessities: The Letters of David Jones to Desmond Chute*, ed. Thomas Dilworth (Toronto: Anson-Cartwright, 1984).
[34] *Mary, the Blessed Virgin: A Child's Rosary Book: Being the Fifteen Mysteries of the Most Holy Rosary of the Blessed Virgin Mary* (Ditchling, Sussex: St. Dominic's Press, 1924).
[35] For a complete list of books Jones illustrated, see *British Wood Engravings of the 20th Century*, ed. Albert Garrett, 73.
[36] The terminology is not always consistent either. 'Wood cutting', as described here, is actually more technically called 'black-line technique' engraving as opposed to 'white-line technique'. But even this terminology already presupposes certain familiarity with basic techniques as we will see.

knife or scalpel which is held perpendicular to the wood and positioned in the hand like a pen or pencil. Wood engraving by contrast uses the end grain of the wood where the rings of growth are exposed. It also demands a particular tree – the boxwood – of which English varieties are considered the best, though frequently the wood is sourced, as it was regularly during Jones's day, from the Caucasus mountain range in Turkey. The primary tool for wood engravers is called the burin, which is cradled in the palm of the hand, its point guided by the thumb. The engraver has a variety of burins to choose from depending on the depth or width of line he or she desires – gravers, spitzstickers, scorpers, tint tools and so on. The hand and burin glide parallel to the wood rather than perpendicular to it. Furthermore, the wood block is positioned on a sandbag which allows the block to be turned into the tool for curves and angles while the artist's hand remains relatively still.

The essential difference however lies in technique. The principle behind woodcuts is the black line on white: the wood on either side of the line by which the artist delineates his or her form is cut away; this upraised area that remains then receives the ink when pressed. By contrast, the principle behind wood engraving is the white line on black, not unlike icon writing: rather than cutting away on either side of the sought for line, the artist makes a single 'burrow' in the wood with his burin; when the block is inked and pressed, this engraved area that does not receive the ink becomes the primary means of conveying form. Carol Leighton summarizes this well: 'Every cut made on a wood block prints white, so that one is always working up from the black towards the light. If the new engraving block were printed, it would be but a rectangle of black ink.'[37]

This somewhat technical introduction, however, overlooks the deeply social and ethical contexts in which such practices were developed. In the medieval West, wood cuts were the primary way of reproducing images. The first playing cards were wood cuts and religious prints collected by pilgrims at holy sites were also frequently produced this way. However, the reproduction of such images was carefully controlled, as Dorothea Braby explains: 'If the woodcutter was not a monk (who alone was permitted to make prints) he worked by stealth against the law, since the Guild of Scribes and Illuminators forbade multiplication of images other than by hand.'[38] Yet, as she continues, 'with the invention of the printing press all of that changed'. Particularly as book production became a commercialized industry in the eighteenth and nineteenth centuries, wood cutting as a craft was increasingly debauched as a merely reproductive technique; an artist would draw an image which was then traced onto the wood block and a group of workers called *formschneiders* would do the manual labour of cutting the wood away from the line. Braby colourfully voices the critique of this development thus: 'The conception was in black lines natural to quill and brush, faithfully rendered in the medium where this was the least natural: imagine the labour of a passage closely cross-hatched, where each small white lozenge left in the interstices had to be removed with soulless dexterity!'[39] Not only is the black-line technique considered ill-fitting to

---

[37] *Wood-engraving and Woodcuts* [How to Do It Series, No. 2] (London: Studio Publications, 1944), 7.
[38] Preface to *British Wood Engraving of the Twentieth Century*, ed. Albert Garrett, 5.
[39] Ibid., 6.

its medium, but the increasing division between artist and workman by commercial industry practices tended to reduce this art to mere *techne*.

The revival of wood engraving in the early twentieth century was formed as a conscious reaction against this weight of commercial industrialism. Artists such as Eric Gill, Gwendolen Raverat and John Nash founded the first Society of Wood Engravers in 1920; by 1922 Jones was already being invited to exhibit with them, and in 1927 he was formally inducted to the Society. Though the reproduction of book illustrations was already being taken over by the cheaper and more efficient means of photography, these early twentieth-century engravers were key in reviving wood engraving as a means of creative expression and as furthering the socialist legacy of the Arts and Crafts movement created by men such as William Morris.[40] The revival flourished also not least because of its adoption of the white-line technique, which, though developed as early as the eighteenth century by Thomas Bewick, only now came into its own. 'Bewick', writes Albert Garrett, 'is remarkable in that he reversed the whole process of wood engraving from the predominantly black-line *formschneider* commercial reproductive technique to the white-line'.[41] Bewick was guided in his development of this technique by his interest 'in the illumination of a surface to disclose details of its structure and texture'.[42] With its revival of Bewick's white-line technique and the reuniting of 'the artist' and 'the craftsmen', Dorothea Braby compares the revival of wood engraving in the early twentieth century to a fairy-tale transformation: 'From Cinderella's dish-clout, wood engraving has become the Princess's robe of glory, displaying the beauty of light emerging from blackness into its full power of creative expression.'[43]

Though counter-intuitive in a culture trained to see in terms of black line on white (not least through the printed page), practitioners of the white line point out that nature draws in white as often as black. It is embraced as the 'more natural and direct method' for this medium versus the 'more laboured and less spontaneous process' of black line.[44] Braby even speaks in terms of the wood itself having been 'all this time … in bondage to an alien means of expression rather than directly creative in its own right'.[45] This technique enables the artist to achieve much finer, delicate lines and thus requires the hard end grain of boxwood, which is 'almost as hard as ivory

---

[40] See Eric Gill's Introduction to John R. Beedham, *Wood Engraving* (Ditchling: St. Dominic's Press, 1921) for a strong assertion of the social and cultural significance of the revival of this craft.

[41] Albert Garrett, *A History of British Wood Engraving* (Tunbridge Wells, Kent: Midas Books, 1978), 129. William Blake, Bewick's contemporary, also ventured into this reversal of the black-line technique, though he did not develop it technically as far as Bewick would. See Garrett, *A History of British Wood Engraving*, 123–9.

[42] Ibid., 131.

[43] Preface to *British Wood Engravings of the 20th Century*, ed. Albert Garrett, 7. Garrett expands, '[Bewick] thought in terms of reproducing the effect of light and of how much to cut away and how much to leave. In so doing he was controlling the total distribution of the light available.' Furthermore, he explains, this technique has 'the double advantage of texture creation, by its being naturally drawn in the white line, with the addition of a natural field of texture arising from the black area left between closely-spaced white line' in Garrett, *British Wood Engravings of the 20th Century*, 36.

[44] Carol Leighton, *Wood-engraving and Woodcuts* (London: Studio Publications, 1944), 7.

[45] Preface to *British Wood Engravings of the 20th Century*, ed. Albert Garrett, 6.

and the only sufficiently close-grained to withstand the minute incisions of detailed engraving without splintering or blurring the line'.[46] The engraver is deeply aware of the preciousness of her material in which mistakes cannot simply be erased or painted over.

The block itself has already undergone intensive processes of preparation. As Braby states, 'The block itself is a beautiful piece of polished craftsmanship; the wood has been seasoned for 3 years, and came from a tree 300 years old.'[47] The primer to wood engraving which Jones likely used while at Ditchling conveys the time and almost visceral sense of these physical processes in which the wood is set in racks to dry 'for many month to season, and during this time sharp cracks are heard which denote the slices of the wood are drying and splitting from the core'. This drying process prevents later splitting of the block after the artist has engraved it. The wood was then cut into even smaller blocks of approximately one inch and then glued together. In its sensitivity to light, texture and the supple fluidity of the line, white-line technique draws nearer to its ancient roots in Palaeolithic engravings. As Albert Garrett claims in *A History of British Wood Engraving*, the British tradition of wood engraving more nearly approximates the peculiar beauty and genius of Palaeolithic engraving. Jones himself paid homage to these ancient artisans and aptly communicates his high regard for them in personal reflections such as this: 'Man, already twenty to forty thousand years ago, whatever his limitations was capable of superb artistry. In some respects we have not equalled that artistry, let alone surpassed it.'[48]

The actual act of engraving may be compared to a religious or spiritual practice akin to the monastic practices of image making which Mary Carruthers describes in *The Craft of Thought*.[49] Carruthers, writing on the material practice of monks in making the beautiful carpet pages of the Lindisfarne gospels, makes this connection between the physical act of inscribing on the tough parchment and the kind of inner or spiritual work that is thereby being performed.

> The prickings, scorings, and 'woundings' of the parchment which were necessary to draw the designs (and which are still visible on some of the pages) bring to mind – in the inventive way of all good composition – the com*punc*tion with which one should begin prayerfully to read the gospel text.[50]

The prickings made on the parchment are tangible visible signs of the internal soul-work from out of which the designs flow and have as their end in building up. So too we might consider how, for an artist like Jones, wood engraving also facilitates this relationship between the material-spiritual aspects of craft-making and the Gospel stories. The wood engraver is given this carefully treated and prepared precious material – for which a tree gave its life – which is of the same material as that upon which Christ died. With an iron burin (not unlike the form of the nails by which

---

[46] Ibid., 5.
[47] Ibid.
[48] Quoted in Garret, *A History of British Wood Engraving*, 31.
[49] Mary Carruthers, *The Craft of Thought: Meditation, Rhetoric, and the Making of Images 400–1200* (Cambridge: Cambridge University Press, 1998).
[50] Ibid., 169.

Christ was crucified), the artist digs grooves into the hard material, long narrow cuts or depressions. The etymology of the word 'engrave' itself is closely bound with burial rites and death, from the Old English 'grave' which means 'to dig' and originates from the German *graben* meaning 'to dig' and *begraben* which means 'to bury'.[51] Carving into the very material on which Christ was crucified with instruments that recall the brutal iron nail that pierced Christ's flesh and the wood of the cross invites the artist to imaginatively enter with the events of the Passion. Whether in a mode of compunction (identifying with those who are the cause of Christ's suffering) or devotion (identifying with those who bear Christ's suffering with him), the visceral act of engraving the furrowed line is always for the artist an act of love, bringing about a transformation and even transfiguration. Especially as the block is finally inked and pressed, its 'wounds' – the cuts in the wood itself – print white, suggesting further this opening of the wounds of Christ to their transfiguration in glory.

The personification of the wood in the ancient Anglo-Saxon poem, *The Dream of the Rood*, is irresistibly recalled here: in this first great English poem, the primal, even chthonic, personage of a tree identifies with the suffering yet also the glorification of Christ.[52] As the Tree speaks, it begins its tale by recalling its felling in the woods until being set up on Calvary where Christ Himself was 'climbing to clasp me'.[53] The visceral woundings of Christ's body are borne by the wood, too. And yet, the Tree rises gloriously ornamented, knowing that it, like the woman Mary, was specially chosen for this singular task:

> One time in days past: I love thereon to think,
> Hewn down I was: from the end of the holt,
> Removed from my roots …
> Felons flung me forth: shouldering me strongly
> Leaving me at last: on a high hill,
> Many fierce foes: fastened me up there.
> Then from there I saw: the Master of mankind
> Striving with much strength: climbing to clasp me …
> Truly then I trembled: as the Youth embraced me. …
> Dark nails they drove me through: the marks may still be seen
> Wicked wounds of malice: nor dared I injure any.
> They reviled us Both together: all with blood was I bedewed
> Begotten of His side: after death came to Him. …
> On me the Son of God: once suffered sore sorrow
> Therefore I glorious now: tower under the heavens,
> And I may heal and bless: each one who hallows me.[54]

---

[51] See entries for 'engrave' and 'grave' in *Oxford English Dictionary*, 2nd edn (Oxford: Clarendon Press, 1989).
[52] Ruth Wainewright, *The Dream of the Holy Rood*, trans. Ruth Wainewright (Ditchling: Dominic's Press, 1931).
[53] Ibid., unpaginated.
[54] Ibid. For a theologically rich reading of 'The Dream of the Rood', see Malcolm Guite, *Faith, Hope and Poetry: Theology and the Poetic Imagination* (Surrey, UK: Ashgate, 2012), 32–51.

The wood becomes, by proxy, the minister of grace – healing and blessing as in a dance of reciprocal exchange with the one who 'hallows' the precious material.

We have perhaps said enough about the general art of wood engraving and the way in which the craft and the guild permit themselves to be read in a theological and almost mystagogical manner. But how did Jones make this medium his own? What kind of engraver was he? The graceful economy and fluidity of Jones's lines as well as his unique ability to capture the effects of light and water distinguish him in this medium as in his drawings and watercolours. In this, as Garrett remarks, 'Jones has understood the art of Palaeolithic man better than most.'[55] His lines are often engraved with such sensitivity and subtlety that they required the equal subtlety and sensitivity which only private printing presses are able to produce.[56] Garrett describes Jones as

> a natural engraver whose burin opens the flow to life and to his images. He is in the grand tradition of painter-engraver and a Jones engraving, whether in wood or copper, could not exist in another medium. With great economy he achieves complex concepts and he uses a pencil beam of delicate white light illuminating and delineating them.[57]

In her introduction to wood engraving, Carol Leighton also presents Jones's work as worthy of study by apprentice engravers. She writes, 'while not thinking as consciously as most artists about the technique of the medium, [he] achieves some extraordinary qualities'.[58] Jones is chosen as a model particularly for his unique ability to capture the play of light. Concerning one of his wood engravings for *The Chester Play of the Deluge*,[59] she writes:

> He gets a very beautiful shimmering quality of light on the water that it is hard to analyse. He has drawn the shape of each wave with light, modelling them by working towards the white outlines with deepening cuts with the graver. His white lines follow the shape of the form he wishes to get.[60]

---

[55] Garrett, *A History of British Wood Engraving*, 179.
[56] However, even among private printers, Jones's work was difficult to reproduce; he even drew this rebuff of this otherwise sympathetic printer, Christopher Sandford: 'I have included the two engravings by David Jones only because I have a passionate admiration of the conceptions of this great artist. Owing to his shallow engraving of the wood, these blocks are virtually unprintable. Artist's please mark my words – when engraving for publishers, scrap your thinnest tools and cut deep', quoted in Garrett, *A History of British Wood Engraving*, 273–4. Jones's art characteristically resists facile reproduction. As photography became the primary means for book illustrations, even this immediacy between the engraved wood block and the printed page became mediated through the lens of the camera. The private printing press was thus especially important for Jones as 'a means of eliminating the intervention of the camera to translate the engraving into the printed page', in Garrett, *A History of British Wood Engraving*, 289.
[57] Ibid., 180.
[58] Leighton, *Wood-engraving and Woodcuts*, 68.
[59] *Chester Play of the Deluge*, ed. J. Isaacs (Berkshire: Golden Cockerel Press, 1927).
[60] Leighton, *Wood-engraving and Woodcuts*, 68.

This technique of Jones to lightly outline many of his subjects in a thin white line is reminiscent of the way objects shimmer in moonlight or after a morning frost, and one is reminded once more of Coleridge's poetry: 'the frost performs its secret ministry', gracing the form of things; and of the 'water-snakes' of *The Ancient Mariner* who 'moved in tracks of shining white' beneath the moonlight, drawing forth the mariner's confession of praise.[61] Perhaps the influence of Maritain's and Jones's understanding of form as *claritas*, a shining forth, also influences his technique here.

As we have come to expect of Jones, he incorporates modernist principles of painting and sculpture even in his practice of this traditional art form.[62] The *Bride* engraving is itself clearly formed by Post-Impressionist principles, as Anne Price-Owen's astute analysis explains:

> There is really no foreground and no background in this engraving. The motifs are absorbed into a fluid pattern so that each image advances and recedes as the eye travels with the prevailing rhythmic forces inherent in the design. Nevertheless, all of the objects remain firmly fixed on the picture plane …. Only by its relevant size does one image apparently predominate over another; yet all contribute to the significance of the manifold allusions which this picture yields.[63]

This respect for the surface or picture plane is an important way of insisting on the 'thingness' of the artwork itself, that is, its existence as a re-incarnation or re-presentation of another thing rather than a mere representation of some other thing.

Importantly, Price-Owen notes that while this is a modernist technique, it in fact has much in common with the traditional practice of writing icons: 'This practice was not new to the visual arts, on the contrary it may be compared to mediaeval iconographic works. Jones combines the techniques of twentieth-century artists and their integrity to the picture plane, with those of pre-Renaissance exponents.'[64] Rowan Williams picks up on this connection in his *Grace and Necessity* when he describes Jones's work as so many 'intersecting and criss-crossing lines on a surface, realities superimposed'.[65] This way of painting, drawing, engraving or even writing poetry, argues Williams, demands a different process of engagement for the viewer/reader. This, he writes, is 'how you paint "excess" ':

---

[61] 'Frost at Midnight', in Samuel Taylor Coleridge, *Poetical Works I, Poems (Reading Text)*, ed. J. C. C. May (Princeton: Princeton University Press, 2001), 453–6; and lines 273–5 in *The Rime of the Ancient Mariner*, ed. Thomas Dilworth, 62.

[62] Albert Garrett's *A History of British Wood Engraving* is an indispensable resource and guidebook to the work of influential modernist engravers including Paul Nash, Leon Underwood, Blair Hughes-Stanton and Gertrude Hermes.

[63] Anne, *Fragments of an Attempted Painting*, 15.

[64] Ibid. For further exploration of the fruitful dialogue possible between David Jones and the Orthodox tradition, particularly here with John Damascene (c. 676–749), cf. also Andrew Louth, 'Image and Reality in David Jones: Some Orthodox Reflections', in *David Jones: The Furrowed Line; Catalogue of an Exhibition*, ed. Rebecca White (Oxford: Fellowship of St. Alban & St. Sergius, 2014), 75–87.

[65] Rowan Williams, *Grace and Necessity: Reflections on Art and Love* (London: Continuum, 2005), 69.

by the delicate superimposing of nets of visual material in a way that teases constantly by simultaneously refusing a third dimension and insisting that there is no way of reading one surface at once. As in the Byzantine icon, visual depth gives way to the time taken to 'read' a surface: you cannot construct a single consistent illusion of depth as you look, and so you are obliged to trace and re-trace the intersecting linear patterns.[66]

In other words, one 'paints "excess"' by creating an artefact that seems to demand a sort of completion that can only be supplied by the dynamic participation of the viewer. One cannot engage such works as a spectator. The movement of the eye is an essential part of its meaning and, like the liturgy itself, a performance of it. Indeed, the wood, the artist and the readers are all gathered and made actors in the liturgical drama of the engraving itself.

'A flowery, starry, intertwined image': The liturgical character of *Bride*

It is worth remembering that liturgy – from the Greek *leitourgia* – refers literally to the work of the people, a folk work, one might even say a craft. Human beings, as Jones frequently reminds, have been liturgical in some sense as long as they have existed – even the Neanderthal, said to be not yet *Homo sapiens*, had burial rites.[67] Liturgies connect the inner and outer life of human beings and connect them once more into the rhythms of their own bodies and the bodies of the world. They facilitate and heal the once natural unity of the material and spiritual aspects of their being. Liturgies are human forms of participation in the cosmic rhythms of the rising and setting of the

---

[66] Rowan, *Grace and Necessity*, 69. Rowan Williams models the way such works invite themselves to be read theologically and meditatively in his two small books, *The Dwelling of the Light: Praying with Icons of Christ* (Norwich: Canterbury Press, 2003) and *Ponder these Things: Praying with Icons of the Virgin* (Norwich: Canterbury Press, 2002). Most importantly, he tends to the way the eye is led around the icon and shows how this movement is integral to its meaning. So, for instance, writing on Rublev's icon in *The Dwelling of the Light*, he shows how the circular motion of the eye from figure to figure is crucial to the trinitarian theology it conveys – it resists any wooden identifications of one figure with a specific person of the Trinity, thus tempting the viewer towards anthropomorphism or tritheism; more importantly, this constant circling movement is an enactment of the divine circling, an ongoing dynamic exchange of love defining the Triune life. '[I]n this image', he writes,

> there is, quite simply, no place to stop; the movement circles around and around. It is impossible to stand and look any of the figures in the eye: no full-face contact is possible. And this immediately says something crucial for our understanding of both Jesus and the Holy Trinity. To look at Jesus is not to enter into a simple one-to-one relation. (Ibid., 53)

Reading the icon in this manner is a performance and form of participation in this Triune life: 'Knowing the Trinity is being involved in this circling movement: drawn by the Son towards the Father, drawn into the Father's breathing out of the Spirit so that the Son's life may be again made real in the world. It is where contemplation and action become inseparable' (ibid., 57).

[67] As Jones himself notes, 'For the zoologist a distinction is made between *homo sapiens* and *homo Neanderthalis*; whereas, seeing the latter was *homo faber* he must, theologically speaking, have been "sapiential", especially when it is remembered that his fabrications were connected with rites for the dead' in 'Art and Sacrament', in *Epoch and Artist*, 147, n. 2.

sun, the waxing and waning of the moon, and the singing of birds at dawn and dusk, marking the seasons and years. Jones captures this beautiful co-inherence of human and cosmic liturgies in his poem, 'Tutelar of the Place' thus: 'As when on known-site ritual frolics keep bucolic interval at / eves and divisions when they mark the inflexions of the year / and conjugate with trope and turn the season's syntax, with / beating feet, with wands and pentagons to spell out the Trisagion.'[68] Jones once more interweaves the pagan or 'Magian' and Christian with bold deliberation here.[69] His verse conveys the strong relationship between these human and natural rhythms, going so far as to suggest that this human dance in some way keeps the cosmic dance going. The relationship is not so much imitative as participatory; liturgy in a very real sense 'keeps time' and the sacredness of place. Conversely, we may infer, desacralization leads to exploitation. As Jones's poems of *The Sleeping Lord* in particular reflect, it is not accidental that as human beings become less sacramental the natural world increasingly suffers at their hands.

This cosmic dimension of the liturgy is perhaps nowhere more beautifully embodied than in the ancient form of the Easter Vigil which traditionally takes place through the night of Holy Saturday until the break of dawn on Easter Sunday.[70] The intimate connection between the liturgy's rich symbolism and the elements of the material world is sustained throughout. I will briefly highlight some of these moments in the liturgy as they recur continuously in Jones's poems and visual art, and will show how thoroughly the *Bride* engraving may be illumined by the meditation upon the Easter Vigil.

In the Good Friday service preceding the Vigil, this rootedness in the earth is enacted in the Adoration of the Cross as the congregants kneel before and even kiss the wood itself. Jones knew these rhythms well and often alluded to them. The Passiontide hymn, *Pange Lingua Proelium Certaminis*, for example, draws out this natural element

---

[68] Jones, *The Sleeping Lord*, 60.
[69] Dilworth recounts Jones's early formative thinking regarding the relationship between Christianity and paganism thus:

> In 1919, Jones's reading of Jessie Watson's *From Ritual to Romance* and especially Frazer's *The Golden Bough* precipitated a religious crisis by revealing similarities between Christianity and paganism. Then, the same year, he read *The Goddess of Ghosts* (1915), a collection of stories by the classicist C. C. Martindale SJ, which resolved his doubts by disclosing the spiritual intimations of paganism as validated by Christianity and what Jones would call 'the Vegetation Rites of the Redeemer'.

in Dilworth, *David Jones*, 63.
[70] Jones's personal library shows his extensive study of the liturgies and rituals of the Catholic Church in general and in particular of Holy Week (cf. *The Library of David Jones, 1895–1974*, ed. Huw C. Jones, especially, 247–56). I have based my reading here on one of these texts, namely, *The Roman Missal in Latin and English According to the Latest Roman Edition*, introduction and liturgical notes by Dom. F. Cabrol, O.S.B., 3rd edn (Tours: A. Mame and Sons, 1921) of which Jones had two copies (though the 8th edition) which show signs of regular use. Cabrol's edition is also wonderfully pedagogical in nature, following his dictum that

> the Missal should not be looked on as intended for the priest alone. The Mass is not a 'devotion' reserved for the clergy – it is the Common Sacrifice of all the Faithful. The laity have their own part to play in this Holy Sacrifice, and they should be able to follow the prayers and ceremonies and to understand their meaning. (Ibid., vii)

of the wood in beautiful passages such as these that, as we will continue to show, have a profound influence on Jones's imagination:

> Faithful Cross, O Tree all beauteous,
> Tree all peerless and divine:
> Not a grove on earth can show us
> Such a leaf and flower as thine.
> Sweet the nails and sweet the wood,
> Laden with so sweet a load.

This Tree is then made animate, embodying the movement of grace as a kind of supple pliancy:

> Lofty Tree, bend down thy branches
> To embrace thy sacred load;
> Oh, relax the native tension
> Of that all too rigid wood:
> Gently, gently bear the members
> Of thy dying King and God.[71]

Moving from the wood of the cross on Good Friday to the Easter Vigil, it is the primordial elements of fire and water which are now elevated. One of the most dramatic moments of the Easter Vigil is the lighting of the new fire, situated in time precisely in this transitional moment between the depth of night and the breaking of dawn, and situated in a similarly liminal place both inside and outside the church itself. Inside, the church is enveloped in total darkness, all candles having been extinguished before the congregants themselves move deeper into this darkness by processing outside the nave into the night air. Here the lighting of the new fire begins, struck from flint at the church entrance and used to kindle coals that are then placed in the thurible. The words accompanying these actions are as striking, recalling the tradition of Christ's descent to the depths of hell and his bursting forth as a light by which all creatures are set free and made anew: 'This is the night in which Christ broke the chains of death, and ascended conqueror from hell.'[72] The night is not something from which one needs to escape but is itself called 'blessed' and even elevated through this address: 'O truly blessed night, which alone deserves to know the time and hour when Christ rose again from hell / This is the night of which is it written: And the night shall be as light as the day, and night is my illumination in my delights.'[73]

The pillar-like paschal candle is lit by a reed with a three-branched candle fixed to it. The paschal candle now becomes the primary symbol of Christ's sacrifice as the form of the cross is etched in its wax and becomes the bearer of the five wounds of Christ

---

[71] *The Roman Missal in Latin and English According to the Latest Roman Edition*, introduction and liturgical notes by Dom. F. Cabrol, OSB, 3rd edn (Tours: A. Mame, 1921), 384–6.
[72] Ibid., 397.
[73] Ibid.

by its piercing with five grains of incense. Even the genesis of the wax 'as made out of the labour of bees' is remembered and lauded by the liturgist: 'Which fire, though now divided, suffers no loss from the communication of its light. Because it is fed by the melted wax, which the mother bee wrought for the substance of this precious lamp.'[74] As the paschal candle leads the procession back inside the enclosure of the nave, its connection to the natural lights of the sky is not severed but instead enriches its Christic symbolism further:

> A night, in which heaven is united to earth, and God to man. We beseech thee therefore, O Lord, that this candle, consecrated to the honour of thy name, may continue burning to dissipate the darkness of this night. And being accepted as a sweet savour, may be united with the celestial lights. Let the morning star find it alight, that star which never sets. Which being returned from hell, shone with brightness on mankind.[75]

The new fire, which bears relation both to the flint of the earth and the celestial star, is now brought back within the enclosure of the church itself and with it the lamps are relit, sustaining this intimate connection between the inner and outer.

Once within the church, the liturgical focus now turns towards the preparation of the catechumens for baptism and so the focus moves from the element of fire to that of water. Consider, for instance, that the account of the Easter Vigil in Jones's Roman Missal recounts how catechumens were traditionally prepared for their baptism during the twelve readings of the 'prophecies' from the Old Testament prefiguring the Church, from the Creation story, to Noah's flood, to Jonah and the prophets. After the readings, the clergy process to the font singing Ps. 42: 'As the hart panteth after fountains of water, so my soul panteth after thee.' The font is itself imagined as an 'immaculate womb' and the Holy Spirit invoked that it may be rendered fruitful so that those who enter it, 'being born again a new creature may come forth a heavenly offspring: and that all that are distinguished either by sex in body, or by age in time, may be brought forth to the same infancy by grace, their spiritual mother'.[76] Just as the wood and the wax bore the sign of the cross, so now the priest divides the water with his hand and even breathes thrice upon it in the form of the cross. The paschal candle itself is sunk three times into the water. Furthermore, just as the lighting of the new fire concludes with a recalling of the connection between this sanctified element and the whole cosmos, so too does the baptismal ceremony culminate in this gesture towards the renewal of all creation. The priest sprinkles water from the font in all four directions of the earth, recalling the rivers of Paradise and the Creator 'who made thee flow from the fountain of paradise and commanded thee to water the whole earth with thy four rivers'.[77] Thus the renewal of the whole cosmos is recalled and bodied forth in the words and matter of the rite.

---

[74] Ibid., 397, 398.
[75] Ibid., 398.
[76] Ibid., 429.
[77] Ibid., 430.

Before looking at the figures of the engraving in detail, we may note how the engraving, like the ritual of the Easter Vigil itself, hovers in this 'in-between' of time and place. The bride herself is situated between the spritely deer with trefoils at his feet, evoking the time of spring and new beginnings, while the dark skull on her far right spells death and mortality. So too is the Easter Vigil situated in this in-between time after Christ's death and before his Resurrection, a transition which mirrors also the changing of seasons from winter to spring. The expression on *Bride*'s face, like the contrast of shadows and glistening white skin, is also simultaneously mournful and lovingly attentive. And though she is situated within the enclosure, the cosmic tapestry of her bodice roots her firmly in the whole earth. The deer who recalls the chanting of Ps. 42.1 in the baptismal ceremony, though formally 'outside' the enclosure, is drawn close by the directness of his gaze and by his nearness to the river-like tresses of the bride's veil which are like the waters for which he longs.

This tensive, liminal character of the engraving – one is tempted, following Plato, to call it 'metaxic'[78] – is reduplicated in the structural dynamisms of the engraving. Anne Price-Owen argues that the structure of the *Bride* engraving is circular, but that the eye is led around the frame by its many diagonal lines, from the candles to the nail and crucified limb, down the line of the bride's hair and veil to her crooked limb reaching across back to the candles. One may trace also a chiasmic structure from the upper left to lower right corners (from the figure of the deer, down the slope of the bride's arm to the harrow below) and from the lower left to the upper right (from the flowering earth to the intimation of the transcendent reaches beyond, crossing a series of parallel diagonal lines from the bride's arm to the bird's body, the nail and finally the suspended limb). Each of these movements lends itself to further glossing. The deer descends towards the harrow as a catechumen for baptism, or even as Christ in his kenotic descent 'even unto death' (Phil. 2.8). Conversely, the movement from the garden of the lower left to the crucified limb on the upper right suggests this movement of return (*reditus*) made by all creatures and ultimately by Christ from the womb of Mary to the throne of heaven. These crossing diagonals form a chiasmus, one of Jones's favoured symbols and also not incidentally a sign of the 'cosmic Christ' as reflected for instance in the beautiful carpet pages of *The Book of Kells*.[79] There are similar tensions created structurally throughout, such as between the agile body of the bird and the rigid body

---

[78] *Metaxu*, literally translating from the Greek as 'between', is presented in Diotima's speech in *The Symposium* as characterizing the philosopher– in between ignorance and knowledge, the ugly and the beautiful. See *The Symposium*, 201e–212a in *Plato on Love: Lysis, Symposium, Phaedrus, Alcibiades with selections from Republic and Laws*, ed. C. D. C. Reeve (Indianapolis: Hackett, 2006); and Simone Weil, 'Metaxu', in *Gravity and Grace*, trans. Emma Craufurd (London: Routledge and Kegan Paul, 1963), 132–4. Cf. also Jacob Holsinger Sherman's discussion of '*Metaxic* Practices' as an alternative paradigm within a participatory metaphysics to liberal and postliberal turns to practice in Jacob Holsinger Sherman, *Partakers of the Divine: Contemplation and the Practice of Philosophy* (Minneapolis, MN: Fortress Press, 2014), 234–41.

[79] Cf. article by Suzanne Lewis, 'Sacred Calligraphy: the Chi Rho Page in the Book of Kells', *Traditio* 36 (1980): 139–59. *The Book of Kells* carpet pages reflect a broader patristic tradition in which the Chi-Cross is interpreted cosmologically following Plato's *Timaeus* 34b10-36d7 in which the composition of the 'world soul' is in the shape of an X. Cf. Justin, *Apologia* 1.60 quoted in Lewis, 'Sacred Calligraphy', 143 fn.12: 'What has been said in the *Timaeus* to explain the world has also been said about the Son of God ... He made him in every way like a Chi.'

of the nail, which are diagonally parallel to one another. Ultimately, all this movement swirls around the voluptuous breasts of the bride herself, themselves suggesting her 'half-celestial'[80] nature as the stark contrast of black and white mirrors the horizon or meeting place of the earth and sky as seen through the windows.[81]

Given this embeddedness of liturgical sign-making in the material elements of the earth, it is perhaps unsurprising that the liturgical character of Jones's *Bride* is inseparable from the *materia* of his own Romano-Britain in all its diversity and multi-layered history. In his essay, published posthumously, 'An Aspect of the Art of England', Jones articulates this cultural aesthetic mirrored in *Bride* as 'this dappled complexity' or 'dappled fairness',[82] a 'flexible, delicate, chequered art', 'on the whole rather gay' and as 'linear rather than an affair of masses'.[83] Perhaps the most beautiful of all descriptions, and one most fitting of *Bride* herself, is his characterization of medieval English poetry: 'Again and again the thing evoked, the image lifted up is a flowery, starry, intertwined image.'[84] For Jones this aesthetic is in continuity with the character of the land and the people of the British Isles themselves. He writes,

---

[80] Cf. Jones's description of the Greek goddess Helen in his poem, 'Epithalmion', in *Wedding Poems*, ed. with foreword and afterword by Thomas Dilworth (London: Enitharmon Press, 2002), 34.

[81] As noted by Dilworth in afterword to *The Rime of the Ancient Mariner*, ed. Thomas Dilworth, 107.

[82] Jones, *The Dying Gaul*, 62.

[83] Ibid., 60. Jones explicitly names Gerard Manley Hopkins as well as William Blake as exemplary examples of this aesthetic. Cf. also a similar description of this aesthetic character in Albert Garrett, *A History of British Wood Engraving*: 'Qualities of linear expression are deeply rooted in Anglo-Saxon and Celtic art (consider the infinite line of the Celtic cross). Blake expressed it as "the bounding line and its infinite inflections and movements"' (ibid., 202) and Sir Herbert Read's description of the art of engraver, John Nash, Jones's contemporary:

> One returns ... to Nash's fidelity to a certain nativeness, a quality representing the historic English tradition in English art ... it is a quality which we find in the delicate stone tracery of an English cathedral, in the linear lightness and fantasy of English illuminated manuscripts, in the silvery radiance of our stained glass. The same quality is expressed, distinctly, in our poetry and our music. It is not a conscious tradition: it is perhaps an emanation of our soil and our climate, as inevitable and as everlastingly vernal as an English meadow. (Ibid., 203)

[84] Jones, *The Dying Gaul*, 59. The Welsh roots of English poetry is further developed by Jones elsewhere in this nod to Hopkins: 'that certain intricate metrical forms of specifically Welsh medieval development had quite a lot to do with the present joy which twentieth-century Englishmen get from the unique poetry of a nineteenth-century and very English Jesuit' in 'Welsh Wales' in *Epoch and Artist*, 54. See also his 'Welsh Poetry' in *Epoch and Artist*, 56–65; and 'Wales and Visual Form' in *The Dying Gaul*, 63–93. Though this connection has not been made before, Jones's *Bride* bears comparison with the fourteenth-century *Wilton Diptych* (National Gallery, London) which he studied in Camberwell Art School. Jones felt it was profoundly '"English" in feeling' and, he recounts, 'as was pointed out to me by my old friend Mr. A. S. Hartrick the wings of the angels are gulls' wings, or at least wings of wave-birds – this seems a very appropriate English "conceit", and an extremely interesting one' (ibid., 60). The panel portraying the heavenly is of the Virgin surrounded by a cohort of feminine angels, all dancing on a bed of blue and pink flowers in bare feet, crowned in wreaths of pink roses and wearing pendants of a white stag on their azure blue robes (the emblem of King Richard for whom the Diptych was made and a symbol of purity and royalty). The stylized shape of the Virgin's hand in the Diptych, with which she grasps the heel of the Christ child in her arms, is also imitated by the hand of the bride of Jones's engraving with which she holds her votive light. This distinctive hand gesture, the overall feel and shared iconography of this medieval work suggest it is at least in the background if not conscious influence on Jones's conception for *Bride*. For a rich theological reading of this Diptych, see John Drury, *Painting the Word: Christian Pictures and Their Meanings* (New Haven, CT: Yale University Press in association with The National Gallery, London, 1999), 9–19 and 23–5.

Not only is our land a most mottled, dappled, pied, partied and brindled land, but so is our character, and so is the physical structure beneath and determining the surface of the land (one of the most interesting, geologically speaking, in the world, I believe), but so also in a curious way is our art, at least one of the characteristics of our art. ... When one tries to conjure up an image signifying this distinguishing quality, a fretted, meandering, countered image emerges.[85]

Jones's poetry and visual art unearth the many-layered cultural history of Britain. As he writes in 'Wales and the Crown', she 'who would re-present this Island must be clothed in a mantle of variety'.[86]

The figures of *Bride*

Having considered the liturgical and cultural character of *Bride* in general, we may now turn to a more detailed engagement with the symbolism of its figures in light of the whole. This reading will be in three movements. I begin with the crucifix-candelabra before turning to the bride herself and then conclude with the figure of the deer. The liturgical and cultural material we have considered thus far, together with Jones's own poetic works, will help us unfold the multivalent significance of these figures. While occasionally drawing from *The Anathemata*, I will primarily read *Bride* alongside passages from Jones's *The Sleeping Lord* collection, especially those poems characterized as 'Celtic' by Dilworth and others.[87] These poems share that quality of '*hud a lledrith*' or magic and fantasy which spellbinds the Wedding Guest of Coleridge's poem and is evoked in Jones's engraving. Throughout this collection, especially 'The Sleeping Lord' poem itself, there are constant if oblique allusions to the Easter Vigil or paschal watch, enabling us to attend to this liturgical connection further.

'*Lumen de lumine* ...'[88]

The vertical sweep of the right-hand column of Jones's engraving enacts the whole drama of the Passion, from the protruding, dark, circular object of the right-hand corner to the sun-like rays of blood streaming from the crucified limb just as it exits the

---

[85] Jones, 'An Aspect of the Art of England', 59.
[86] Jones, *Epoch and Artist*, 47. As Jeremy Hooker writes in his essay, 'Brut's Albion': 'David Jones restores this island to the Britons, the Britons to their European and Christian inheritance; to the English he restores a sense of what actually lies under their feet and under their tongues, in the land, in words themselves' in *David Jones*, ed. Roland Mathias, 134. Hooker's essay is commendable for distinguishing Jones's embrace of 'the corporate inheritance of this island' (ibid., 126) from the nationalism of the British Empire and for his account of Jones's embrace of Welsh culture as a form of resistance to these imperialist impulses.
[87] 'The Tutelar of the Place'; 'The Hunt'; and 'The Sleeping Lord'. Thomas Dilworth, *The Shape of Meaning in the Poetry of David Jones* (Toronto: University of Toronto Press, 1988), 238–359; Kathleen Henderson Staudt, *At the Turn of a Civilization: David Jones and Modern Poetics* (Ann Arbor: University of Michigan Press, 1994), 159–82; and Christine Pagnouelle, *David Jones: A Commentary on Some Poetic Fragments* (Cardiff: University of Wales Press, 1987).
[88] Jones, 'The Sleeping Lord', 77.

frame. Jones's own brief but leading comments on this engraving provide a way into this rich liturgical imagery: 'The bride is putting a votive candle on one of the sharp iron spikes of a "hearse" or "harrow" (from French herse) applied to those contraptions placed before shrines or statues for us to put up a votive light.'[89] Jones's focus on the technical names of the candelabra here is jolting, especially the underlined 'herse' which immediately is associated with funeral rites and processions. Yet this is clearly intentional, as though he does not want the dark side of wisdom to be elided by the loveliness of the scene. His notes also act as subtle clues as to its liturgical significance. A hearse is the technical name of a particular kind of frame – traditionally made of wood and triangular in shape – which holds twelve candles for the service of *Tenebrae* during Holy Week.[90] *Tenebrae* – meaning 'shadows' or 'darkness' in Latin – is one of the most hauntingly beautiful rituals of the church during which passages from the Old Testament are read consecutively, from the Creation story to Noah's flood to Jonah and the prophets. After each reading, a candle is extinguished, culminating in the complete darkness of Holy Saturday. The traditionally triangular form of the hearse is taken from the agricultural tool named a harrow, 'a heavy frame of timber (or iron) with iron teeth or tines, which is dragged over ploughed land to break clods, pulverise and stir the soil, root up weeds, or cover in the seed'.[91] And a *herse*, in French (and older usages in English), can mean not only this agricultural harrow but also a portcullis. Jones's comments thus tie this figure closely to the events of Holy Saturday as Christ descends to hell, breaks open its gates and 'harrows' the dead. All those that died before the coming of Christ, recalled by the readings of the Old Testament, are thus taken up with Christ, his life and death being salvific for all. The liturgy thus looks forward and backward – back to those who followed Christ even before they knew his Name, and those who now, through the baptismal rite, enter into this new life.

It is worth noting here that in the cancelled engraving for *The Ancient Mariner*, which is likely a direct precursor to this engraving, the bride is also kneeling before a hearse which is there represented in this traditional form as a wooden and triangular structure.[92] Why, in returning to these themes in this later engraving, does Jones change the shape of the candelabra to this circular form? This circular shape perhaps not only allowed him greater fluency in the overall form of the engraving but also deepens its richness as sign. In this form, it now also evokes the crown of thorns that Christ bore on the cross and its sharp spikes are also reminiscent of the spear points which pierced his side. Even more suggestively, the round shape of the harrow suggests

---

[89] Jones continues, 'The stag at the left hand side seen through the open window is partly because I like stags, but mainly because of the very many associations: "the playing of the merry organ and the running of the deer", and also the psalm, "like as a hart desireth the water-brooks". I am indebted to Anne Price-Owen's recovery of this fragment from the National Library of Wales, David Jones Papers, 1978 deposit, Box II/49 and quoted in her dissertation, *Fragments of an Attempted Painting*, 20. She further notes, 'Owing to the other material in this collection of papers, this undated fragment may have been written in the 1950s' in Anne Price-Owen, *Fragments of an Attempted Painting*, 43 fn. 19. Note that the underlining in the fragment is Jones's.

[90] This is still the primary meaning of 'hearse' in the *Oxford English Dictionary*.

[91] 'harrow' Def. 1 in *Oxford English Dictionary*. Anne Price-Owen perceptively notes this inversion too: 'in order for the harrow in the picture to fulfil its function as a candelabra, it is inverted' in *Fragments of an Attempted Painting*, 22.

[92] See Coleridge, *The Rime of the Ancient Mariner*, ed. Thomas Dilworth, 85, fig. 4.

those 'roundy wells' of the baptismal fonts themselves.[93] Indeed, in looking more closely at the harrow of Jones's engraving, signs of life spring up from its centre in the form of three curling ferns. These leafy flora of native Britain and denizens of lush, watery woodlands suggest there is a life-force and vitality even in these depths. The trio of ferns may furthermore be a symbol of the Trinity, the Father, the Son and the Holy Spirit, in whose Name the catechumens are baptized.

Perhaps then it is also not incidental that the spikes mounted on the harrow number twelve, remembering the twelve prophecies read during the preparation of the catechumens for baptism at the Easter Vigil and recalling also those twelve black diamonds punctuating and binding the Latin words of the painted inscription. More broadly, they recall the first twelve disciples of Christ, the tiny seed from which the Tree of the Church grows. The twelve days of Christmas links this Passion liturgy also to the Nativity, which we have seen is essential for Jones. By situating the dark hearse next to the fertile womb-garden of the bride, Jones's engraving further communicates this unity between the nativity and the passion of Christ: As Christ first descends from heaven to take on the flesh of all creation through the womb of Mary, so he redeems all creation through his second descent into hell and rising again from the tomb. The paradoxical form of the harrow, understood also as baptismal font, also embodies this dual significance of baptism as both a death and a birth: 'We were buried therefore with him into death in order that, just as Christ was raised from the dead by the glory of the Father, we too might walk in newness of life' (Rom. 6.4).[94] The ancient practice of baptizing new catechumens on the night of Holy Saturday was itself a strong reminder that this renewal of life comes by passing with Christ through the cross.

Christ's resurrection from the dead is boldly suggested in Jones's engraving by the forefront candle rising with strength from the iron harrow. The white of the candles and their supple flames draw out this contrast with the dark and rigid spikes of the harrow that pierces them.[95] A remarkable passage in 'The Sleeping Lord' poem communicates the 'theology in wax'[96] that is here in visual form. Jones compares the wick to the pliable limbs of woodland trees, which in turn recall the wood of the cross, and he draws out the analogy between Christ's sacrifice on the cross and the candle itself:

> might his Candle-bearer be standing
> to hold and ward
> against the rising valley-*wynt*
> his iron-spiked guttering light
> The twisted flax-wick

---

[93] Cf. Hopkins' 'Kingfisher' poem, 'As tumbled over rim in roundy wells / Stones ring', in *Gerard Manley Hopkins: A Critical Edition of the Major Works* (Oxford: Oxford University Press, 1986), 129. Jones alludes to this image explicitly in *The Anathemata*: 'Mandater of all the roundy-wells / *totius orbis mundi*', 235.

[94] For discussion of this paradoxical nature of baptism, see Andrew Davison, *Why Sacraments?* (London: SPCK, 2013), 13–16.

[95] We might note also the practice of giving the newly baptized a white candle. The traditional form of making a candle by dipping the wick in hot wax is itself a vivid image of baptism.

[96] This wonderful phrase in from Martin Laird's discussion of the paschal candle in his *Into the Silent Land: The Practice of Contemplation* (London: Darton, Longman & Todd, 2006), 120.

>   (without which calcined death
> no uprising, warm, gold-rayed *cannwyll*-life)
>   bends one way
> with the wind-bowed elder boughs
> and the pliant bending of the wild elm
>   (that serves well the bowyers)
> and the resistant limbs
>   of the tough, gnarled *derwen* [oak] even
> lean all to the swaying briary-tangle
> that shelters low
>   in the deeps of the valley-wood
> the fragile *blodyn-y-gwynt* [flower of the wind][97]

Jones's Bride also acts as Candle-Bearer here, 'to hold and ward' this 'iron-spiked guttering light' and sheltering the 'deeps of the valley-wood'. Commentary can hardly do justice to the condensed power of such images as 'iron-spiked guttering light'. This wonderful word, guttering, has multiple meanings. It can simply mean 'to flicker or burn unsteadily', suggesting the vulnerability of the flame, akin to the fragile flowers which grace the woodland floor. But guttering also means 'to make a channel, furrow; cut grooves in' whether by downpours of water or by the wax of a rapidly melting candle or, particularly salient here, by an engraver in wood. The image thus mixes all these elements into one and evokes a picture of Christ on the cross as one whose pierced body flows over not only in tears of pain and grief but ultimately in the life-giving blood itself by which the Church is birthed and nurtured. The wick of the candle in turn symbolizes this ongoing sacrifice at the heart of the Church and the Liturgy itself: '(without which calcined death/no uprising, warm, gold-rayed *cannwyll*-life)'. From the brutal imagery of 'iron-spiked guttering light', Jones returns us to the warmth of the hearth around which the life of the household proceeds. Just as at the very heart of this life-giving flame there is an ongoing 'calcined death', so too is the Eucharist this ongoing sacrifice at the heart of the household of God.

These images marvellously illuminate the candles of Jones's engraving, five of which are pierced at their base by the spikes of the harrow, while the ascending lines of their bodies culminate in lively flames in the shape of tree leaves.[98] The candles appear to form an embrace, gathering in close communion with one another.[99] Given Jones's interest in sacred numbers, the number of candles and their flames may also be significant. In *The Anathemata*, Jones relates the number five to the five shining wounds of Christ, 'terrible lovely, starring the wide steer-board' of the ship called Mary.[100] However, as one looks more closely at the engraving, there appear in fact to be seven candle flames in all. Perhaps Jones's intention is thus to prompt us to think of the seven lamps of the churches in Rev. (1.4; 4.5; 5.6) or the seven charisms of the Spirit in Isa. (11.1-3) or

---

[97] Jones, *The Sleeping Lord*, 74.
[98] As Anne-Price Owen notes in *Fragments of an Attempted Painting*, 18.
[99] Ibid., 18.
[100] See, for example, *The Anathemata*, 141; also noted by Anne Price in *Fragments of an Attempted Painting*, 17.

even the seven Sacraments.[101] As the bride lifts up her own candle to join this embrace, so, too, is she tethered to their grace-filled movement.

These flames coalesce under the crucifix itself, which recapitulates the symbolism of the harrow. As the iron spikes pierce the candles, so here an iron nail pierces the bare and vulnerable flesh of Christ, opening a wound that overflows in a downpour of life-giving blood. The skull recalls the meaning of Golgotha as 'place of decaying bones', which Jones glosses in *Anathemata* as the wedding place of the Son of Mary, 'yoked for his nuptials on Skull Ridge'.[102] The support of the ridge on which the skull rests echoes the triune form of curling ferns, once again suggesting that a deeper love is at work even in these most seemingly unambiguous signs of death and desolation. The almost surrealist figuring of the body here, enlivened further by the bounding lines of smoke rising from the candles below, conveys a sense of the immediacy of this sacrifice, and so perhaps of the real presence of Christ in the ongoing Eucharistic offerings of the Church.

The contrast between the skeleton of the skull and the fleshly feet of Christ signifies the paradoxical triumph of the cross, recalling the Pauline imagery: 'For as all die in Adam, so all will be made alive in Christ. ... For he must reign until he has put all enemies under his feet. The last enemy to be destroyed is death. For "God has put all things in subjection under his feet" ' (1 Cor. 15.20-22, 27).[103] As the gaze rises with the ethereal, bounding lines of smoke from the candles below, it is met by the drops and streams of blood which flow down from the crucified Christ until they morph into sun-like rays, intimating the resurrected Christ, reigning from his 'Axile Tree'.[104]

Before moving on from this exploration of the liturgical and theological significance of Jones's candelabra and crucifix, as a way of transition to the central figure of the bride herself, I'd like to turn to a motif in *The Sleeping Lord* collection which both draws out further the cosmic, ecological and social significance of the Passion of Christ and bears remarkable affinity with the multiple aspects of the *Bride* engraving. In 'The Sleeping Lord' poem itself, Jones imagines these forces of death and violence, exemplified in the engraving through the iron spikes and nail, to be embodied in the mythical creature from the Arthurian tales named 'Boar Trwyth'.[105] This malevolent beast appears in this poem's lament for the ravaged woods and for all the men who have fallen 'in the

---

[101] Such references are far from exhaustive of the symbolism of this sacred number. For a contemporary philosophical theological discussion of the sacred meaning of numbers, see Stratford Caldecott, *Beauty for Truth's Sake: On the Re-enchantment of Education* (Grand Rapids, MI: Brazos Press, 2009), 55–8.

[102] Jones, *The Anathemata*, 241.

[103] Cf. also Heb. 2.8-9:

'What are human beings that you are mindful of them, or mortals, that you care for them? You have made them for a little while lower than the angels; you have crowned them with glory and honour, subjecting all things under their feet.' Now in subjecting all things to them, God left nothing outside their control. As it is, we do not yet see everything in subjection to them, but we do see Jesus, who for a little while was made lower than the angels, now crowned with glory and honour because of the suffering of death, so that by the grace of God he might taste death for everyone.

[104] Jones, *The Anathemata*, 243.

[105] See the story of 'How Culhwych Won Olwen', in *The Mabinogion*, trans. Sioned Davies (Oxford: Oxford University Press, 2007), 179–213.

trackway of the long tusked great hog'.[106] The lament begins, characteristically of Jones, in the interrogative mode:

> And the trees of the *llanerch*? [glade]
> >   Why are they fallen? [...]
> >   but by the riving tusks
> of the great hog
> >   are they felled.
> It is the Boar Trwyth
> >   that has pierced through
> the stout-fibred living wood
> >   that bears the sacral bough of gold.
>
> It is the hog that has ravaged the fair *onnen* [ash tree] and the hornbeam and the Queen of the Woods. It is the hog that has tusk-riven the tendoned roots of the trees of the *llwyn* whereby are the tallest with the least levelled low and lie up-so-down.[107]

In relation to Jones's wood engraving, it is not difficult to imagine the sharp spikes of the hearse as the 'riving tusks' of the hog, its circular mouth as jaws flung open, rending a chasm in this cosmic tapestry. His lament is for the woodlands of Wales, which in the Arthurian tales are laid to waste by his running from the pursuing cohort of Arthur and his men. But Jones's recollection of this tale in the context of his poem is also for the actual woodlands of Wales that have been ravaged by the insatiable hunger of industrial and commercial growth. When these great mighty trees are felled by the 'tusks of the hog', they are levelled to the same heights; diversity is obliterated. By contrast, the poet's litany recalls the trees of the forest by name, almost as though by the agency of the poetic word their powers may be restored and the forest re-enchanted.

> And the trees of the *llanerch*? [glade]
> >   Why are they fallen?

What of the *llwyn* where the fair *onnen* grew and the silvery queen of the *coedwig* [a wood] (as tough as she's graced & slender) that whispers her secrets low to the divining hazel, and the resistant oak boughs that antler'd dark above the hornbeam?

> >   *Incedunt arbusta per alta*
> > >   *rapacibus caedunt*
> >   *Percellunt sacra quercus…*
> >   *Fraximus frangitur …*[108]

---

[106] Jones, *The Sleeping Lord*, 90.
[107] Ibid., 89–90.
[108] 'They [tusks] move through high trees / fell them with tearers / over throw sacred oaks / the ash shattered', Jones, *The Sleeping Lord*, 90; translation provided by Dilworth, *The Shape of Meaning in the Poetry of David Jones*, 215.

The litany culminates with this passage from Ennius' *Annals* Bk iv, which, as Jones relates, 'has become as it were part of a liturgy whenever the destruction of a woodland is involved'.[109] The verb *'frangitur'* is incidentally not the same used of the Eucharistic host as it is broken at the moment of consecration. By analogy with the Eucharistic host of which Christ says, 'This is my body,' so the poet suggests that we see in the ravaging of the trees, by analogy, the very wounding of the body of Christ himself. The poet thus strongly suggests that the suffering with which Christ identifies on the cross is not only human suffering but that of the creation more broadly.

Throughout 'The Sleeping Lord' poem, Jones regularly returns to the image of the lord 'who weeps for the land'.[110] The image is suggestive and ambiguous, especially insofar as the lord Arthur is analogous to the Lord God. How are we to understand the preposition 'for' here? Is it a simple dative (the lord weeps on account of the land)? Or does it function as a kind of subjective substitutionary genitive (the lord weeps on behalf, in place of the land)? Or is it stronger yet? Jones carefully suggests – but never insists – upon the latter: the lord does not just weep for the land, but, as the poet asks, might the land be the lord weeping?[111]

> Is the Usk a drain for his gleaming tears
> who weeps for the land
>   who dreams his bitter dreams
> for the folk of the land
> does Tawe clog for his sorrows
> do the parallel dark-seam drainers
>   mingle his anguish-stream
> with the scored valleys' tilted refuse.[112]

In this in-between time, the relationship between the lord and the land is suggestively reciprocal. Do the trees ward the lord from evil or does the lord ward the trees? Are

---

[109] Jones, *The Sleeping Lord*, 89, n. 1.

[110] Ibid., 96.

[111] It is significant that Jones never actually phrases the identification in this form: 'the lord *is* the land' but always only in the interrogative, 'is the land that very lord?' The interrogative suggestively presses forward this identification yet with a subtlety that resists wooden or dogmatic interpretations, for example, that Jones is a pantheist. He hints at the importance of this poetic subtlety in an interview in 1973:

> you see, theologians are like a lot of other trades, you can't, if you start nailing things down, you find they *won't* have it, and quite rightly, I mean. I always like the things said about Tennyson. There were three figures in some poem by Tennyson, and someone said, 'Oh, Tennyson, I take it that these figures stand in some way for Faith, Hope and Charity?' And Tennyson said 'Well, you can think what you *bloody well like* as far as I'm concerned. They can stand for what you say, I don't object to that. You know, I mean I won't be *bound down*'

in 'David Jones, Mabon Studios Interview, 31 August–3 September 1973', ed. Jasmine Hunter and Anne Price-Owen in *Unpublished Prose*, ed. Thomas Berenato, Anne Price-Owen and Kathleen Henderson Staudt (London: Bloomsbury, 2018), 300.

[112] Jones, *The Sleeping Lord*, 91.

the strong oaks his guard or is he the secret of their strength? If the lord and the land exchange wounds, so too do they exchange sources of healing:

> Do the small black horses
>   grass on the hunch of his shoulders?
> are the hills his couch
>   or is he the couchant hills?
> Are the slumbering valleys
>   him in slumber
>   are the still undulations
> the still limbs of him sleeping?
> Is the configuration of the land
>   the furrowed body of the lord
> are the scarred ridges
>   his dented greaves
> do the trickling gullies
>   yet drain his hog-wounds?
> Does the land wait the sleeping lord
>   or is the wasted land
> that very lord who sleeps?[113]

Perhaps nowhere does Jones achieve a more unified vision of the cosmic significance of the Incarnation and Passion of Christ than in his portrait of King Arthur, in pursuit of the Boar Trwyth himself. By the very passion of Arthur's riding, he is himself gradually transfigured, becoming as one flesh with the woodlands themselves. This incarnate becoming entails wounding, but, as we have come to expect with Jones, such wounds always also anticipate a transfigured glory:

> (indeed, was it he riding the forest-ride
> or was the tangled forest riding?)
> for the thorns and flowers of the forest and the bright elm-
> shoots and the twisted tangle wood of stamen and stem clung and
> meshed him and starred him with variety
> and the green tendrils gartered him and briary loops galloon
> him with splinter-spike and broken blossom twining his royal
> needlework
>   and ruby petal-points counter
> the countless point of his wounds.
> and from his lifted cranium where the priced tresses dragged
> with sweat stray his straight brow-furrows under the twisted
> diadem …
> and like a stricken numen of the woods

---

[113] Ibid., 96.

>   he rode
> with the trophies of the woods
>   upon him
> who rode
>   for the healing of the woods
> and because of the hog.[114]

In his riding through the woods of the land, Arthur becomes one with them, taking up their very flesh in his own and healing them along the way. The sumptuous imagery of this passage is remarkably evocative of *Bride* herself with her star-studded floral ornamentation, the very fibres of her clothing as the tendons and roots of trees themselves, and the tresses of her hair as rivers gliding through a valley.

It is thus to the bride herself I now turn. By means of this particular form of the bride, Jones evokes or calls up an almost endless stream of holy or sacred women and of the divine in feminine form. From the ordinary 'Marys' and 'Marthas' for whom the only 'veined alabaster was a carton to be / torn at the dotted line' to 'those half-celestial' goddesses of antiquity to the 'Queen of Heaven' herself, Jones invites us to meditate at length upon this 'mantle of variety'.[115] I will explore her character, first, in light of ancient myths of earth-mothers and mother goddesses. I will then explore her identity as Mary, the Mother of Christ and the second Eve. Finally, I conclude with Jones's own re-telling of the myth of 'Mary Maudlen', the woman who breaks an alabaster jar at the feet of Christ and whom Jones deems 'the mistress of all contemplatives and the tutelary figure of all that belongs to poiesis'.[116] Our primary source for illuminating these meanings of the bride will continue to be Jones's own poetry and essays in which many feminine tutelars appear, both mythical and historical – though more often, as we might have come to expect, somewhere in between.[117]

The feminine tutelar

Incarnate in this female form, Jones's *Bride* reaches back to traditions even prior to the beloved myths of Arthur and his men. As he suggests in his essay, 'Art in Relation to

---

[114] Ibid., 67. Cf. the Arthurian tale of *Sir Gawain and the Green Knight*, trans. Simon Armitage (London: Faber & Faber, 2007). For a reading of this passage relating to Jones's artistic vision as a whole, see Malcolm Guite, 'Imagination, Bodies and Locality: The Incarnational Thrust of David Jones' Art', in *Flashpoint* 18 (2016).

[115] 'Epithalamion', in *Wedding Poems*, ed. Thomas Dilworth, 36, 34; *The Anathemata*, 60, n. 1; 'Wales and the Crown', in *Epoch and Artist*, 47.

[116] Jones, 'Use and Sign', in *The Dying Gaul*, 183.

[117] Cf. J. R. R. Tolkien, 'On Fairy Stories', in *Tree and Leaf* (London: Harper Collins, 2001), especially 27–33, for an exposition of the relation of myth and history which illumine Jones's own practice. Tolkien colourfully describes the relationship as a process in which a historical figure gets thrown into 'the Soup' or 'Cauldron of Story' or Myth: 'a considerable honour', he writes, 'for in that soup were many things older, more potent, more beautiful, comic, or terrible than they were in themselves (considered simply as figures of history)' in Tolkien, 'On Fairy Stories', 29. We don't know what essays or stories Jones had read of Tolkien, though he names him as an important influence on his thinking in the preface to *The Anathemata*, 37.

War', 'all our tradition is of war, and the hero at his tasks, either to gain or defend a land or to gain the "giant's daughter", but behind this we are half-conscious of traditions more "cosmic" – less wholly warlike, more magical'.[118] Jones at least entertains the possibility of a ' "golden age" of primitive peace', of some

> dim remembrance in the race-consciousness of an actual pre-power-politic state, when Mars was still the god of agriculture and not yet the god of war, when 'our Arthur' was hardly the Bear, still less the *Dux*, was not yet a Celtic battle-deity, let alone a Roman cavalry leader, was not even a male, but as yet, perhaps, some female goddess of fruition – not the warrior, but the creatrix.[119]

Jones pays homage to the ancient image of the earth goddess in his *Anathemata* through that 'first plastic-in-the-round known to us', namely, the Venus of Willendorf:

> But already he's at it
> the form-making proto-maker
> busy at the fecund image of her.
> Chthonic? why yes
> but mother of us.
> Then it is these abundant ubera, here, under the species
> of worked lime-rock, that gave suck to the lord? She that
> they already venerate (what other could they?)
> her we declare?
> Who else?[120]

---

[118] Jones, *The Dying Gaul*, 126.
[119] Ibid., 125.
[120] Jones, *The Anathemata*, 59–60. The claims concerning a matriarchal prehistory are contested. Rosemary Radford Ruether, *Goddesses and the Divine Feminine: A Western Religious History* (Berkeley: University of California Press, 2005) is a rejoinder to, for example, the second-wave feminist, Wicca, and Jungian-inspired reconstructions. For a representative and highly readable example of the latter tradition, see Jules Cashford and Anne Baring, *The Myth of the Goddess: Evolution of an Image* (London: Viking Arkana, 1991). Although these historical claims have been rather decisively laid to rest, as has the politically and symbolically naive suggestion that the presence or absence of goddess figures could be easily equated with a greater attention to women's dignities, it remains the case that hypostatization of the divine feminine is extraordinarily ancient, surprisingly ubiquitous and deeply under-theorized in recent theology. For an account of the prevalence of medieval 'goddesses' in Orthodox Christendom, see Barbara Newman, *God and the Goddesses: Vision, Poetry and Belief in the Middle Ages* (Philadelphia: University of Pennsylvania Press, 2003). Cf. the constructive reflection on this motif by Orthodox theologian Sergius Bulgakov, *Sophia: The Wisdom of God: An Outline of Sophiology* (Hudson, NY: Lindisfarne Press, 1993). Cf. also Christopher Pramuk's study, *Sophia: The Hidden Christ of Thomas Merton* (Collegeville, MN: Liturgical Press, 2009). The myth of matriarchal prehistory, whose recent roots are deeply bound up with James Frazer's *The Golden Bough: A Study in Magic and Religion* (London: Macmillan, 1933) had a deep effect upon many characteristically modernist writers such as D. H. Lawrence, W. B. Yeats, T. S. Eliot and Jones himself. The historical debunking of the myth is now almost complete but, as we can see in both Jones and Bulgakov, this needn't render a final verdict on the myth itself but only on an overly literalist reading of the myth. I am grateful to Jacob Sherman's guidance through this literature.

He sees in her not only the first of many earth goddesses but a prefiguring of the mother Mary, in whom, for Jones, all such figures coalesce. While taking on vast and varied form, as Miranda Green writes, within the Celtic tradition 'the overwhelming feature, perhaps common to all the female divinities, is a fundamental concern with life, fertility, and regeneration';[121] there are no goddesses of war in the Celtic tradition. Instead, 'they are serene benefactresses, with a "dark" aspect in their association with the "womb" of earth and with death. But even in their underworld aspect, rebirth and renewal are frequently promised.'[122] Many Celtic goddesses are the spirits of a natural local habitation of springs and rivers considered to be sacred. For this Celtic tradition, as for Christian sacramental theology, nature is never just matter but possesses its own inviolable grace.

Wherever she is found, the feminine is a healing and renewing force in Jones's poetic world. She is aligned with the creative pulse in human culture and so too with the gratuitous and sacramental. As Jones declares in his essay 'The Viae', 'the truth is that whether we are Greeks or barbarians, Celts or Romans or whoever we are, we cannot for long suppose a creativity without the female principle. There is always a Virgo Potens to direct the *via*.'[123] As Desirée Hirst elegantly surmises, her form, even within Jones's own work, is remarkably diverse: 'The Feminine can be august and awe-inspiring, sublimely protective and also tender, familiar and itself protective of what is vital, precious and frail, the earth mother and the queen of heaven.'[124]

This memory of origins – most primordially not only in the mother's womb but also in one's native land and culture – is intimately tied up for Jones with the memory of what it is to be a fundamentally sacramental being, that is, with what it is to be fully human. In his poem, 'The Tribune's Visitation', it is precisely the renunciation of this primordial connection that is the necessary requirement for the formation of the 'Fact-Man' and his army of 'levellers', summed up in this dismissal:

>   Only the neurotic
> look to their beginnings.
> We are men of now and must strip as the facts of now would have
> it. Step from the caul of fantasy even if it be the fantasy of sweet
> Italy.
> Spurn the things of Saturn's Tellus?
> Yes, if memory of them
>   (some pruned and bearing tree
>   our sister's song)
> calls up some embodiment
>   of early loyalty
> raises some signum

---

[121] Miranda J. Green, *Dictionary of Celtic Myth and Legend* (London: Thames and Hudson, 1992), 43.
[122] Ibid., 36.
[123] Jones, *Epoch and Artist*, 195.
[124] Desirée Hirst, 'Fragility and Force: A Theme in the Later Poems of David Jones', in *David Jones*, ed. Roland Mathias, 107.

>   which, by a subconscious trick
> softens the edge of our world intention.¹²⁵

The tribune's speech is a bittersweet renunciation of all that has made the men anything other to or in excess of their oath to Caesar: 'If then we are dead to nature,' he concludes, 'from Caesar's womb we issue / by a second birth.'¹²⁶ Their innate love for local stories and rituals, rivers and songs known to them since childhood must be trod down within them. Fidelity to one's kin or 'some such dolorous anamnesis' threatens the ruthless levelling power necessary to carrying out the commands of Caesar: 'Lest, thinking of our own, our bowels turn when we are commanded to storm the palisades of others and the world-plan be undone by plebeian pity.'¹²⁷

Jones's deeply liturgical, almost hymnic poem, 'The Tutelar of the Place', is a profound rejoinder to 'The Tribune's Visitation' which it immediately follows in *The Sleeping Lord* collection. Throughout, the poet intimates that to remember one's origins in the mother's body is not, as Freud would have it, regressive, but is the heart of an alternative social order. Here the memory of one's origins reaches through one's own material mother and 'homeland' to the transcendent Mother who even now protects and guides them. 'The Tutelar' poem, perhaps the poem most resonant with Jones's *Bride* engraving, begins with this invocation:

> She that loves place, time, demarcation, hearth, kin, enclosure,
> site, differentiated cult, though she is but one mother of us all:
> one earth brings us all forth, one womb receives us all, yet to each
> she is other, named of some name other.¹²⁸

This goddess is both far and near, outside all times and places yet known only through particular sites and peoples. He sings of her transcendence thus:

> Though she inclines with attention from far fair-height outside
> all boundaries, beyond the known and kindly nomenclatures,
> where all names are one name, where all stones of demarcation
> dance and interchange.¹²⁹

---

¹²⁵ Jones, *The Sleeping Lord*, 51–2.
¹²⁶ Ibid., 58.
¹²⁷ Ibid., 55. Jones makes a point of recalling in *The Anathemata* his personal experience as a soldier in the First World War of the Christmas morning in which the front-fighters crossed the enemy line – literally and figuratively – leaving weapons behind, 'exchanging tokens' and even playing games together. 'These things', he writes, 'were done BECAUSE OF THE CHILD' (*The Anathemata*, 216). This spontaneous and free act, born of charity, was also the most politically transgressive. Thomas Dilworth makes the important argument that Jones's inclusion of this story in his book was itself a resistance to attempts to suppress it. As Dilworth says, '[Jones] writes with special emphasis. He is setting the record straight. Consorting with the enemy at Christmas had been widespread in 1914 and widely reported, though subsequently forbidden. News of its sporadic recurrence in 1915 was suppressed and not entered into the historical record' in *Reading David Jones* (Cardiff: University of Wales Press, 2008), 169.
¹²⁸ Jones, *The Sleeping Lord*, 59.
¹²⁹ Ibid., 60. A comparative reading of Jones's 'Tutelar' poem and Dionysius's 'On the Divine Names', in *Pseudo-Dionysius: The Complete Works*, ed. Colm Lubheid and Paul Rorem (Mahwah, NJ: Paulist Press, 1987) could reveal many illuminating parallels in both form and content. Consider just these

And yet, as his opening introit proclaims, this transcendence is enshrined only in the particular: 'Tellus of the myriad names answers to but one name: ... / she's a rare one for locality.'[130] He encapsulates her wisdom in the warning: 'you must not call her but by that name / which accords to the morphology of that place'.[131] Unlike Caesar's issue, the One does not depend on the destruction of the many. Nor is the valorization of the many – the particular, individuated and specific – an endless fragmented splintering.[132] Jones insists on the 'in-between' space of a differentiated unity in this 'in-between' time of becoming: 'As between sister and brother at the time of beginnings. ... after the weaning and before the august / initiations, in the years of becoming.'[133] And again, 'brother by sister / under one *brethyn* / kith of the kin warmed at the one hearth-flame'.[134]

Jones's 'Tutelar' poem culminates in the invocation of Mary the Mother of God ('Womb of the Lamb spoiler of the Ram'[135]) and he elsewhere frequently delights in the fluid exchange of identity between Mary and Wisdom. As he notes in *The Anathemata*,

> 'Before the hills was I brought forth', Prov. VIII, 25, said of Wisdom and applied in the Liturgy to the Mother of God who represents Wisdom. She was quickened by the Spirit and the bringer forth of the Logos-made-Flesh. Or, to use a mythologer's terms, she is both bride and mother of the cult-hero.[136]

Amidst these many allusions, Jones's engraving also unmistakably names Mary through the iconography of the lily and the rose garland. This beautiful passage in the Song of Songs is attributed to Mary: 'I am a rose of Sharon, a lily of the valley. As a lily among brambles, so is my love among maidens' (2.1). The horizontal thrust of the lily in the engraving recalls Gabriel's fertile annunciation while the rose garland points towards the Passion which 'will pierce [her] soul also' (Lk. 2.35). She is the tutelar of tutelars because through her the scandal of particularity in the mystery of salvation unfolds – that God's own Son comes to *this* young girl in *this* time, yet for all times and all places.

---

few lines from Dionysius: '[T]he theologians praise it by every name – and as the Nameless One ... This surely is the wonderful "name which is above every name" and is therefore without a name ... And yet on the other hand they give it many names, such as "I am being", "life", "light", "God", the "truth"'; and 'that while remaining ever within himself he is also in and around and above the world' in *Pseudo-Dionysius*, ed. Colm Lubheid and Paul Rorem, 54–5.

[130] Ibid., 59.
[131] Jones, *The Sleeping Lord*, 61.
[132] Compare Paul Fiddes's argument that 'Jones's sacramental modernism offers us ... a guide for taking the best and rejecting the worst from the mood of a late-modernity which understands the whole world as a text, a network of signs, to be read again and again in new situations' in Paul Fiddes, 'The Sacramental Modernism of David Jones and the World as Text', in *David Jones*, ed. Rebecca White, 53.
[133] Jones, *The Sleeping Lord*, 59.
[134] Jones, *The Sleeping Lord*, 60. This recovery of the feminine in Jones's poetry raises some interesting parallels with the ethics of sexual difference in the feminist philosophy of Luce Irigaray. See, for example, Luce Irigaray, *An Ethics of Sexual Difference*, trans. Carolyn Burke and Gillian C. Gill (Ithaca, NY: Cornell University Press, 1993); and 'Divine Women', in *Sexes and Genealogies*, trans. Gillian C. Gill (New York: Columbia University Press, 1993), 55–72.
[135] Jones, *The Sleeping Lord*, 64.
[136] Jones, *The Anathemata*, 234, n.1.

Mary's role in salvation is voiced in Jones's *Anathemata* through a colourful character named Marged, described by scholars as 'a feminist witch'.[137] She makes the boast on behalf of all women that God elects to redeem all creation by means of Mary's flesh – a rebuff, she proclaims, to any gnostic and Docetic heretical leanings. Through Mary, she rallies her sisters to a relationship of solidarity and participation rather than competition. The election of Mary among women to bear the Son of God does not exclude or lessen the worth of other women but gathers them all up in the saving flow of grace, thus further elevating and glorifying them too. God's way of saving is 'medial', acting by means of the materiality and free will of His creatures:

> Sisters, not so jealous! *Someone* must be chosen and fore-
> chosen – it stands to reason! After all there should be
> solidarity in woman. No great thing but what there's a
> woman behind it, sisters. Begetters of all huge endeavour
> we are. The Lord God may well do all without the aid of
> man, but even in the things of god a woman is medial – it
> stands to reason. […]
> It all hangs on the fiat. If her fiat was the Great fiat, neverthe-
> less, seeing the solidarity, we participate in the fiat – or can
> indeed, by our fiats – it stands to reason.[138]

Mary's 'fiat', her 'yes', ushers in the new creation and gathers up in one redeeming voice the responding desire of all creation.

The garland of roses which adorns the bride of Jones's engraving is itself a gratuitous artefact and replete with liturgical and theological significance. In 'Art and Sacrament', Jones dwells on the multivalent rose thus: 'A man cannot only smell roses … but he can and does and ought to pluck roses and he can predicate of roses such and such. He can make a *signum* of roses. He can make attar of roses. He can garland them and make anathemata of them.'[139] A whole vision of humanity's 'becoming beauty' through their participation in the graces of wisdom resides in this tender artefact. The garland of roses recalls at once the Virgin Mary whose name is 'the Mystical Rose' and also Lady Wisdom who promises those who respond to her call: 'I will place on your head a fair garland; she will bestow on you a beautiful crown' (Prov. 4.9).[140] Furthermore, rosary beads are themselves called *chaplets* (wreaths of flowers) or *coronas* (crowns) and the *aves* prayed with them are like so many roses strung into a garland with which Mary as bride is crowned.[141]

---

[137] Thomas Dilworth, *Reading David Jones* (Cardiff: University of Wales Press, 2008), 168.
[138] Jones, *The Anathemata*, 213–14. Cf. Anne Price-Owen, 'Feminist Principles in David Jones's Art', in *Diversity in Unity: Studies in His Literary and Visual Art*, ed. Belinda Humfrey and Anne Price-Owen (Cardiff: University of Wales Press, 2000).
[139] Jones, 'Art and Sacrament', 166.
[140] Cf. also Prov. 1.9, 'Hear, my child, your father's instruction, and do not reject your mother's teaching; for they are a fair garland for your head and pendants for your neck.'
[141] Cf. Jones's beautiful drypoint, *Nativity with Beasts and Shepherds* (1928), in which Mary herself is holding rosary beads in Bankes and Hills, *Art of David Jones*, 108, fig. 104.

By crowning Mary with this garland of roses, Jones suggests that in her the plight of Eve is reversed. In John Milton's *Paradise Lost* (a work well-known to Jones since childhood), Eve is honoured as the first 'mother of flowers',[142] a title which Jones himself uses in 'The Tutelar of the Place' for the Virgin Mary: 'Mother of Flowers save them then where no flower blows.'[143] In Milton's tale, while Eve is treading the spiral staircase of serpentine reason 'to mischief swift', Adam sets off to find her in the garden, carrying in his hand a wreathe of roses. But of course Adam is too late to the scene and the loss of innocence is intimated thus: 'From his slack hand the garland wreathed for Eve / Down dropped, and all the faded roses shed: / Speechless he stood and pale.'[144] With Jones's Marian tutelar figure, however, all is not lost; the call of Lady Wisdom prevails. If in Christ we are given the second Adam, so in Mary we find the second Eve.

The desire between Adam and Eve, and so between all human beings, is also redeemed by the desire exchanged between Christ and Mary. Jones frequently delights in *The Anathemata* on the interchangeable roles between Christ and Mary and unabashedly plays with what a post-Freudian era knows only as the Oedipal complex but which the pre-modern Church delighted in as the overdetermination of identities and roles in the eternal love song between God and His people. So Jones boldly opens his recounting of the Passion in 'Sherthursdaye and Venus Day':[145] 'He that was her son / is now her lover.'[146] This reciprocal desire between Christ and Mary is expressed in this vignette from 1430 titled, 'Our Lady Mary's Rose Garden', a German Dominican poem/song associated by theme and practice with the praying of the rosary:

[Christ] followed the noble fragrance until he came to the beautiful rose… For the Son of the Most High saw this lovely, tender, fragrant rose blooming among the thorns of the sinful world and the sweet fragrance of her earnest desire wafted up to him unceasingly. He was caught up by her eager love and so enraptured that he leapt from his Father's lap down to this rose among thorns and was so sorely pierced that his hands and feet bled.[147]

---

[142] John Milton, *Paradise Lost*, ed. Scott Elledge, A Norton Critical Edition (New York: W. W. Norton, 1993), IX.837-40/220. Jones knew Milton's work well though he distanced himself from him theologically.

[143] Jones, *The Sleeping Lord*, 63.

[144] John Milton, *Paradise Lost*, ed. Scott Elledge, IX.892-93/221.

[145] Part VIII, *The Anathemata*, 224-43. This isn't to deny the relevance of a Freudian interpretation, but only to resist reductive uses of it. Jones had been conversant with Freudian theory since at least the late 1920s and later received treatment from the Freudian psychoanalyst, William A. H. Stevenson, during his time at Bowden House in the late 1940s and for which he would remain grateful throughout his life. In his biography, Dilworth traces Jones's 'apprenticeship' in Freudian thought as well as his ambivalence to it: '[Jones] wrote more naturally when sceptical of Freud's simple-minded, reductive, "part-for-the-whole" inclination. … In later years, he would say of his Oedipal diagnosis, "I just can't really believe it." … [H]e would always respect Freud, while remaining wary of much of his theory' in *David Jones*, 243-4. Cf. also Dilworth, *David Jones*, 108, 127-8, 243-6.

[146] Ibid., 234.

[147] I was introduced to this through the Blackfriars Oxford pamphlet on Dominican devotion to Mary. For more on this vignette cf. Anne Winston-Allen, *Stories of the Rose: The Making of the Rosary in the Middle Ages* (Philadelphia: Pennsylvania State University Press, 1997).

Though it is uncertain whether Jones was himself familiar with it, the passage captures the movement of desire in his engraving, as one can visualize the stag in the upper left corner as Christ Himself, leaping through the lattice in response to the 'buxom will' of the bride and then falling on the crown of thorns in the lower right.

Moving from the figure of the Mother of Christ to his Lover leads us to consider one final feminine tutelar whom Jones names as 'the mistress of all contemplatives and the tutelary figure of all that belongs to poiesis'.[148] Jones paints his own portrait of the alabaster jar pericopes from both John and the synoptics in this lyrical piece of carefully crafted prose, interweaving the biblical material with his beloved Celtic myths:[149]

> When Mary Maudlen fractured the alabaster of nard over the feet of the hero of the Christian cult, the Sir Mordred at the dinner-party asked: To what purpose is this waste? But the cult-hero himself said: Let her alone. What she does is for a pre-signification of my death, and wherever my saga is sung in the whole universal world, this sign-making of hers shall be sung also, for a memorial of her. A totally inutile act, but a two-fold anamnesis (that is, a double and effectual re-calling). First of the hero Himself and then of the mistress of all contemplatives and the tutelary figure of all that belongs to poiesis. The woman from Magdala in her golden hair, wasting her own time and the party funds: an embarrassment if not a scandal. But an act which is of the very essence of all poetry and, by the same token, of any religion worth consideration.[150]

This intimate and radical act is held up by Jones as the paradigm of the artist – a gratuitous gesture of love, an offering and a remembering. Jones's re-telling also has the effect of drawing attention to the way this most personal of acts is also the most profoundly political. She disrupts and overturns the seemingly prudent and rational logic of Judas which, the gospel tells us, is after all just a facade (cf. Jn 12.6). He would ultimately exchange the life of Christ Himself for much less, as George Herbert in his own poem discerns: 'For thirte pence he did my death devise / Who at three hundred

---

[148] 'Use and Sign', in *The Dying Gaul*, 183.

[149] Cf. Mary of Bethany (Jn 12) and Mary Magdalene (Jn 20) and the unnamed woman of the synoptics (Mk 14, Mt. 26 and Lk. 7). For a historical account of the figure of Mary Magdalene and other named women in the gospels, see Richard Bauckham, *Gospel Women: Studies of the Named Women in the Gospels* (Grand Rapids, MI: Eerdmans, 2002).

[150] 'Use and Sign', in *The Dying Gaul*, 183. This passage from Jacques Maritain's *Art and Scholasticism* is likely to have inspired Jones here:

> That great Contemplative, learned by the gift of Knowledge, has deep discernment of all the needs of the human heart: she knows the unique value of art. Therefore she has given it such powerful protection in the world. Ever so much more, she has summoned Art to the opus Dei, and asks Art to make perfumes of great price which she scatters on the head and feet of her Master. *Ut quid perditio ista?* murmur the philosophers. She continues to embalm the body of her Beloved, whose death she proclaims every day, *donec veniat*

in trans. J. F. Scanlan (London: Sheed & Ward, 1946), 63. Thomas Dilworth notes that Jones had marked this passage of his copy of *Art and Scholasticisim* in 'David Jones and the Maritain Conversation', in *David Jones*, ed. Belinda Humfrey and Anne Price-Owen, 52.

did the ointment prize, / Not half so sweet as my sweet sacrifice: / Was ever grief like mine?'[151]

This woman's radical gesture of love makes her vulnerable to scorn, accusation and dismissal. There is no apparent necessity for taking such a risk, but she does it anyway and for no apparent reason other than love. This wholly gratuitous and personally costly act is thus hailed as the most profound anticipation and recalling of Christ's sacrifice on the cross. In a culture defined by 'The Break', 'Mary Maudlen' might be the apotheosis of divine women. She is herself broken (maculate rather than immaculate) and yet this brokenness becomes the very medium for grace.[152] In her own brokenness, the brokenness of the jar and the broken body of Christ, the beauty of Christ is revealed most truly as a 'spilled beauty',[153] not perfectly kept and preserved but poured out, shared and given away.

All of these women are lovers of Christ and so lovers of Truth: philosophers.[154] They see and know the Light and this shining forth is beautiful. The Light within them recognizes the Light without and they allow themselves to be drawn in. This drawing and letting be drawn is the movement of love. But part of the way of love is that there aren't any absolute arrivals. They are 'in-between' and there is as much anguish as delight. All these women are lovers of Christ, but this loving breaks them all open: Mary's '*gladius*-piercings';[155] Mary Magdalene's weeping in the garden when she cries, 'where is his bed and / where has he lain him?',[156] and Mary of Bethany's public ridicule by Judas. For each of these women, their recognition and love of Truth issues a call to which they must respond. To love is to be vulnerable and to risk the possibility – or even likelihood – of wounding. However, by giving themselves over, all thus become mediators: Mary Magdalene is the first apostle, sent to tell the world the truth of the Resurrection; Mary of Bethany's gratuitous gesture proclaims Christ's death 'until he

---

[151] 'The Sacrifice', in *The Complete English Poems* (London: Penguin Books, 1991), 24.
[152] Cf. Ben Quash's chapter, 'Maculation' in his *Found Theology: History, Imagination and the Holy Spirit* (London: Bloomsbury, 2013), 55–85.
[153] The evocative phrase is from Jones's poem, 'The Fatigue', in *The Sleeping Lord*, 34: 'the spilled beauty on the flowering transom'.
[154] Mary is presented as the image of philosophy throughout the monastic Middle Ages and by John Paul II Encyclical Letter, *Fides et Ratio: On the Relationship Between Faith and Reason* (Rome: St. Peters, 1998), par. 108:

> Between the vocation of the Blessed Virgin and the vocation of true philosophy there is a deep harmony. Just as the Virgin was called to offer herself entirely as human being and as woman that God's Word might take flesh and come among us, so too philosophy is called to offer its rational and critical resources that theology, as the understanding of faith, may be fruitful and creative ... May Mary, Seat of Wisdom, be a sure haven for all who devote their lives to the search for wisdom. May their journey into wisdom, sure and final goal of all true knowing, be freed of every hindrance by the intercession of the one who, in giving birth to the Truth and treasuring it in her heart, has shared it forever with all the world.

[155] Jones, 'The Sleeping Lord', 71. Jones makes note here of the passage in the gospels which says that 'the *gladius* would pierce the heart of the God-bearer'; cf. Simeon's prophecy to Mary in the temple: 'a sword will pierce your own soul too' (Lk. 2.34).
[156] Jones, 'The Sleeping Lord', 71, but also recalling Mary Magdalene's plea to the soldiers and then, unwittingly, to the resurrected Christ Himself: 'They have taken him away and I do not know where they have laid him' (Jn 20.13) and 'Sir, if you have carried him away, tell me where you have laid him' (Jn 20.15).

comes again'; and Mary's 'yes' – to the joys and the agonies of both birth and death – invites all to become God-bearers with her.

As re-presentative of these women in search of wisdom, the visage of the bride in Jones's engraving is both in shadow and bathed in light, her expression bearing a mourning and attentive love. Directly within her line of sight is the gothic skull; however, she does not stare into its face directly for she too has a mediator. Christ's body intercepts the taunting gaze of the skull, covering it with his own body and thus opening the way for the agile body of the bird to become her eternal interlocutor, singing songs of love.[157] The rigid iron nail which pierces his skin pierces also this skull in the 'third eye', dealing a final blow to not only physical but spiritual death, the corruption of inner eyes and heart. In absorbing this violence on the cross, Christ destroys death. All the loves and griefs of not just these women but all the world are mediated by this Passion story.

We turn now to one final figure, that of the 'young stag' which peers through the window of the enclosure. This transition is perhaps best hailed by the song of the bride herself in the Song of Solomon:

> The voice of my beloved! Look, he comes, leaping upon the mountains, bounding over the hills. My beloved is like a gazelle or a young stag. Look, there he stands behind our wall, gazing in at the windows, looking through the lattice. My beloved speaks and says to me: "Arise, my love, my fair one, and come away; for now the winter is past, the rain is over and gone. The flowers appear on the earth; the time of singing has come, and the voice of the turtle-dove is heard in our land. (2.9-12)

In turning to the figure of the stag, we will continue to unfold his significance primarily through Jones's prose and poetic writings. I will then conclude this exploration of the figures of *Bride* by turning to a passage in *The Anathemata* in which all the figures thus far are drawn together in a stunning unity and kind of theological apotheosis.

The hart's desire

In his essay 'Use and Sign', Jones explicitly ties the figure of the deer and Ps. 42.1 to the desire for the sacramental that for him is the heart of what it is to be human:

> We must assert with the greatest emphasis that this demand for the sacramental is not like the demand for a health-giving medicine. It is not because it affords him some consolation. Still less is his addiction to the extra-utile that of the drug or drink addict. His incurable thirst is best expressed by the Psalmist: 'Like as the hart desireth the water-brook' without which, as the English carol says, there could be no 'running of the deer' nor 'playing of the merry organ' nor 'singing in the choir', concelebrating with angels and archangels and the whole war-band of heaven.[158]

---

[157] Cf. Jn 16.7: 'I tell you the truth, it is to your advantage that I go away, for if I do not go away, the Advocate will not come to you; but if I go, I will send him to you.'

[158] Jones, *The Dying Gaul*, 182.

The deer is a recurring motif in Jones's visual art throughout his life. The deer appears in many forms: the pastoral grazers of *Resting Animals (four deer)* (1927);[159] the mysterious half-human, wandering deer of *Horned Man*;[160] the thirsty deer of *Kneeling Animals* (1927)[161] and *The Artist* (1927);[162] and the slain stag in his illustration for T. S. Eliot's *The Cultivation of Christmas Trees* (1954)[163] as well as finally in *Y Cyfarchiad i Fair* (The Greeting to Mary) (1963).[164] The figure also appears in verbal form in Jones's 'The Sleeping Lord' poem where the deer joins the sacred flame of the candle and the creatures of the woodland forest in their graceful bending towards the Good:

> over the high *gwaundir* [moorland]
>   and below in the *glynnoedd* [glen]
> where the *nentydd* [brooks] run
>   to conflow with the *afon* [river]
> where too is the running of the deer
> whose desire is toward these water-brooks.[165]

But the particular form of the deer in Jones's wood engraving is of yet another type, prancing and virile, a confident and happy creature. This deer is akin to a small wood engraving made the same year as *Bride*, simply titled, *Stag*,[166] which depicts a similarly prancing, virile and confident creature and may have been a study for this engraving. Just a year earlier he also made a pencil, ink and watercolour miniature titled, *A stag in its natural habitation*, which also bears a similar character.[167] The title of this latter drawing is instructive since, for Jones, the rich religious significance of this creature of the woods never overshadows or eclipses the sheer delight of the animal in its own right. As Jones himself comments on this figure in the *Bride* engraving: 'The stag at the left hand side ... is partly because,' simply put, 'I like stags.'[168] The naturalness of the deer is essential to Jones's thesis that the deer is a sign of the human 'demand for the sacramental'. Human beings just *are* the kind of creatures who long for 'the more than', the gratuitous, which is ultimately the longing for no less than God Himself. The strange essence of human nature, as the Catholic theologian Henri de Lubac argues, is this paradoxical naturalness of longing for the supernatural: 'My finality, which is

---

[159] Drypoint on paper in Kettle's Yard reserve collection [DJ 31].
[160] Pencil on paper (date unknown) reprinted in Jonathan Miles and Derek Shiel, *The Maker Unmade* (Brigend, Wales: Seren Press, 1995), 294, fig. 2.
[161] Kettle's Yard reserve collection [DJ32]. *To Petra with Love: The Petra Tegetmeier Collection of Works by David Jones: Paintings, Drawings, Engravings, Inscriptions and Carvings* (London: Wolseley Fine Arts, 2001), 67, catalogue no. 100.
[162] Wood engraving frontispiece for Eric Gill, *Christianity and Art* (Capel-y-ffin, Abergavenny: Francis Walterson, 1927); reprinted in Jonathan Miles and Derek Shiel, *The Maker Unmade*, 71, fig. 21.
[163] T. S. Eliot, *The Cultivation of Christmas Trees* (London: Faber & Faber, 1954).
[164] Pencil, crayon and watercolour, Amgueddfa Cymru – National Museum of Wales in Bankes and Hills, *Art of David Jones*, 165, fig. 151.
[165] Jones, *The Sleeping Lord*, 74–5.
[166] Print in Kettle's Yard reserve collection [DJ 37] and *To Petra with Love*, 67, catalogue no. 104.
[167] *To Petra with Love: The Petra Tegetmeier collection of works by David Jones: Paintings, drawings, engravings, inscriptions and carvings* (London: Wolseley Fine Arts, 2001), 42, catalogue no. 28.
[168] N. L. W., David Jones Papers, 1978 deposit, Box II/49 quoted in Price-Owen, *Fragments of an Attempted Painting*, 20.

expressed by this desire, is inscribed upon my very being as it has been put into this universe by God.'[169] In Jones's own words,

> The zoological description of man as a creature of the highest order of the class *mammal* of the genus *homo* of the species *sapiens* is of interest to us, for simply as a definition it takes us some distance ... toward the definition proposed by theology. For theology supposes man to be, first and foremost, a sapiential mammal. Further that this *sapientia*, by which man proceeds, implies, by a further chain of reasoning, that this mammal has an end other than that of the other mammals, or, as they say, this creature, because he is endowed with rationality (i.e. has a 'rational soul') must have a supernatural end. In catechismal terminology this is expressed by asserting that the natural end of man (i.e. the end conformable to man's nature) is eternal felicity.[170]

To long for 'eternal felicity', Jones sees, is as natural to being human as the body's thirst for water. Or rather, the thirst for God is felt even in the physical thirst for water. Human beings do not leave behind their material dependence as the rational soul ascends to God, but such physical gifts take on ever more degrees of significance. 'One does not live by bread alone' (Mt. 4.4); nevertheless, by means of bread, God in Christ makes us his own: 'This is my body which is given for you' (Lk. 22.19).

This emphasis upon nature, thick and dynamic – which grace does not destroy but rather perfects, completes and fulfils – is powerfully thematized and embodied in the stag.[171] The stag of the *Bride* engraving is seen through the open window as a living creature in its natural habitat. His antlers ascend like the fecund woods of the forest over which, according to Celtic mythology by association with the god, Cernunnos, he is king.[172] The white trefoils on the grass create a festive mood and resemble crowns, echoing in their triune form those leafy ferns of the harrow and of Skull Ridge. His body is poised as though about to leap, his dappled coat and full antlers convey both strength and suppleness, like the living woods and swaying branches themselves. His exaggerated breast presses eagerly towards the bride as towards 'the water-brooks'. As we have explored in relation to the harrow and the bride, the deer is both 'everyman' – born by 'grace, their spiritual mother', having crossed through the waters of the

---

[169] As Henri de Lubac continues: 'And, by God's will, I now have no other genuine end, no end really assigned to my nature or presented for my free acceptance under any guise, except that of "seeing God"' in *The Mystery of the Supernatural*, trans. Rosemary Sheed (New York: Herder and Herder, 1967), 70; cf. John Milbank, *The Suspended Middle: Henri de Lubac and the Debate concerning the Supernatural* (Grand Rapids, MI: Eerdmans, 2005).

[170] Jones, 'Art and Sacrament', 147–8.

[171] Cf. Jones's nod to (and delightful rephrasing of) the Thomistic saying that grace does not destroy nature, it perfects it: 'All the while "grace follows nature" (or however it is one says it)' in 'Eric Gill: An Appreciation' in *Epoch and Artist*, 299.

[172] Cernunnos is the lord of the animals and, akin to Celtic female deities, is a figure of 'fertility, abundance and regeneration' and his body is in human form, often seated in cross-legged position and his head decked with antlers. As Miranda Green writes, he too is 'one of those beings who regularly underwent transmogrification or shape-shifting from human to animal form' in Green, *Dictionary of Celtic Myth and Legend*, 60.

'immaculate womb of this divine font'[173] – and Christ Himself who in first desiring us opened the way before us.

We may now bring this reading of the engraving to a close by relating it to one final passage from *The Anathemata* in which the poet meditates on the final hours and words of Christ on the cross. This passage draws together all the figures of the *Bride* engraving and articulates the theological unity of its paradoxical, bittersweet character. At the heart of this section of the poem we encounter Ps. 42.1 once more, 'As a deer longs for flowing streams, so my soul longs for you, O God', sung at the baptism of catechumens at the Easter Vigil. When this psalm is sung on Holy Saturday, the congregants would have fresh in their ears the cry of Christ from the cross, read on Good Friday, from the Gospel of John:

> Afterwards Jesus knowing that all things were now accomplished, that the Scripture might be fulfilled, said: I thirst [*Sitio*]. Now there was a vessel set there full of vinegar. And they putting a sponge full of vinegar about hyssop, put it to his mouth. Jesus, therefore, when he had taken the vinegar, said: It is consummated. And bowing his head, he gave up the ghost.[174]

This penultimate moment before his death is interlaced by Jones with the imagery of the thirsty deer in Ps. 42:

> As the bleat of the spent stag
>   toward the river-course
> he, the *fons*-head
>   pleading, *ad fontes*,
> his desiderate cry:
>   SITIO.[175]

On the cross, the Creator – Christ as Word and Wisdom – has become a creature of longing and subject to the anguish, as well as the joys, of temporal becoming. The irony at the heart of this tragedy is here drawn to the fore: this One from whom all waters of the earth flow and to whom they return has no one and nothing in this particular time and place to slake this very real thirst (both literal *and* figurative, as the Gospel John suggests, this cry fulfils the Scriptures).

---

[173] This invocation of the Holy Spirit in the blessing of the baptismal waters in the Easter Vigil reads in full:

> Who by a secret mixture of his divine virtue may render this water fruitful for the regeneration of men, to the end that those who have been sanctified in the immaculate womb of this divine font, being born again a new creature may come forth a heavenly offspring: and that all that are distinguished either by sex in body, or by age in time, may be brought forth to the same infancy by grace, their spiritual mother.

in *The Roman Missal*, 429.

[174] *The Roman Missal*, 375. Cf. Ps. 69.21: 'They gave me poison for food, and for my thirst they gave me vinegar to drink.'

[175] Jones, *The Anathemata*, 237. Cf. Jones's inscription in watercolours and ink (1951) of the 'Chant to the Passion according to St. John' reprinted in *The Anathemata*, 235.

In his note to the phrase, 'his desiderate cry', Jones cites no less than three different translations of Ps. 42.1:

Cf. the psalm. '*Quaemadmodum desiderat cervus ad fontes aquarum.*' (Vul. Ps. 41.)
'*Like as the hart desireth the water-brooks.*' (Bk. of Com. Pr. Ps. 42.)
Fel y brefa'r hydd am yr afonydd dyfroedd. As the bleat of the stag for the rivers of waters. (Welsh Psalter).[176]

These translations, drawn from the Latin Vulgate, the English Book of Common Prayer and the Welsh Psalter, once more re-present the layered cultural history of the British Isles, Jones's particular place.[177] God takes on the voice of all humanity in Christ, yet, as 'the Tutelar of the Place' reminds, 'she's a rare one for locality'.[178] Christ speaks to and through this specific, finite and vulnerable body on the cross – a point brought home by the Gospels' recording of his final words on the cross, '"*Eloi, Eloi, lema sebachthani*" – "my God, my God, why have you forsaken me?"'[179]

In the passage just preceding this, the poet extols Christ as the '*fons*-head' or Creator thus: 'Of all the clamant waters / firthing forth from the Four Avons / himself the *afon*-head.'[180] The 'Four Avons' recall that baptismal imagery of the final sprinkling of the water in the four directions of the earth, and 'firthing forth' recalls the 'guttering light' of the paschal candle.[181] With these gestures to the cosmic significance of the crucified Lord, Jones's poetry reminds his readers that when Christ suffered on the cross, the groaning of all creation coursed through him. In turn, the cry of the 'spent stag' issues in a litany of voices that commune with him in his suffering, bearing his grief as their own. The many lovers of Christ the Truth here once more take the form of these feminine tutelars of the sacred woodland, for as we have seen, if Christ is the 'Lord of lords', he is also the Lord of Faerie:

> What will the naiads
> do now, poor things:
>   the lady of the *ffynnon* [fountain]
> *Es sitt* that moves the *birket*, fay *del lac*, the donnas of the
> lyn, the triad-*matres*, the barley-tressed *mamau* and the
> grey-eyed *nymphae* at the dry *ffynhonnau* whose *silvae*-office
> is to sing:
>   VNVS HOMO NOBIS
>   (PER AQVAM)
>   RESTITVIS REM.[182]

---

[176] Jones, *The Anathemata*, 237 n. 2.
[177] For further theological reflection on the topic of translation see the chapter, '"I will happen as I happen" (Exod. 3.14)' in Quash, *Found Theology*, 33–53.
[178] Jones, *The Sleeping Lord*, 59.
[179] Mk 15.34 and cf. Mt. 27.46; notably this cry is also from the Ps. (22.1). This Greek transliteration of Aramaic reflects the cultural 'layering' of Jesus's own time and place.
[180] Jones, *The Anathemata*, 236–7.
[181] Jones, 'The Sleeping Lord', 74.
[182] Jones, *The Anathemata*, 237–8.

These monumental, inscription-like words are from Virgil's *Eclogue* IV which Jones translates in his note thus: '"One man, by water, restores to us our state" (i.e. continues to restore).'[183] Jones wonderfully highlights the tense of *restituis* so as to press home the ongoing reality of this restoration, for him and his present-day readers. By first choosing the waters of Mary and subsequently drinking the bitter waters of the cross, Christ turns ours sweet.[184]

Thus this most deepest of ironies gives way to the truest of love songs: the mystery of the unity of Christ and the Church. The bleat of the deer echoes the cry of humanity and all creations' groaning. In all the Gospels' accounts of the death of Christ, he speaks in the voice of the Psalmist.[185] In adopting our nature and the full range of our voice, from the heights of triumphant praise to the depths of despair, God begins to mend even through this rending. The Christian practice of reading the Psalms, particularly in times or places of suffering and need, is grounded in this understanding of the unity of Christ and the Church. As Rowan Williams perceptively summarizes,

> The meaning of our salvation is that we are included in his life, given the right to speak with his divine voice, reassured that what our human voices say out of darkness and suffering has been owned by him as his voice, so that it may in some way be opened to the life of God for healing or forgiveness.[186]

If the Psalms are the prayer book of the Church, so too are they its wedding song.

As the ethereal nightingale of Jones's wood engraving does not let its viewers forget, this exchange of voices between human and divine is through the mediation of the

---

[183] Jones, *The Anathemata*, 238, n.5. Water bears perhaps the greatest analogical breadth of all in Jones's work and is closely associated with the feminine. From the physical waters which surround and define the British Isles, to the intimate waters of the womb, to the waters of the Sacraments of the Church through which the life of grace flows. Water, like light, is a living element or creature in Jones's work which freely conducts this passage between time and eternity. Cf. Jones's footnote in *The Anathemata*, 236 n.1. Jeremy Hooker aptly summarizes the significance of this element for Jones: 'Water therefore unites the historical, physical, and mythological or religious meanings of the voyage; it is life-giving under all these forms and as both element and sign it carries a complex but unified significance' in *David Jones: An Exploratory Study of the Writings* (London: Enitharmon Press, 1975), 47.

[184] Turning the bitter waters sweet is one of Jones's favourite images for redemption, for example, 'the hydromel / that moists the mortised arbor' in *The Anathemata*, 140. Cf. Exod. 22.15-22: 'The LORD showed [Moses] a piece of wood; he threw it into the water, and the water became sweet.' Cf. also Jones's unfinished wood engraving, *He Frees the Waters* (1931), of a unicorn dipping its horn into a stream, reproduced as an illustration in *The Anathemata*, 213.

[185] Mt. 27.46 and Mk 15.34: '"*Eli, eli, lena sebachtani*", that is, "my God my God why have you forsaken me?"' (Ps. 22.1); Lk. 23.46 'Father, into your hands, I commend my spirit' (Ps. 31.5); and Jn 19.28, as quoted above. In the conversion of the Apostle Paul, Christ appears once more with the words of the Psalmist on his lips: '"Saul, Saul, why do you persecute me?"... "I am Jesus, whom you are persecuting"' (Acts 9.4; Ps. 31.5), revealing on an extraordinary level the identification of Christ with his Bride the Church. Cf. Tarsicius van Bavel, 'The "Christus Totus" Idea: A Forgotten Aspect of Augustine's Spirituality' in *Studies in Patristic Christology*, ed. Thomas Finan and Vincent Twomey (Portland: Four Courts Press, 1998), 84–94. See also Kevin Grove, CSC, 'The Word spoke in our words that we might speak in his: Augustine, the Psalms and the poetry of the incarnate Word' in *Poetic Revelations: Word Made Flesh Made Word: The Power of the Word III*, ed. Mark S. Burrows, Jean Ward, Malgorzata Grzegorzeska (Abingdon, Oxon: Routledge, 2017).

[186] Rowan Williams, 'Augustine and the Psalms', 20.

Spirit, the breath of Love who speaks in many tongues. As the Spirit hovered over the fecund waters of the first Creation, so now she conducts its renewal. As 'John the Divine' proclaims in Revelation, so too we might translate as the visible voice of *Bride*:

> The Spirit and the Bride say, 'Come.'
> And let everyone who hears say, 'Come.'
> And let everyone who is thirsty come.
> Let anyone who wishes take the water of life as a gift.[187]

Conclusion: 'Magdalenian splendours'

The oldest artefact found in any British museum dates to around 11,000 BC, towards the end of the last Ice Age called the Magdalenian Era.[188] This is the kind of artefact Jones would have loved had he known about it. The form of two reindeer, a male and a female, swimming across a river in a chain-line formation is delicately carved from the narrow length of a mammoth tusk. The upward tilt of the hart and hind and their outstretched limbs create, as curator Neil MacGregor remarks, 'a marvellous impression of stream-lined movement'.[189] The skilful engraving reveals ribs and sternum, a full set of antlers and the texture of full coats. These details convey even the time of this couple's crossing as autumn, another 'in-between' time marking the turn from summer to winter. For the Palaeolithic artist (or artists) who made this engraving, autumn meant preparation for the freezing winter months and reindeer were essential to their survival. And yet, springing up from such harsh conditions is this gratuitous sign, a masterpiece of craftsmanship revealing a powerful imagination and sympathetic engagement with the forces of life and death around them. As Rowan Williams in commenting on this artefact remarks, 'You can feel that somebody's making this who was projecting themselves with huge imaginative generosity into the world around, and saw and felt in their bones that rhythm …, trying to enter fully into the flow of life around them.'[190] This evolving capacity to imaginatively enter the patterns and processes of the world, Williams goes on to suggest, is at the same time the capacity to enter the sacred. 'Art' and 'Religion', he reflects, may in the modern world seem to be deeply alienated from one another, but the testimony of the ancients is quite other. The theological point is clear: The religious impulse in humanity does not originate in a flight from the world of nature but takes root in these processes and acts by which we become *more* incarnate, *more* at one with the world around us. As human beings discover their capacity to create, he suggests, so too do they begin to

---

[187] Rev. 22.17. Cf. Jones's dry point engraving, *Animals and Shepherds* (1929), of a woodland scene and winding river with deer, shepherds and other creatures on which Jones has inscribed this verse in Latin: 'Qui Vult Accipiat Aquae Vitae Gratis'. The original is in the reserve collection of The Ditchling Museum of Art and Craft and reprinted in *Engravings of David Jones*, ed. Douglas Cleverdon, plate no. 89.
[188] Jones, *The Anathemata*, 37.
[189] Neil MacGregor, *A History of the World in 100 Objects* (London: Penguin Books, 2012), 18.
[190] Neil MacGregor, *A History of the World in 100 Objects* [Audio CD] (BBC Audiobooks, 2011).

discover their Creator, the Supreme Artist. As Catherine Pickstock elegantly argues, 'our attempt to "return" to our divine origin is not so much a journey towards God, as a journey towards God's entry into our body'.[191] Or, to hearken back to Kathleen Raine's beautiful summary of Jones's artistic vision, 'What is "capable of being loved and known" is God incarnate.'[192] If originally conceived as an illustration of Coleridge's *Ancient Mariner*, the *Bride* engraving clearly does more than depict its allusive and elusive themes. Jones's *Bride* is itself a conduit of the Mariner's ancient wisdom:

> Farewell, farewell, but this I tell
> To thee, thou Wedding Guest!
> He prayeth well, who loveth well
> Both man and bird and beast.[193]

---

[191] Pickstock, *After Writing*, 273.
[192] Raine, *David Jones and the Actually Loved and Known*, 25.
[193] Lines 610–14 in *The Rime of the Ancient Mariner*, ed. Thomas Dilworth, 80.

Conclusion

'Yours is the day, yours the night, / a sign from you sends minutes speeding by; / spare in their fleeting course a space for us / to ponder the hidden wonders of your law.'[1] In this prayer from Augustine's *Confessions*, he praises the Creator – maker of day and night – for a world ripe with signification; not mute things, but signs of 'something other', which 'send minutes speeding by'. He prays for dwelling places, like sacred sites, to open within this flux of signs, 'to ponder', as he writes, 'the hidden wonders of your law', a law which can only find its fulfilment in love. He likens this kind of sign-reader or 'dweller' to those 'harts and hinds [who] seek shelter in those woods, / to hide and venture forth, / roam and browse, lie down and ruminate'.[2] For Augustine, 'those woods' are the words of Scripture, the liturgy and the whole created order which harbour, like nuts and seeds, the secret of their existence, their relation to the Creator. Like the deer of Ps. 42, the desire propelling this hunt through the woods is for that 'living water' – the '*fons* head' from which flows the whole 'sign-stream'[3] – a taste of the Eternal in time that prefigures the Sabbath rest towards which, for Jones and Augustine alike, creation moves 'in common travail'[4] together.

If this 'fleeting course' of signs is the place of emergence for the contemplative's prayer, so too, for Jones, is it the beginning of the artist's work. In his preface to *The Anathemata*, he also reflects on the speed of human thought which such signs may set in motion:

> The speed of light, they say, is very rapid – but it is nothing to the agility of thought and its ability to twist and double on its tracks, penetrate recesses and generally nose about. You can go around the world and back again, in and out the meanders, down the history-paths, survey *religio* and *superstitio*, call back many yesterdays, but yesterday week ago, or long, long ago … during the few seconds taken by the presbyter to move from the Epistle to the Gospel side, or while he leans to kiss the board or stone … or when he turns to incite the living *plebs* to assist him.[5]

---

[1] Augustine, *Confessions* XI.2.3, trans. Maria Boulding, OSB (Hyde Park, NY: New City, 2000), 286.
[2] Ibid., 287.
[3] David Jones, *The Anathemata* (London: Faber & Faber, 1952), 236, 237.
[4] David Jones, Introduction to *The Rime of the Ancient Mariner*, ed. Thomas Dilworth (London: Enitharmon Press, 2005), 16.
[5] Preface to *The Anathemata*, 32.

Jones likens his thoughts in this unabashed confession of daydreaming to those of a wanderer, not unlike those foragers of the woods, through far-off lands and down the recesses of history. He locates his own meanderings as arising 'as often as not "in the time of the Mass"': 'The mental associations, liaisons, meanderings to and fro ... have been as often as not initially set in motion, shunted or buffered into near sidings or off to far destinations, by some action or word, something seen or heard, during the liturgy.'[6] These liturgical actions and words, like an engine or a railroad switch, conduct his train of thought and deliver the cargo needed for his poetic works.

This lighting-like speed of thought is not, however, the fulcrum of the artist's work. Jones contrasts this 'agility of human thought' with the slow plodding of making a work: 'But if the twists and turns that comprise thought are quicker than light, the action of making anything – any artefact or work of any sort – from those thoughts, is, as the tag says, longer. ... Now making a work is not thinking thoughts but accomplishing an actual journey.'[7] Even those slight movements of 'the presbyter ... from the Epistle to Gospel side', 'to kiss the board or stone' or 'to incite the living *plebs*' for assistance, in contrast to the meandering 'mental associations' they put into play, are themselves kinds of made works that accomplish 'an actual journey'. By wedding himself to his material, the artist weds himself to time. To make a work is to accept the contingencies and limitations of the artist's horizon and the weighty reality of forms which exceed, relativize and more often than not frustrate, as Jones puts it, 'the order of your mental itinerary'.[8] They are material gestures, carefully formed to, quite literally, 'make sense'. The word 'liturgy' itself, as we discovered, means just this, a folk-work or, even, a craft. So the priest is said to 'con-fect', *conficere*, the Mass – from the Latin *con* (with) and *facere* (to make). 'Something has to be made by us,' Jones observes, 'before it can become for us a sign of him who made us.'[9]

Like the narrowing of the meaning of the words 'art' and 'sacrament' which Jones sets out to dismantle in his essay, 'Art and Sacrament', the word 'craft' in modern parlance has similarly come to be identified with a *sphere* of human making – like pottery, weaving, woodwork or even scrapbook making. So, too, it may be in need of some of Jones's etymological therapy. Its origins, however, are obscure, and Jones turns instead to another Latin word, *disciplinae* (synonymous with *ars*), to explore this 'whole gamut of man's making'.[10] Buried in a footnote in his preface to *The Anathemata*, he performs his own joinery across an almost dizzying assortment of activities. He sets side by side children's games and achievements of the finest artistry; military orders and spiritual treatises; domestic work and the highest orders of the court; work on the farm and art school. The final juxtaposition of images likens the rites of a papal inauguration to the singing of nursery rhymes – each, according to their own mode, minding child and high priest alike of their belonging to a wider web of relations and not just to themselves. All are summarized by this admonition: 'This is a way to make a thing, that way won't do at all.'[11]

---

[6] Ibid., 31–2.
[7] Ibid., 33.
[8] Ibid., 32.
[9] Ibid., 31.
[10] David Jones, 'Art and Sacrament', in *Epoch and Artist* (London: Faber & Faber, 1959), 176.
[11] Ibid., 34, n.1.

To learn a craft, as Jones's heap of *disciplinae* testifies, cannot be readily reducible to a list of rules or techniques. To make the judgement 'this is the way to make the thing' is to speak with knowledge that hasn't been *codified* so much as *incorporated* – into one's hands, gestures, language and cast of mind. To learn how, for instance, to bake an apple pie, is to be incorporated into a tradition of bakery peculiar to the customs and habits of one's own time and place.[12] And yet, these customs could not be but for the wider web of relations which stretch out from them endlessly as concentric circles across time and place. Both the difficulty and the joy of making something resides in the crafting of our own senses, gestures and ways of thinking in response to and in collaboration with the inherited *materia*. To shape a thing according to a certain *disciplinae* is to become oneself, at least in part, shaped by it. It is at least implicitly to recognize that 'no man is an island' and that to be a law unto oneself is illusory at best.

This is why for Jones the poet is not most like a prophet or visionary but like a priest or 'Servus Servorum'.[13] She does not rise above the world in order to re-present it, nor does her *materia* arrive as an interruptive divine gesture from outside it. The poet-vicar is 'of a parish', so to speak, enmeshed in the strata of time and the 'water-stream' of signs. He is made up of the deposits even as he makes with them – these are the only things he has to make with. And yet by means of this offering or re-presenting again under another form, they become sites in and through which the 'more than' may be seen. 'No wonder', Jones writes,

> the proud column leaned / to such a board / even before the Magian handling and the Apollinian word / that shall make of the waiting creatures, in the vessels on the / board-cloths over the Stone, his body who said, DO THIS / for my Anamnesis.[14]

The bread and wine, like the many 'waiting creatures', are that before which all lean in anticipation that they may become places of '*hud a lledrith*', this magic of metamorphosis. They are sites of fragile anticipation.[15]

Like art, craft is just another word for telling us what it means to be human: 'sapiential mammals' who belong to this fragile, material world – no less than the bear, the beaver and the blackbird – and who make things with it. We, too, have our dens, dams and nests which can only be made by attending to the way things work, becoming attuned to their own '*sapientia*' – from dirt, water and sticks to steel, hydroelectrics and fibreglass. It is this innate wisdom of things with which the artist must take care, as standing before the divine Artist, this 'Master of Harlequinade, Himself not made, / maker of sequence and permutation in all things made'.[16] In this sense, each creature and the diverse range of human artefacture bear this theological character, inhabiting in their very form an implicit word about God. If all crafts or *disciplinae* cultivate particular habits,

---

[12] Ibid. Cf. Stanley Hauerwas, 'Discipleship as a Craft, Church as a Disciplined Community'. *The Christian Century* (October 1991): 881–4.
[13] Preface to *The Anathemata*, 35.
[14] Jones, *The Anathemata*, 204–5.
[15] Cf. Jean-Yves Lacoste, 'Place and Nonplace', in *Experience and the Absolute: Disputed Questions on the Humanity of Man*, trans. Mark Raftery-Skehan (New York: Fordham University Press, 2004).
[16] Jones, *The Anathemata*, 63.

gestures and ways of life, perhaps there is one which joins them all: these admonitions to lovingly attend. The artist's work returns us to the contemplative's prayer with which we began, 'spare ... a space for us / to ponder the hidden wonders of your law'.[17]

The poem, 'A, a, a, DOMINE DEUS', is itself a prayer, a kind of Good Friday litany made from the garden of Gethsemane to the hill of Golgotha. The '*Quia per incarnati*' inscription similarly embodies a prayer, this Preface of the Mass repeated from Nativity to Epiphany, a celebration of the birth of this ancient Light from before the beginning of time into that dark night in Bethlehem. In the *Bride* wood engraving, the ordinary gesture of lighting a candle is set as a participation in the 'whole argosy' of the Redeemer and of all creation as gallantly performed in the drama of the Easter Vigil. The despair of exile is not banished here but becomes itself a form of being-before-God, a portal for 'making whole' and the receiving as one's own the name that is no Name. The sheltering embrace of *Bride* as archetypal Mother Earth and the Church is not itself 'the whole' but held open within this (m)othering grace. The inscription standing at the centre of this work is witness that being-before-God is nothing if not a being before creatures in all their incompleteness and particularity – there is no other sense of 'God-with-us'.

If prayer is a form of attention or, Simone Weil counsels, *is* attention directed to God, each of these three artefacts directs us also in the way such attention itself may be shaped in relation to the divine and holy in things. 'A, a, a, DOMINE DEUS' can even be read in terms of the *conversion* of the artist's attention.[18] The pilgrim-poet exercises his energies in every direction; he enquires, looks, feels, watches, guards, tests and tires. But it is only as the confident 'I' transmutes into the '*Eia*' of confession – as both plea for forgiveness *and* praise – that he reaches his journey's end and finds hope of a new beginning. By becoming himself a character in the poem, the 'I' of the author enters into and becomes subject to its dramatic unfolding. By yielding himself to the time of the poem, the subject himself becomes capable of change or turning, and if he is capable of turning, so, too, may the civilization for which he is tempted to despair. In imitating the boast of Taliesin, that master of shape-shifting forms in Welsh literature, he at last stumbles – even falls – upon that greatest boast of all: this mysterious I AM at the heart of being as the living source of all his conjugations.[19] This apparent point of

---

[17] Augustine, *Confessions* XI.2.3, trans. Maria Boulding, OSB, 286.
[18] Simone Weil, *Gravity and Grace*, trans. Emma Craufurd (London: Routledge and Kegan Paul, 1963).
[19] Cf. Rowan Williams's description of Taliesin as

> the identity of a speaker who is, like the 'Dai Greatcoat' of *In Parenthesis*, displaced, buried, absorbed and dispersed in what he witnesses or remembers; the speaker's exuberant and apparently egotistical boasting is in fact a claim to have successfully *let go* of conventional selfhood in the absorbing journey into the past, into the life of another, even into the elusive and miraculous processes of the surrounding world – 'Why silver glitters / And the brook runs dark,' 'the mist's bones? And the wind's twin waterfalls'

> in *The Book of Taliesin: Poems of Warfare and Praise in an Enchanted Britain* (London: Penguin Classics, 2019), xlv–xlvi. In Jones's footnote to this boast of 'Dai Greatcoat', he notes, 'I was not entirely unmindful of the boast of John viii.58' in *In Parenthesis* (London: Faber & Faber), 207 n.37. The gospel passage to which Jones alludes, reads, ' "Very, truly, I tell you," Jesus answered, "before Abraham was born, I am!" '

failure, of admitting his own 'uselessness' in the great bardic quest, is thus infused with grace and the words of his poem become one of its 'manifold lurking-places'.

In a civilization that values the imminently 'useful' and discards the apparently 'useless', the poet, in taking on the position of the latter, becomes himself a kind of redemptive figure. So writes Jean-Pierre Caussade in his spiritual classic, *The Sacrament of the Present Moment*, a work to which Jones frequently returned throughout his life:

> These simple souls often find themselves discarded in some forgotten corner, like pieces of broken crockery for which no further use can be found. … The world will think them useless. Indeed appearances will favour this judgement, though that truth is that secretly and through unknown channels these souls pour out infinite blessings on people who may never have heard of them, of whose existence they are themselves unaware.[20]

What many see as useless, the saint, says Caussade, humbles herself before, even taking on their form, a holiness moulded after their likeness.

In conversation with a friend, Jones described the letters of his painted inscriptions as looking like 'soldiers marching across the page'.[21] As Lily-Gurton-Wachter explores in her book, *Watchwords*, 'attention!' is the archetypal military command for 'exact uniformity in all movements'.[22] This kind of 'militarised attention', she argues, is the inheritance of the Romantic period which extended from military personnel to civilians who were urged to stay vigilant and keep watch as a way of safeguarding against the imminent threat of invasion. If the soldier standing to attention is the epitome of control, rigour and erasure of the particular, Jones transgresses such abstract idealizations by attending to the inevitable unconformities even among these archetypal uniforms. As Gurton-Wachter writes, '*how* we attend might alter, *what* we notice'.[23] Akin to the soldiers of his *In Parenthesis*, the beauty of Jones's letter forms resides precisely in their refusal of this 'perfect form', as 'not mathematically dead or true' but who also may 'look to their neighbour for support'.[24]

In *Bride*, it is a tiny blackbird who has her ear, this little creature a conduit and sign of the Spirit and Muse who speaks through the small and familiar, the breath which hovers over the pregnant waters, and upon whom the maker depends. She, too, stands to attention but in a mode of delicate listening, akin to that of Isa. 50.4: 'Morning by morning he awakens; / he awakens my ear / to hear as those who are taught.' It is by being rooted in and listening to the life and beauty of all things – even those, as Jones insists, which feel most resistant – that our own creations, including our words, find this living breath and light.

---

[20] Jean-Pierre Caussade, *The Sacrament of the Present Moment*, trans. Kitty Muggeridge (San Francisco, CA: Harper Collins, 1989), 6.
[21] Thomas Dilworth, *David Jones: Engraver, Soldier, Painter, Poet* (London: Jonathan Cape, 2017).
[22] Lily-Gurton-Wachter, *Watchwords: Romanticism and the Poetics of Attention* (Redwood City, CA: Stanford University Press, 2016), 11.
[23] Ibid.
[24] René Hague, *David Jones* (Cardiff: University of Wales Press, 1975), 31.

Perhaps because they are so intimate and near to us, our use of words is especially prone to the 'merely utile', to becoming channels for nothing but use. As Sergius Bulgakov reflects,

> in human usage, along with general utilitarian pragmatism, there encroaches prosaic expression, insensitivity to the beauty of the word which becomes vapid. Words, when they are deprived of life and beauty, wither and ... turn into bank-notes which replace coinage of full weight. ... They are dry leaves, rustling like paper but not ringing sonorously.[25]

The three artefacts we have immersed ourselves in here have repeatedly concentrated our attention on the potential for human words, written or spoken, 'to channel graces'.[26] Jones's poem takes us back to the genesis of writing in the stuttering babe's first grasping for speech, these early exercises in the art of *mimesis*. By feeling the shapes and hearing the sounds from the mouths of our carers, that 'A, a, a,' of 'Ma' and 'Da', one already begins to learn the wisdom embodied in the cry, 'A, a, a, Domine Deus'. The painted inscription returns us to the hand of the scribe in which these typeset letters also find their shapes and forms. As 'shaped in response to the others'[27] and 'look[ing] to their neighbour for support',[28] they give material form to the communal and borrowed nature of speech. It is one of the paradoxes of Jones's inscriptions that though they are considered the most original of all his art forms, they are the most immersed in borrowing from others, whether letter forms from palaeographical textbooks or whole texts from church liturgies and 'Magian' sources. Though wordless, the wood engraving, *Bride*, shows forth how intricately interwoven is the sign-making of humans in the wider ecology of the material world. The poet, translator and typographer Robert Bringhurst thinks about words in a manner very akin:

> Words are tracks left by the breath of the mind as it intersects with the breath of the lungs. Words are for shining, like apple blossoms, like stars, giving a sign that life is lived here too, that thought is happening here too, among the human beings, just as it is out there in the orchard and up there in the sky, and in the forest, in the oceans, in the mountains, where no humans are around.[29]

These living roots of word-craft mean there will be no code, set recipe or mould by which we may guarantee their beauty, but they will be as diverse as the lives of those who pen them. But, in adopting this posture of loving attention to what is proximate,

---

[25] Sergei Bulgakov, *Jacob's Ladder: On Angels*, trans. Thomas Allan Smith (Grand Rapids, MI: Eerdmans, 2010), 123.
[26] David Jones, 'A Christmas Message 1960', in *The Dying Gaul and Other Writings*, ed. Harman Grisewood (London: Faber & Faber, 2008), 174.
[27] Ariane Bankes and Paul Hills, *Art of David Jones: Vision and Memory* (Farnham: Lund Humphries, 2015), 155.
[28] René Hague, *David Jones* (Cardiff: University of Wales Press, 1975), 31.
[29] Robert Bringhurst, 'Poetry and Thinking', in *Tree of Meaning: Language, Mind and Ecology* (Berkeley, CA: Counterpoint Press, 2008), 144.

we may be best poised to discover how 'shéer plod makes plough down sillion / Shine'.[30] For even the most rigid of forms may flex when flowing from this molten source where the 'Word is made fire'.[31] 'Love aright,' echoes Augustine, 'and do what you will.'[32]

Even the 'angelic doctor', Aquinas, insists that the theologian, no less than any other craftsman, must tether himself to the ground when seeking the things above:

> Sacred Scripture fittingly teaches about divine and spiritual things by means of likenesses drawn from physical things. For God provides for all things according to their nature. Now it naturally belongs to us to reach invisible things through sensible ones, for all our cognition originates from the senses. ... This is what Dionysius says, 'The divine rays cannot enlighten us except wrapped up in many sacred veils.'[33]

The practitioner of the *disciplinae* of theology must above all learn what it is to 'lean low to his high office'.[34] This gesture of humility embodies the principal warning for this discipline. Not only because, as Aquinas writes, 'in this life what [God] is not is clearer to us than what [God] is'[35] but also because it is only by this sustained attention or love for things 'small and familiar' that she can hope to perceive the living God. For 'grace,' in the disarming words of Aquinas, 'makes God to be in [the substance of things] as a known and loved object'.[36] In doing theology in and with these three artefacts, we have limited ourselves to the proximate, to what is small, particular and limited, and seen how such attention leads to connections that stretch far into the past, the future, the near and the very far. They themselves have acted as dwelling places in which the 'hidden wonders' of wisdom shine forth. Together with them we have made a work of our own from the multiple 'associations, liaisons, meanderings' they have put into play. This sustained dialogue has called up many voices of the past and asked us to tune

---

[30] Gerard Manley Hopkins, 'The Windhover', in *Gerard Manley Hopkins: A Critical Edition of the Major Works* (Oxford: Oxford University Press, 1986), 132. Robin Kirkpatrick reflects on the relation of this phrase to the craft of academic writing thus: 'The ploughshare glitters through the friction of the furrow. Grace shines, however unexpectedly and unconstrainedly, on our pedestrian works. Not perhaps on works that are "good" on any human standard but on the working evidence of human potentiality, on those textured manifestations of being which demonstrate that we are alive' in Robin Kirkpatrick, 'Polemics of Praise: Theology as Text, Narrative, and Rhetoric in Dante's *Commedia*', in *Dante's Commedia: Theology as Poetry*, ed. Vittorio Montemaggi and Matthew Treherne (Notre Dame, IN: University of Notre Dame Press, 2010), 20.

[31] Jones, 'The Sleeping Lord', 72.

[32] Augustine, *Homilies on the First Epistle of John*, trans. Boniface Ramsey (Hyde Park, NY: New City Press, 2008), VII.8. The context of this oft-quoted phrase is equally illuminating: 'People's deeds are indistinguishable apart from the root of charity. For there are many things which can come about that have a good appearance and don't proceed from the root of charity. After all, thorns also have flowers ... . The root of love must be within; nothing but good can come forth from this root', in Augustine, *Homilies on the First Epistle of John* VII.8.

[33] *Summa Theologiae* I. q. 1, a. 9 in *Summa Theologiae, Questions on God*, ed. Brian Davies and Brian Leftow (Cambridge: Cambridge University Press, 2006), 16.

[34] Jones, 'The Sleeping Lord', 73.

[35] *Summa Theologiae* I. q. 1, a. 9 in *Summa Theologiae, Questions on God*, ed. Brian Davies and Brian Leftow, 17.

[36] *Summa Theologiae* 1.8.3 in *Summa Theologiae, Questions on God*, ed. Brian Davies and Brian Leftow, 84.

our ear to those perhaps less frequently expected to speak – 'nozzles and containers', letters 'like soldiers marching', woodland trees, alabaster jars and many more besides. In this apprenticeship, Jones has modelled for us an alternative practice of a modern theology that recuperates liturgy, spiritual formation and a richly orthodox vision of theology as a way of life. Above all, we have found it is in the cultivation of 'sensitive creatureliness'[37] or 'this deep and delicate listening',[38] in the words of St John of the Cross, that the living centre of each artefact resides, the font out of which they, and we with them, may become beauty along the way.

---

[37] Jim Ede, from an undated manuscript for a lecture about Jones's *In Parenthesis* quoted in *Kettle's Yard and Its Artists: An Anthology*, ed. Sebastiano Barassi (Cambridge: Kettle's Yard, University of Cambridge, 1995), 38. Cf. Thomas Berenato on the significance of this word 'sensitivity' to Jones's poetic practice: 'Sensitivity is the cardinal quality of man-the-artist's influence, and it is achieved when he goes with the flow, submits himself to influence without reserve, blesses unaware the world within which he works' in 'David Jones and the Ancient Mariner: A History of Forgiveness', *Religion and Literature* 49.1 (2017): 147.

[38] St John of the Cross, 'The Living Flame of Love', in *The Collected Works of St John of the Cross*, trans. Kieran Kavanaugh O.C.D. and Otilio Rodriguez O.C.D. (Washington, DC: ICS Publications, 1991), 687.

Bibliography

Alldritt, Keith. *David Jones: Writer and Artist*. London: Constable & Robinson, 2003.
Anderson, James F., ed. and trans. *An Introduction to the Metaphysics of St. Thomas Aquinas*. Washington, DC: Regnery, 1953.
Annwn, David. *From A to Eia: A Small Book of David Jones's 'A, a, a, DOMINE DEUS'*. Wakefield, West Yorkshire: Is Press, 1999.
Annwn, David. 'On A, a, a, DOMINE DEUS'. *David Jones Journal* 4.1/2 (2003): 7–8.
Armitage, Simon, trans. *Sir Gawain and the Green Knight*. London: Faber & Faber, 2007.
Astell, Ann W. *Eating Beauty: The Eucharist and the Spiritual Arts of the Middle Ages*. Ithaca, NY: Cornell University Press, 2006.
Augustine. *City of God against the Pagans*. Edited by R. W. Dyson. Cambridge Texts in the History of Political Thought. Cambridge: Cambridge University Press, 1998.
Augustine. *Confessions*. Translated by Maria Boulding, OSB. London: Hodder & Stoughton, 1997.
Augustine. *De Doctrina Christiana*. Edited and translated by R. P. H. Green. Oxford: Clarendon Press, 1995.
Augustine. *Earlier Writings*. Edited by J. H. S. Burleigh. The Library of Christian Classics. Philadelphia, PA: Westminster Press, 1953.
Augustine. *Expositions of the Psalms 33–50*. Translated by Maria Boulding, OSB. Works of Saint Augustine: A Translation for the 21st Century. No. 3. Hyde Park, NY: New City, 2000.
Augustine. *Homilies on the First Epistle of John*. Translated by Boniface Ramsey. Hyde Park, NY: New City, 2008.
Augustine. *The Trinity* (De Trinitate). Translated by Edmund Hill, O. P. Hyde Park, NY: New City, 1991.
Bakhtin, M. M. *Speech Genres and Other Late Essays*. Translated by Vern W. McGee. Edited by Caryl Emerson and Michael Holquist. Austin: University of Texas Press, 1986.
Bamford, Christopher, and William Parker Marsh, eds. *Celtic Christianity: Ecology and Holiness*. Hudson, NY: Lindisfarne Press, 1982.
Bankes, Ariane, and Paul Hills. *The Art of David Jones: Vision and Memory*. Farnham: Lund Humphries, 2015.
Barassi, Sebastiano, ed. *Kettle's Yard and its Artists: An Anthology*. Cambridge: Kettle's Yard, University of Cambridge, 1995.
Barfield, Owen. *The Rediscovery of Meaning and Other Essays*. Middletown, CT: Wesleyan University Press, 1977.
Bauckham, Richard. *Gospel Women: Studies of the Named Women in the Gospels*. Grand Rapids, MI: Eerdmans, 2002.
Beedham, R. John. *Wood Engraving*. Ditchling. St. Dominic's Press, 1921.
Begbie, Jeremy. *Beholding the Glory: Incarnation through the Arts*. London: Darton, Longman & Todd, 2000.

Benjamin, Walter. *The Work of Art in the Age of Mechanical Reproduction*. London: Penguin Books, [1935] 2007.

Berenato, Thomas. 'David Jones and the Ancient Mariner: A History of Forgiveness'. *Religion and Literature* 49.1 (2017): 140–9.

Blamires, David. *David Jones: Artist and Writer*. Manchester: Manchester University Press, 1971.

Blissett, William. *The Long Conversation: A Memoir of David Jones*. Oxford: Oxford University Press, 1981.

Boersma, Hans. *Heavenly Participation: The Weaving of a Sacramental Tapestry*. Grand Rapids, MI: Eerdmans, 2011.

Bradley, Ian. *The Celtic Way*. London: Dartman, Longman & Todd, 1993.

Bringhurst, Robert. *The Elements of Typographic Style*, 4th edn. Seattle: Hartley and Marks, 2012.

Bringhurst, Robert. *Everywhere Being Is Dancing: Twenty Pieces of Thinking*. Berkeley, CA: Counterpoint Press, 2008.

Bringhurst, Robert. *Tree of Meaning: Language, Mind and Ecology*. Berkeley, CA: Counterpoint Press, 2008.

Brooks, Francesca. 'Liturgy, Performance, and Poetry of the Passion: David Jones and *The Dream of the Rood*'. *Religion and Literature* 49.1 (2017): 91–101.

Buber, Martin and Franz Rosenzweig, *Scripture and Translations*. Bloomington: Indiana University Press, [1936] 1994.

Bulgakov, Sergei. *Jacob's Ladder: On Angels*. Translated and introduced by Thomas Allan Smith. Grand Rapids, MI: Eerdmans, 2010.

Bulgakov, Sergei. *Sophia: The Wisdom of God: An Outline of Sophiology*. Hudson, NY: Lindisfarne Press, 1993.

Burrows, Mark S., Jean Ward and Malgorzata Grzegorzeska, eds. *Poetic Revelations: Word Made Flesh Made Word: The Power of the Word III*. Abingdon, Oxon: Routledge, 2017.

Byassee, Jason. *Praise Seeking Understanding: Reading the Psalms with Augustine*. Grand Rapids, MI: Eerdmans, 2007.

Caldecott, Stratford. *Beauty for Truth's Sake: On the Re-enchantment of Education*. Grand Rapids, MI: Brazos Press, 2009.

Callison, James, Anna Johnson and Erik Tonning, eds. *David Jones: A Christian Modernist? Studies in Religion and the Arts*. Leiden: Brill, 2017.

Cameron, Michael. *Christ Meets Me Everywhere*. Oxford: Oxford University Press, 2012.

Candler, Peter M. *Theology, Rhetoric, Manuduction, or Reading Scripture Together on the Path to God*. London: SCM Press, 2006.

Carruthers, Mary. *The Book of Memory: A Study of Memory in Medieval Culture*. Cambridge: Cambridge University Press, 1990.

Carruthers, Mary. *The Craft of Thought: Meditation, Rhetoric, and the Making of Images, 400–1200*. Cambridge: Cambridge University Press, 1998.

Cashford, Jules, and Anne Baring. *The Myth of the Goddess: Evolution of an Image*. London: Viking Arkana, 1991.

Catherine of Siena. *The Dialogues of St. Catherine of Siena, Seraphic Virgin and Doctor of Unity*. Translated by Algar Thorold. Vancouver: Eremitical Press, 2009.

Chrétien, Jean-Louis. *Hand to Hand: Listening to the Work of Art*. Translated by Stephen E. Lewis. New York: Fordham University Press, 2003.

Christman, Angela Russell. *'What Did Ezekiel See?': Christian Exegesis of Ezekiel's Vision of the Chariot from Irenaeus to Gregory the Great*. Leiden: Brill, 2005.

Claudel, Paul. *The Satin Slipper*. Translated by John O'Connor. Frontispiece by David Jones. London: Sheed & Ward, 1931.
Cleverdon, Douglas, ed. *The Engravings of David Jones: A Survey*. London: Clover Hill Editions, 1981.
Cohen, Leonard. 'Anthem'. *The Future*, Columbia Records, 1992.
Coleridge, Samuel Taylor. *Biographia Literaria* I. Edited by James Engell and W. Jackson Bate. Princeton, NJ: Princeton University Press, 1983.
Coleridge, Samuel Taylor. *The Collected Works of Samuel Taylor Coleridge*. Vol. 16.1: Poetical Works: Part 1; Poems (Reading Text). Edited by J. C. C. May. Princeton, NJ: Princeton University Press, 2001.
Coleridge, Samuel Taylor. *The Rime of the Ancient Mariner*. Illustrated by David Jones. Bristol: Douglas Cleverdon, 1929.
Coleridge, Samuel Taylor. *The Rime of the Ancient Mariner*. Illustrated and introduction by David Jones. Clover Hill Editions. New York: Chilmark Press, 1964.
Coleridge, Samuel Taylor. *The Rime of the Ancient Mariner*. Illustrated and introduction by David Jones. Edited (with Preface and Afterword) by Thomas Dilworth. London: Enitharmon Press, 2005.
Coomaraswamy, Ananda K. *Christian & Oriental Philosophy of Art*. Mineola, NY: Dover, 1956.
Coomaraswamy, Ananda K. *Figures of Speech or Figures of Thought? The Traditional View of Art*. Rev. edn. Bloomington, IN: World Wisdom, 2007.
D'Souza, Robin. 'From Egalitarian to Sacramental Community: Re-writing William Morris's Social Romance in David Jones's *In Parenthesis*'. *Religion and Literature* 49.1 (2017): 102–10.
Daly, Carson. 'Transubstantiation and Technology in the Work of David Jones'. *Notre Dame English Journal* 14.3 (1982): 217–230.
Daniélou, Jean. *Primitive Christian Symbols*. Translated by Donald Attwater. London: Burns & Oats, 1964.
Dauphinais, Michael, David Barry and Matthew Levering, eds. *Aquinas the Augustinian*. Washington, DC: Catholic University Press of America, 2007.
Davies, Sioned, trans. *The Mabinogion*. Oxford World's Classics. Oxford: Oxford University Press, 2007.
Davison, Andrew. *Why Sacraments?* London: SPCK, 2013.
De Caussade, Jean-Pierre. *The Sacrament of the Present Moment*. Translated by Kitty Muggeridge. San Francisco, CA: Harper Collins, [1966] 1989.
De la Taille, Maurice. *The Mystery of Faith and Human Understanding Contrasted and Defined*. Translated by J. P. Schimpf. London: Sheed & Ward, 1930.
De Lubac, Henri. *The Mystery of the Supernatural*. Translated by Rosemary Sheed. New York: Herder and Herder, 1967.
Derrida, Jacques. *Dissemination*. Translated by Barbara Johnson. London: Bloomsbury, 2004.
Dilworth, Thomas. 'Antithesis of Place in the Poetry and Life of David Jones'. In *Locations of Literary Modernism: Region and Nation in British and American Modernist Poetry*, edited by Alex Davis and Lee M Jenkins, 67–88. Cambridge: Cambridge University Press, 2000.
Dilworth, Thomas. *David Jones: Engraver, Soldier, Painter, Poet*. London: Jonathan Cape, 2017.
Dilworth, Thomas. *David Jones in the Great War*. London: Enitharmon, 2012.

Dilworth, Thomas. *The Liturgical Parenthesis of David Jones*. Ipswich: Golgonooza Press, 1979.
Dilworth, Thomas. *Reading David Jones*. Cardiff: University of Wales Press, 2008.
Dilworth, Thomas. *The Shape of Meaning in the Poetry of David Jones*. Toronto: University of Toronto Press, 1988.
Dix, Gregory. *The Shape of the Liturgy*. London: Dacre, 1945.
Domestico, Anthony. *Poetry and Theology in the Modernist Period*. Baltimore, MD: Johns Hopkins University Press, 2017.
Drury, John. *Painting the Word: Christian Pictures and their Meanings*. New Haven: Yale University Press in association with the National Gallery, London, 1999.
Dubois, Martin. 'Siegfried Sassoon's Release, David Jones's Formation'. *Literature and Theology* 25.1 (2011): 79–91.
Dye, Jenifer M. 'David Jones: Artist, Writer, Theologian?' *Chesterton Review* (1997): 135–7.
Ede, H. S. 'David Jones', *Horizon* VIII.44 (August 1943).
Ede, H. S. *A Way of Life: Kettle's Yard*. Cambridge: Cambridge University Press, 1984.
Eliot, T. S. *The Cultivation of Christmas Trees*. Illustrated by David Jones. London: Faber & Faber, 1954.
The Four Gospels of the Lord Jesus Christ According to the Authorised Version of King James I. Illustrated by Eric Gill. Waltham St. Lawrence: Golden Cockerel Press, 1931.
Frazer, Sir James George. *The Golden Bough: A Study in Magic and Religion*. London: MacMillan, 1933.
Freccero, John. *Dante: The Poetics of Conversion*. Cambridge, MA: Harvard University Press, 1986.
García-Rivera, Alejandro. *The Community of the Beautiful: A Theological Aesthetics*. Collegeville, MN: Liturgical Press, 1999.
Garrett, Albert. *A History of British Wood Engraving*. Tunbridge Wells, Kent: Midas Books, 1978.
Garrett, Albert. *British Wood Engravings of the 20th Century: A Personal View*. London: Scholar Press, 1980.
Gill, Eric. *Beauty Looks after Herself*. 1933. Tacoma, WA: Angelico Press, 2012.
Gill, Eric. *An Essay on Typography*. 1931. London: Penguin Classics, 2013.
Gray, Nicolete. *The Painted Inscriptions of David Jones*. London: Gordon Fraser, 1981.
Gray, Nicolete. *The Paintings of David Jones*. Hatfield: John Taylor/Lund Humphries in association with the Tate Gallery, 1989.
Gray, Nicolete. 'Palaeography of Latin Inscriptions in the Eighth, Ninth and Tenth Centuries in Italy'. *Papers of the British School at Rome*. New Series III, no. 16 (1948): 38–162.
Green, Miranda J. *Dictionary of Celtic Myth and Legend*. London: Thames and Hudson, 1992.
Greggs, Tom, Rachel Muers and Simeon Zahl, eds. *The Vocation of Theology Today: A Festschrift for David Ford*. Eugene, OR: Cascade Books, 2013.
Guest, Lady Charlotte, trans. *Mabinogion*. Everyman's Library. London: Dent, 1906.
Guite, Malcolm. *Faith, Hope and Poetry: Theology and the Poetic Imagination*. Surrey: Ashgate, 2012.
Guite, Malcolm. 'Imagination, Bodies and Locality: The Incarnational Thrust of David Jones's Art'. *Flashpoint* 18 (2016).
Hague, René. *A Commentary on* The Anathemata *of David Jones*. Toronto: University of Toronto Press, 1977.

Hague, René. *David Jones*. Cardiff: University of Wales Press, 1975.
Hanke, John W. *Maritain's Ontology of the Work of Art*. The Hague: Martinus Nijhoff, 1973.
Hart, David Bentley. *The Beauty of the Infinite: An Aesthetics of Christian Truth*. Grand Rapids, MI: Eerdmans, 2003.
Hartman, Geoffrey. *The Geoffrey Hartman Reader*. Edinburgh: Edinburgh University Press, 2004.
Hauerwas, Stanely. 'Discipleship as a Craft, Church as a Disciplined Community'. *The Christian Century* (October 1991): 881–4.
Herbermann, Charles, ed. *The Catholic Encyclopedia*. 15 vols. New York: Appleton, 1913.
Herbert, George. *The Complete English Poems*. London: Penguin Books, 1991.
Hills, Paul, ed. *David Jones: Artist and Poet*. Aldershot: Scholar Press, 1997.
The Holy Bible. *New Revised Standard Version*. Anglicized ed. Oxford: Oxford University Press, 1998.
Hooker, Jeremy. *David Jones: An Exploratory Study of the Writings*. London: Enitharmon Press, 1975.
Hopkins, Gerard Manley. *A Critical Edition of the Major Works*. Oxford: Oxford University Press, 1986.
Hugh of St. Victor. *The Didascalicon of Hugh of St Victor: A Medieval Guide to the Arts*. Translated by Jerome Taylor. New York: Columbia University Press, 1991.
Hughes, John. *The End of Work: Theological Critiques of Capitalism*. Oxford: Blackwell, 2007.
Huk, Romana. 'Sacrament as *Ars* in the Down-to-Earth Poetics of David Jones (pursued through a reading of his ars[e]-poetica, "A, a, a, Domine Deus")'. *Religion and Literature* 49.1 (2017): 181–201.
Humfrey, Belinda, and Anne Price-Owen, eds. *David Jones: Diversity in Unity – Studies in His Literary and Visual Art*. Cardiff: University of Wales Press, 2000.
Hunter-Evans, Jasmine. 'Bridging the Breaks: David Jones and the Continuity of Culture'. *Flashpoint* 18 (Summer 2016). Available at: http://www.flashpointmag.com/hunterevans.pdf (accessed 21 April 2020).
Hunter-Evans, Jasmine. 'You're Awfully Unorthodox, David'. *New Welsh Review* 104 (2014): 24–31.
Illich, Ivan. *In the Vineyard of the Text: A Commentary to Hugh's* Didascalicon. Chicago, IL: University of Chicago Press, 1993.
Irenaeus of Lyons. *Against the Heresies* (Book 3). Ancient Christian Writers, No. 64. Translated and annotated by Dominic J. Unger. New York: The Newman Press, 2012.
Irigaray, Luce. *An Ethics of Sexual Difference*. Translated by Carolyn Burke and Gillian C. Gill. Ithaca, NY: Cornell University Press, [1984] 1993.
Irigaray, Luce. *Sexes and Genealogies*. 1987. Translated by Gillian C. Gill. New York: Columbia University Press, 1993.
Irvine, Christopher. *The Cross and Creation in Christian Liturgy and Art*. London: SPCK, 2013.
Isaacs, J., ed. *The Chester Play of the Deluge*. Illustrated by David Jones. Berkshire: Golden Cockerel Press, 1927.
James, Merlin. *David Jones 1895–1974: A Map of the Artist's Mind*. London: Lund Humphries Publishers in association with National Museums & Galleries of Wales, 1995.
John, Jeffrey, ed. *Living Tradition: Affirming Catholicism in the Anglican Church*. London: Darton, Longman & Todd, 1992.

John of the Cross. *The Collected Works of St John of the Cross*. Translated by Kieran Kavanaugh O. C. D. and Otilio Rodriguez O. C. D. Washington, DC: ICS Publications, 1991.

John Paul II. *Fides et Ratio. The Vatican*. The Holy See. 14 September 1998. Web. 25 March 2020.

Jones, David. 'Art and Sacrament: An Enquiry Concerning the Arts of Man and the Christian Commitment to Sacrament in Relation to Contemporary Technocracy'. In *Catholic Approaches*, edited by Elizabeth Pakenham, 143–82. London: Weidenfeld & Nicolson, 1955.

Jones, David. *The Anathemata: Fragments of an Attempted Writing*. London: Faber & Faber, 1952.

Jones, David. 'Beauty in Catholic Churches'. *Blackfriars: A Monthly Review* (July 1926): 438–41.

Jones, David. *Dai Greatcoat: A Self-Portrait of David Jones in his Letters*. Edited by René Hague. London: Faber & Faber, 2008.

Jones, David. *The Dying Gaul and Other Writings*. Edited and introduced by Harman Grisewood. London: Faber & Faber, 2008.

Jones, David. *Epoch and Artist: Selected Writings*. Edited by Harman Grisewood. London: Faber & Faber, 1959.

Jones, David. *Inner Necessities: The Letters of David Jones to Desmond Chute*. Edited and introduced by Thomas Dilworth. Toronto: Anson-Cartwright, 1984.

Jones, David. *In Parenthesis*. London: Faber & Faber, 1937.

Jones, David. *Introducing David Jones: A Selection of His Writings*. Edited by John Matthias. London: Faber & Faber, 1980.

Jones, David. *To Petra With Love: The Petra Tegetmeier Collection of Works by David Jones: Paintings, Drawings, Engravings, Inscriptions and Carvings*. Introduction by Dr. Jonathan Miles with a contribution by Lottie Hoare. London: Wolseley Fine Arts, 2001.

Jones, David. *The Roman Quarry and Other Sequences*. Edited by Harmon Grisewood and René Hague. New York City: Sheep Meadow Press, 1981.

Jones, David. *The Sleeping Lord and Other Fragments*. London: Faber & Faber, 1974.

Jones, David. *Unpublished Writings of David Jones: On Politics and Christian Modernism*. Modernist Archives. Edited by Thomas Berenato, Anne Price-Owen and Kathleen Henderson Staudt. London: Bloomsbury, 2018.

Jones, David. *Wedding Poems*. Edited (with Foreword and Afterword) by Thomas Dilworth. London: Enitharmon Press, 2002.

Jones, Huw C. *The Library of David Jones, 1895–1974: A Catalogue*. Aberystwyth: National Library of Wales, 1995.

Julian of Norwich. *The Showings of Julian of Norwich*. Edited by Denise N. Baker. Norton Critical Editions. London: W.W. Norton, 2004.

Kilby, Karen. *God, Evil and the Limits of Theology*. London: T&T Clark, 2020.

Lacoste, Jean-Yves. *Experience and the Absolute*. Translated by Mark Raftery-Skehan. Fordham University Press, 2004.

Laird, Martin. *Into the Silent Land: The Practice of Contemplation*. London: Darton, Longman & Todd, 2006.

A Latin Dictionary. Edited by Charlton T. Lewis and Charles Short. Oxford: Oxford University Press, 1879.

Leighton, Clare. *Wood-engraving and Woodcuts*. How to Do It Series No. 2. London: Studio Publications, 1944.

Levering, Matthew. *Participatory Biblical Exegesis: A Theology of Biblical Interpretation*. Notre Dame, IN: University of Notre Dame Press, 2008.
Lewis, Gwyneth, and Rowan Williams, trans. *The Book of Taliesin: Poems of Warfare and Praise in an Enchanted Britain*. London: Penguin Classics, 2019.
Lewis, Suzanne. 'Sacred Calligraphy: The Chi Rho Page in the Book of Kells'. *Traditio* 36 (1980): 139–59.
Lombardi, Elena. *The Syntax of Desire: Language and Love in Augustine, the Modistae, Dante*. Toronto: University of Toronto Press, 2007.
Lubheid, Colm, and Paul Rorem, eds. *Pseudo-Dionysius: The Complete Works*. Classics of Western Spirituality. Mahwah, NJ: Paulist Press, 1987.
MacGregor, Neil. *A History of the World in 100 Objects*. London: Penguin Books, 2012.
MacGregor, Neil. *A History of the World in 100 Objects*. London: BBC Audiobooks, 2011. Audio CD.
Mâle, Émile. *Religious Art in France of the Thirteenth Century*. 1913. Translated by Dora Nussey. Mineola, NY: Dover, 2000.
Maloney, Brian. *Francis of Assisi and His 'Canticle of Brother Sun' Reassessed*. The New Middle Ages Series. New York: Palgrave Macmillan, 2013.
Marion, Jean-Luc. *The Reason of the Gift*. Translated by Stephen E. Lewis. Charlottesville: University of Virginia Press, 2011.
Maritain, Jacques. *Art and Scholasticism with Other Essays*. Translated by J. F. Scanlan. London: Sheed & Ward, 1946.
Maritain, Jacques. *The Philosophy of Art: being 'Art et scholastique'*. Translated by John O'Connor. Introduction by Eric Gill. Ditchling: St. Dominic's Press, 1923.
Mary, the blessed Virgin. A Child's Rosary Book; Being the Fifteen Mysteries of the Most Holy Rosary of the Blessed Virgin Mary. Illustrated by David Jones. Ditchling: St. Dominic's Press, 1924.
Matthias, John. 'David Jones: Letters to H. S. Ede'. *Notre Dame English Journal* 14.2 (Spring 1982): 145–6.
Matthias, John, ed. *David Jones: Man and Poet*. Orono, ME: National Poetry Foundation, 1989.
Mathias, Roland. *David Jones: Eight Essays on His Work as Writer and Artist*. Llandysul: Gomer Press, 1976.
Milbank, Alison. *Chesterton and Tolkien as Theologians: The Fantasy of the Real*. London: T&T Clark, 2008.
Milbank, John. *Being Reconciled: Ontology and Pardon*. Radical Orthodoxy Series. London: Routledge, 2003.
Milbank, John. On 'Thomistic Kabbalah'. In *Modern Theology* 27.1 (2011): 147–85.
Milbank, John. *The Suspended Middle: Henri de Lubac and the Debate Concerning the Supernatural*. Grand Rapids, MI: Eerdmans, 2005.
Milbank, John. *The Word Made Strange: Theology, Language and Culture*. Oxford: Blackwell, 1997.
Milbank, John, Graham Ward and Edith Wyschogrod, eds. *Theological Perspectives on God and Beauty*. Harrisburg, PA: Trinity Press International, 2003.
Miles, Jonathan. *Backgrounds to David Jones: A Study in Sources and Drafts*. Cardiff: University of Wales Press, 1990.
Miles, Jonathan, and Derek Shiel. *The Maker Unmade*. Brigend, Wales: Seren Press, 1995.
Miles, Margaret. 'Vision: The Eyes of the Body and the Eye of the Mind in St Augustine's *De Trinitate* and *Confessions*'. *Journal of Religion* 63 (1983): 125–42.

The Missal in Latin and English, Being the Text of the Misalle Romanum with English Rubrics and a New Translation. Edited and translated by John O'Connell, H. P. R. Finberg and R. A. Knox. London: Burns Oates and Washbourne, 1949.

Milton, John. *Paradise Lost*. Edited by Scott Elledge. Norton Critical Edition. 2nd edn. New York: W.W. Norton, 1993.

Miner, Robert. *Truth in the Making: Creative Knowledge in Theology and Philosophy*. New York: Routledge, 2004.

Montemaggi, Vittorio. *Reading Dante's* Commedia *as Theology: Divinity Realized in Human Encounter*. Oxford: Oxford University Press, 2016.

Montemaggi, Vittorio, and Matthew Treherne, eds. *Dante's 'Commedia': Theology as Poetry*. Notre Dame, IN: University of Notre Dame Press, 2010.

Newman, Barbara. *God and the Goddesses: Vision, Poetry and Belief in the Middle Ages*. Philadelphia: University of Pennsylvania Press, 2003.

The Nicene Creed. Anglicans Online. http://anglicansonline.org/basics/nicene.html.

Nichols, Aidan. *Redeeming Beauty: Soundings in Sacral Aesthetics*. Ashgate Studies in Theology, Imagination and the Arts. Aldershot: Ashgate, 2007.

O'Rourke, Fran. *Pseudo-Dionysius and the Metaphysics of Aquinas*. Leiden: Brill, 1992.

Oxford English Dictionary. 2nd edn. Oxford: Clarendon Press, 1989.

Pagnoulle, Christine. *David Jones: A Commentary on Some Poetic Fragments*. Cardiff: University of Wales Press, 1987.

Pattison, Stephen. *Seeing Things: Deepening Relations with Visual Artefacts*. London: SCM Press, 2007.

Patri, Gabriel Diaz. 'Poetry in the Latin Liturgy'. In *The Genius of the Roman Rite: Historical, Theological, and Pastoral Perspectives on Catholic Liturgy*, edited by Uwe Michael Lang, 45–82. Chicago, IL: HillenbrandBooks, 2010.

Pechey, Graham. 'Pointed Remarks: Scholasticism and the Gothic in the English Counter-Enlightenment'. *Christianity and Literature* 57.1 (2007): 3–33.

Pickstock, Catherine. *After Writing: On the Liturgical Consummation of Philosophy*. Oxford: Blackwells, 1998.

Pickstock, Catherine. 'What does Othering Make? David Jones's "A, a, a, Domine Deus"'. *Religion and Literature* 49.1 (2017): 167–80.

Pieper, Josef. *Faith, Hope, Love*. Translated by Richard and Clara Winston and Mary Frances McCarthy. San Francisco, CA: Ignatius Press, 1997.

Pieper, Josef. *Only the Lover Sings: Art and Contemplation*. Translated by Lothar Krauth. San Francisco, CA: Ignatius Press, [1988] 1990.

Plato. *Plato on Love: Lysis, 'Symposium', 'Phaedrus', 'Alcibiades' with selections from "Republic" and "Laws"*. Edited by C. D. C. Reeve. Indianapolis: Hackett, 2006.

Plato. *Timaeus*. Translated by Donald J. Zeyl. Indianapolis: Hackett, 2000.

Pramuk, Christopher. *Sophia: The Hidden Christ of Thomas Merton*. Collegeville, MN: Liturgical Press, 2009.

Price-Owen, Anne. *Fragments of an Attempted Painting: An Investigation of the Pictorial Concepts in David Jones's 'The Anathemata'*. PhD dissertation. Lampeter: University of Wales, 1992.

Price-Owen, Anne. 'From Medieval Manuscripts to Postmodern Hypertexts in the Art of David Jones'. In *Writing and Seeing: Essays on Word and Image*, edited by Rui Carvalho Homem and Maria de Fátima Lambert, 355–68. Amsterdam: Rodopi, 2006.

Prickett, Stephen, ed. *The Edinburgh Companion to the Bible and the Arts*. Edinburgh: Edinburgh University Press, 2014.

Quash, Ben. *Found Theology: History, Imagination and the Holy Spirit*. London: Bloomsbury, 2013.
Quiller-Couch, Sir Arthur, ed. *The Oxford Book of English Verse: 1250–1918*. Oxford: Oxford University Press, 1940.
Raine, Kathleen. *David Jones and the Actually Loved and Known*. Ipswich: Golgonooza Press, 1978.
Raine, Kathleen. *David Jones: A Solitary Perfectionist*. Ipswich: Golgonooza Press, 1975.
Reddaway, Chloë. *Transformations in Persons and Paint: Visual Theology, Historical Images, and the Modern Viewer*. Turnhout: Brepols, 2016.
Ricoeur, Paul, and André LaCocque. *Thinking Biblically: Exegetical and Hermeneutical Studies*. Translated by David Pellauer. Chicago, IL: University of Chicago Press, 1998.
Robichaud, Paul. *Making the Past Present: David Jones, the Middle Ages and Modernism*. Washington, DC: Catholic University Press, 2007.
The Roman Missal in Latin and English According to the Latest Roman Edition. Introduction and liturgical notes by Dom. F. Cabrol, OSB. 3rd edn. Tours: A. Mame and Sons, 1921.
Rowland, Christopher. 'Ezekiel's *Merkavah* in the Work of William Blake and Christian Art'. In *The Book of Ezekiel and Its Influence*, edited by Henk Jan de Jonge and Johannes Tromp, 183–200. Aldershot: Ashgate, 2007.
Ruether, Rosemary Radford. *Goddesses and the Divine Feminine*. Berkeley: University of California Press, 2005.
Ruskin, John. 'The Nature of Gothic'. In *The Stones of Venice*. Vol. 2, 1851–53. London: Dent, 1907.
Ryan, Fáinche. *Formation in Holiness: Thomas Aquinas on Sacra Doctrina*. Leuven: Peeters, 2007.
Schwartz, Adam. *The Third Spring: G. K. Chesterton, Graham Greene, Christopher Dawson, and David Jones*. Washington, DC: Catholic University Press, 2005.
Schwartz, Regina. *Sacramental Poetics at the Dawn of Secularism: When God Left the World*. Stanford, CA: Stanford University Press, 2008.
Selborne, Joanna and Lindsay Newman. *Gwen Raverat, Wood engraver*. London: British Library, 2003.
Sellner, Edward C. *Wisdom of the Celtic Saints*. Notre Dame, IN: Ave Maria Press, 1993.
Shakespeare, William. *As You Like It*. Updated edition. Edited by Michael Hattaway. Cambridge: Cambridge University Press, 2009.
Shakespeare, William. *A Midsummer Night's Dream*. Updated edition. Edited by R. A. Foakes. Cambridge: University of Cambridge Press, 2003.
Sherman, Jacob Holsinger. *Partakers of the Divine: Contemplation and the Practice of Philosophy*. Minneapolis, MN: Fortress Press, 2014.
Sherry, Patrick. *Spirit and Beauty: An Introduction to Theological Aesthetics*. London: SCM Press, 2002.
Shewring, Walter. *Hermia and Some Other Poems*. Ditchling: St. Dominic's Press, 1930.
Shiel, Derek, ed. *David Jones in Ditchling: 1921–1924*. Ditchling: Ditchling Museum, 2003.
Shorter Oxford English Dictionary. 5th ed. Oxford: Oxford University Press, 2002.
Soskice, Janet M. '*Creatio ex nihilo*: Its Jewish and Christian foundations'. In *Creation and the God of Abraham*, edited by David B. Burrell, Carlo Cogliati, Janet M. Soskice and William R. Stoeger, 24–39. Cambridge: Cambridge University Press, 2010.
Soskice, Janet M. *The Kindness of God: Metaphor, Gender, and Religious Language*. Oxford: Oxford University Press, 2007.

Staudt, Kathleen Henderson. *At the Turn of a Civilization: David Jones and Modern Poetics*. Ann Arbor: University of Michigan Press, 1994.
Steiner, George. *Real Presences: Is There Anything* in *What We Say?* London: Faber & Faber, 1989.
Svendsen, Anna, and Jasmine Hunter Evans, eds. *David Jones: Towards a Theology of History*. Special Issue. *Religion and Literature* 49.1 (2017).
Thomas, Aquinas Saint. *Summa Theologiae*. 61 vols. Cambridge: Blackfriars, 1964–81.
Thomas, Aquinas Saint. *Summa Theologiae, Questions on God*. Edited by Brian Davies and Brian Leftow. Cambridge Texts in the History of Philosophy. Cambridge: Cambridge University Press, 2006.
Tolkien, J. R. R. *Tree and Leaf*. London: Harper Collins, 2001.
Torevell, David. *Liturgy and the Beauty of the Unknown: Another Place*. Aldershot: Ashgate, 2007.
Torevell, David. '"Wounded by the Arrow of Beauty": The Silent Call of Art'. *The Heythrop Journal* 54 (2013): 932–41.
Toulmin, Stephen. *Cosmopolis: The Hidden Agenda of Modernity*. Chicago, IL: University of Chicago Press, 1990.
Trapani, John G., Jr. *Poetry, Beauty and Contemplation: The Complete Aesthetics of Jaques Maritain*. Washington, DC: Catholic University of America Press, 2011.
Van Bavel, Tarsicius. 'The "Christus Totus" Idea: A Forgotten Aspect of Augustine's Spirituality'. In *Studies in Patristic Christology*, edited by Thomas Finan and Vincent Twomey, 84–94. Portland: Four Courts Press, 1998.
Velde, Rudi te. *Participation and Substantiality in Thomas Aquinas*. Leiden: Brill, 1995.
Venard, Olivier-Thomas, O. P. '"Theology and Literature": What Is It about?' In *Religion and Literature* 41.2 (2009): 87–95.
Villis, Tom. 'When Was "the Break"? David Jones and Catholic Ideas of Rupture in British History'. *Religion and Literature* 49.1 (2017): 9–18.
Wainewright, Ruth, trans. *The Dream of the Holy Rood*. Ditchling: Dominic's Press, 1931.
Ward, Elizabeth. *David Jones, Mythmaker*. Manchester: Manchester University Press, 1983.
Webster's New Universal Unabridged Dictionary. New York: Random House, 1996.
Weil, Simone. *Gravity and Grace*. Translated by Emma Craufurd with an Introduction by Gustave Thibon. London: Routledge and Kegan Paul, [1947] 1963.
White, Rebecca, ed. *David Jones: The Furrowed Line; Catalogue of an Exhibition*. Oxford: Fellowship of St. Alban & St. Sergius, 2014.
Wilken, Robert Louis. *The Spirit of Early Christian Thought: Seeking the Face of God*. New Haven: Yale University Press, 2003.
Wilcockson, Colin. '"I Have Journeyed Among the Dead Forms": David Jones and the Wasteland Motif'. *Flashpoints* (Spring 2010). Web Issue 13.
Wilcockson, Colin. 'Mythological References in Two Painted Inscriptions of David Jones'. *Journal of Modern Literature* 23.1 (1999): 173–82.
Wilcockson, Colin. 'Presentation and Self-Presentation in *In Parenthesis*'. In *Presenting Poetry: Composition, Publication, Reception: Essays in Honour of Ian Jack*, edited by Howard Erskine-Hill and Richard A. McCabe, 235–56. Cambridge: Cambridge University Press, 1995.
Williams, Rowan. 'Augustine and the Psalms'. *Interpretation* (2004): 17–27.
Williams, Rowan. *The Dwelling of the Light: Praying with Icons of Christ*. Norwich: Canterbury Press, 2003.
Williams, Rowan. *Grace and Necessity: Reflections on Art and Love*. London: Continuum, 2005.

Williams, Rowan. '"New Words for God": Contemplation and Religious Writing'. In *A Silent Action: Engagements with Thomas Merton*, 43–51. Louisville, KY: Fons Vitae, 2011.

Williams, Rowan. *On Augustine*. London: Bloomsbury, 2016.

Williams, Rowan. *Ponder these Things: Praying with Icons of the Virgin*. Norwich: Canterbury Press, 2002.

Williams, Rowan. *Silence and Honey Cakes: The Wisdom of the Desert*. Oxford: Lion Books, 2003.

Winston-Allen, Anne. *Stories of the Rose: The Making of the Rosary in the Middle Ages*. Philadelphia: Pennsylvania State University Press, 1997.

Wood, Juliette. *The Holy Grail: History and Legend*. Cardiff: University of Wales Press, 2012.

Index

Page numbers in *italics* denote figures.

'A, a, a, DOMINE DEUS' (poem) 9, 10, 11, *18*, 17–20, 22–3, 25–49, 83, 132, 134
Adoration of the Cross 98–9
The Anathemata 7 n.7, 12, 21–2, 23, 28 n.71, 40, 46, 52, 62 n.44, 67, 68, 69 n.71, 87–8, 103, 106–7, 111 n.115, 112–13, 115, 116, 117, 123, 124 nn.176, 180 and 182, 125 nn.183 and 184, 126 n.188, 129, 130, 131 nn.13, 14 and 16
Anderson, James F. 70 n.74
Animals and Shepherds (drypoint engraving) 126 n.187
Aquinas, Thomas 42, 69–70, 71, 135
  Summa Theologiae 71 n.80, 72–8, 79 nn.114 and 115, 135 nn.34–6
Aristotle xii, 70 n.77, 73
ars 20, 24
'Art in Relation to War' (essay) 2 n.8, 11 n.1, 15 n.16, 34 n.93, 111–12
'Art and Sacrament' (essay) 3–4, 4–5, 9 n.37, 14, 15 nn.14 and 15, 16 nn.17–20, 17, 20 n.38, 29, 30, 34 n.94, 40 n.117, 42, 44 n.136, 68, 83 n.4, 97 n.67, 116, 122 n.170, 130
Arthurian myths 11–13, 107, 108, 110
The Artist (wood engraving) 121
Arts and Crafts movement 2, 92
'asking the question' 11–17, 23
'An Aspect of the Art of England' (essay) 102
attention 9, 17, 23, 24, 26, 59, 60, 132, 133, 134–5
Augustine xii, xiii, 71, 79, 88 n.26, 135 n.32
  Confessions 129, 132 n.17
  De Doctrina Christiana 77–8
  The Trinity (*De Trinitate*) 78

Bakhtin, M. M. 6–7
baptism 100, 101, 104, 105

Barfield, Owen 35–6, 44
'Beauty in Catholic Churches' (essay) 1 nn.1 and 3–5, 2 nn.6 and 8, 75 n.94
beauty/the beautiful xiii, 1, 2–3, 4, 5, 8, 38, 54–5, 69, 71, 74–5, 81
  three classical attributes of 71–2, 74, 79
being (*esse*) 2, 4, 5, 13, 14, 15
Benjamin, Walter 20
Boar Trwyth 107–8, 110
The Book of Balaam's Ass 47, 83 n.2
The Book of Kells 101
'The Break' 2
Bride (wood engraving) 9, 10, 84–5, *86*, 87, 89, 96, 132, 133, 134
  bride figure 111–20
  crucifix-candelabra figure 103–11
  deer figure 120–6
  liturgical character of 101–3
Bringhurst, Robert 25, 134
Bulgakov, Sergei 112 n.120, 134

Carruthers, Mary 40 n.116, 58–9, 60, 93
Catherine of Siena 69
Caussade, Jean-Pierre 133
Celtic mythology 88, 89, 113, 122
Cernunnos (Celtic god) 122
The Chester Play of the Deluge 95
Chesterton, G. K. 22
Child's Rosary Book, A. 90
Chrétien de Troyes 12 n.5
Christmas inscriptions 60, 66. *See also* Preface to the Christmas Mass
Christological participation 80–1
Church 1, 2, 3, 10, 32, 60, 63, 84, 87–9, 90, 105, 106, 107, 117, 125, 132
claritas 53–4, 70–1, 72, 74, 75, 79, 96
Coleridge, Samuel Taylor 44
  The Rime of the Ancient Mariner 31 n.83, 47 n.147, 83 n.1, 85, 86, 87, 88, 96, 104, 127

Index

commodification 14
craft 130–2
   everyday 4
   of theology 5–8, 11
creation 100, 104, 109, 116, 129
   doctrine of 28
   as gift 2, 5, 13, 15, 79
Crucifixion (painting) 56 n.18
Crucifixion with Inscription (painting) 56 n.18

Dai Greatcoat: A Self-Portrait of David Jones in His Letters 49 n.154, 51 n.1, 52 nn.2 and 3, 83 n.3
De la Taille, Maurice 42, 43
De Lubac, Henri 121–2
defamiliarization 22
Delacroix, Eugène 48
Derrida, Jacques 13n. 6
the diagonal 66–7
dialogue 6, 7
Ditchling arts and crafts community 20, 90
divine being 72–9
Dix, Gregory 3 n.12
'The Dream of Private Clitus' (poem) 39 n.111, 66 n.57, 68 n.62
The Dream of the Rood 94
The Dying Gaul and Other Writings xii n.2 and 3, xiii n., 2 n.8, 85 n.14, 102 n.84, 111 n.116, 112 nn.118 and 119, 120 n.158, 134 n.26

Easter Vigil 98, 99–101, 103, 123, 132
Ede, H. S. (Jim) 1 n.2, 8, 15 n.14, 136 n.37
Eliot, T. S. 12 n.2
   The Cultivation of Christmas Trees 121
Epiphany 52, 63–4
'Epithalmion' (poem) 102 n.80, 111 n.115
'Eric Gill: an Appreciation' 56 n.17, 122 n.171
Eucharist 3, 12 n.5, 15 n.15, 21, 29, 31, 42, 52, 60, 62, 85, 106, 107, 109

'The Fatigue' (poem) 119 n.153
feminine tutelar 111–20, 124
Francis of Assisi 37
Freud, Sigmund 117 n.145

gift
   creation as 2, 5, 13, 15
   metaphysics of 13, 14–15, 22
Gill, Eric 20, 55, 56, 57, 81, 90, 92, 122 n.171
   The Four Gospels 66
God 73, 74, 76, 78, 80
   beauty of 2, 71
   love of xiii
goddess figures 62, 64, 112–13, 114–15
the Good 13, 14, 16, 23
goodness xiii, 2, 4
Gospels 32, 36 n.102, 125
grace 8, 39, 40, 47, 49, 53, 95, 99, 100, 113, 116, 119, 122, 125 n.183, 133, 135
grail quest 12 n.2
gratuitous 13, 14, 16, 113
gratuitous sign-making 2–3, 5, 7, 24, 49
Guest, Lady Charlotte 12 n.4

harmony, as condition of beauty 74, 79
Herbert, George 118–19
Holy Spirit 73, 74, 77, 126
homo faber 15
Hopkins, Gerard Manley 29, 63, 68, 102 n.83, 105 n.93, 135 n.30
Horned Man (pencil on paper) 121
Human Being (self-portrait) 8

In Parenthesis 14 n.10, 16 n.16, 21, 30, 32–3, 34, 132 n.19, 133
Incarnation 23, 53, 62, 66, 73, 84, 110
inner word (verbum cordis) 75–6, 80
inscriptions 54–60
   Christmas 60, 66. *See also* Preface to the Christmas Mass
instrumentalization 14
integrity, as condition of beauty 71, 74, 79
Irenaeus 36 n.102
Irigaray, Luce 115 n.134

John of the Cross 136 n.38

Kneeling Animals (drypoint on paper) 121

language, materiality of 24, 55
Latin 58–9
lettering 53, 54–60. *See also* typography

liturgy 21, 59, 88–9, 90, 97–103, 104, 106, 109, 115, 129, 130, 136
love xii, 77, 78, 79, 80, 81
   of God xiii

The Mabinogion 12, 107 n.105
The Maid at No. 37 (watercolour) 45
Maritain, Jacques 2, 15 n.14, 52, 70, 75, 96
   Art and Scholasticism 4, 17 n.26, 19, 20, 22, 40, 54–5, 65, 71, 80, 118 n.150
   Philosophy of Art 71, 72
Mary 115–18, 119
Mary of Bethany 118 n.149, 119–20
Mary Magdalene 118 n.149, 119
Mass 9, 21, 29, 39, 51, 52, 59, 83–4, 87, 98 n.70, 130. *See also* Preface to the Christmas Mass
mass production 14
Mies van der Rohe, Ludwig 37–8
modernism 21, 22
monologic discourse 6–7
Morris, William 92
Moses 26, 27 n.66, 28

Nash, John 92, 102 n.83
Nativity with Beasts and Shepherds (drypoint) 116 n.141

'Our Lady Mary's Rose Garden' (German Dominican poem/song) 117

Pange Lingua Proelium Certaminis 98–9
participation
   christological 80–1
   metaphysics of 2, 4, 15 n.14, 22
paschal candle 99–100
Passover 29–30
Peredur, myth of 12–13
poiesis 15, 44, 53
   as Christological participation 80–1
Preface to the Christmas Mass (painted inscription) 52–3, 60–72, *61*, 78–9, 132
printed page, window casement analogy 24–5
profane 15, 23
projection 35–6
Pseudo-Dionysius
   Celestial Hierarchy 36

   Divine Names 36, 47, 69, 114–15 n.129
   Mystical Theology 70

'Quia per Incarnati'. *See* Preface to the Christmas Mass

Raine, Kathleen 83–4, 127
Raverat, Gwendolen 92
re-presentation 3, 4, 8, 9, 10, 23, 24, 53, 66, 81, 84, 86, 96, 120, 124, 131
reading, as performative act 23–4
'Religion and the Muses' (essay) 32 n.87, 36, 38
Resting Animals (four deer) (drypoint on paper) 121
Ricoeur, Paul 88, 89 n.30
The Roman Missal in Latin and English According to the Latest Roman Edition 42 n.126, 68 nn.64 and 65, 98 n.70, 99 nn.71–3, 100 nn.74–7, 123 nn.173 and 174
The Roman Quarry and Other Sequences (poems) 9 n.37

sacrament 3–4, 10, 11, 14–15, 16, 17, 31, 33, 34, 43, 46, 49, 53, 60, 84, 89, 113, 120, 121, 130
Shakespeare, William
   As You Like It 39–40 n.114
   A Midsummer Night's Dream 28, 30
'Sherthursdaye and Venus Day' (poem) 117
signifer/signified 22–3
signs/sign-making 2–4, 15–16, 129
   gratuitous 2–3, 5, 7, 24, 49
Sir Gawain and the Green Knight 111 n.114
'The Sleeping Lord' (poem) 31, 42 n.128, 46, 57, 81 n.125, 103, 105–6, 107–11, 119 nn.155 and 156, 124 n.181
The Sleeping Lord (poems) 10 n.42, 38, 39, 46, 98, 103, 107, 114–15, 124 n.178
Society of Wood Engravers 92
Stag (wood engraving) 121
A stag in its natural habitation (miniature) 121

Taliesin 132
theology
   craft of 5–8, 11
   as human practice 7–8

Thomism 13, 15 n.14
Tolkien, J. R. R. 22, 41, 43 n.129, 111 n.117
'The Tribune's Visitation' (poem) 38 n.108, 113–14
Trinity 53, 71, 72–9, 80, 105
truth xiii, 2, 4, 81
'The Tutelar of the Place' (poem) 31 n.82, 46 n.143, 47 n.146, 98, 103 n.87, 114–15, 117, 124
typography 25, 55–6

'Use and Sign' (essay) 12, 16 n.23, 111 n.116, 118 n.150, 120
the utile 11, 13–14, 16, 32, 34, 49

verbum cordis (inner word) 75–6, 80
'The Viae' (essay) 113

'The Wall' (poem) 31 n.79
water, significance to Jones 125 n.183
Wedding Poems 102 n.80, 111 n.115
Weil, Simone 132
Williams, Rowan 2 n.9, 6–7, 10 n.41, 15 n.14, 17, 81, 88 n.26, 89 n.27, 96–7, 97 n.66, 125, 126, 132 n.19
Wilton Diptych 102 n.84
Wisdom 29, 53, 115, 117
wood engraving
  tradition of 89–97. See also *The Artist*; *Bride*; *Stag*

Y Cyfarchiad i Fair (The Greeting to Mary) 121